THE TACTICS OF SMALL BOAT RACING

By the same author

THE TECHNIQUES OF SMALL BOAT RACING
THE TACTICS OF SMALL BOAT RACING

THE TACTICS

OF SMALL BOAT

RACING

By

STUART H. WALKER, M.D.

Illustrated by CAROL H. LITTLE

W · W · NORTON & COMPANY · INC · *New York*

SBN 393 03132 2

5 6 7 8 9

*To my wife Frances—who loves sailing
in order to love me and accepts my racing
all day and writing all night.*

Contents

IV. Reaching—The Acquisition of Maximum Speed

V. Running—The Search for Clear Air

VI. Finishing—The Resolution of the Contest

VII. Synthesis—The Organization of a Plan for Victory

Foreword

This is a collection of anecdotes derived from my own experiences in sailing International 14's during the last few years. Many were published in *One-Design Yachtsman Magazine* but have been modified and extended for inclusion here. Each chapter is based upon a particular experience or group of related experiences and constitutes an analysis of the causative factors determining a situation as well as the techniques appropriate to its successful solution. As each representation is specifically related to a specific set of circumstances, universality of application is not to be expected. Clarifying discussion and classification is included, however, to demonstrate the relation of a particular circumstance to the general problems expected in small-boat racing. Understanding derived from racing in the open sea, in harbors, rivers, and lakes, in strong winds and light, in smooth water and rough, and in various current conditions in the United States, Canada, Bermuda, and England permit a relatively complete coverage of every sailor's common experiences.

It is presumed that the reader to whom these stories are told is interested in developing an improved understanding of small-boat racing, of his own behavior, and of the likely behavior of his competitors. It is presumed that he wants to win, wants to assure himself and his competitors that he is one of them, equaling or bettering their skills and so worthy of their respect. He must then learn the art of maneuvering one boat in relation to other boats so as to complete the course in the lead. This necessitates strategic utilization of the fastest possible course and manipulation of interboat relationships to emerge victorious. No two racing situations are ever identical, and thus no manual of general principles can be of much value to a skipper. Only experience can indicate which of the many considerations applicable at a given racing moment is the determinant of success. The anecdotes included herein should provide additional experience and when personally applied can be incorporated into an individual's own repertoire.

The book as a compilation of experience is meant to be instructive. As a teacher (of pediatric medicine) I recognize that information is of little value; understanding is needed. Understanding is dependent upon the application of information to a testing situation, remembered or to be expected. It is hoped that the reader will recall situations similar to those recounted in this book and project himself into similar ones yet to come. Only an experienced sailor will synthesize understanding into a functioning ability to modify his behavior in future unfamiliar situations. But every sailor will find familiar experiences that, added to his own, will enhance his understanding and utilization of appropriate techniques. Perhaps he will return from a race with a half-recognized explanation of the outcome in mind, turn to a chapter in this book with his feet up in the evening, and reach an understanding of future benefit. A spoonful of stimulus to learning is more effective than a platterful of fact. There is no intention here to present all that could be said or all that is known concerning the tactics of small-boat racing. No apology is made for the obvious repetition; there are but a few major principles that underly all racing solutions. It will be enough if these chapters stimulate a more thorough evaluation of another race on another day, which may then be extended into an understanding beyond any presented herein.

The format was chosen to be entertaining as well as instructive, however, and it is hoped that the reader will find pleasure in it. Racing a small boat and developing a standard of excellence determined by one's competitors is a means of finding oneself. This development brings a satisfaction like few others. The people who compete and the boats they sail transport us into a simple world where absolutes exist, where all is possible, where hopes of yesterday and today can become realities tomorrow. Small-boat racing is what we make of it. Although dependent upon what we bring to it, it seems often to transcend our workaday defects and limitations and displays us bigger than life. The danger is not in losing or failing to fulfill our expectations but in no longer caring whether we win or lose. For this stimulation we depend upon our competitors— and their standards. Here, then, to my competitors—may they read and enjoy this and continue to beat me!

Acknowledgments

I would like particularly to express my appreciation to Mrs. Edwin Lowe for her faithful and unflagging efforts to type and retype the manuscript. I would also like to thank Dr. Nathan Schnaper for his assistance in analyzing the psychological implications of personal behavior in sailboat racing.

THE TACTICS OF SMALL BOAT RACING

I. *General Principles —*

The Nature of Small Boat Racing

A. The Essentials

*"The man who takes the trouble to inspect the course
. . . the day before has a tremendous advantage. If he adds
to this knowledge of what the wind is likely to be doing
at the time the race will be run—he's half-way there. In fact
I'm inclined to agree with those who say that two-thirds
of the work of winning a race is done before going afloat."*
—STEWART MORRIS

Although this is intended to be a book on racing tactics, it seems reasonable at the start to place tactics in proper perspective. Despite intense interest in discussions of tactics, rarely do tactical decisions alone determine the winning of races. Success in racing is not merely consequent to knowing the right thing to do (or we'd all be winners). It is a matter of knowing *which* right thing to do. Factors relating to boat handling, boat speed, and strategy outweigh tactical considerations in many circumstances.

The ultimate basis of success in racing is the skipper's decisive command of *himself, his boat,* and *the situation.* Self-control depends upon psychological maturity that permits conscious management of activity in accordance with conscious intent, unimpeded by unconscious needs; the effectiveness of self-control is not subject to significant modification by study and thus must be accepted in whatever state it exists. Command of the boat depends upon the experience, familiarity, and development of the boat and its crew to become extensions of the skipper's intentions. Facility is required only through practice and application of learned techniques in all possible weather and race conditions. It is obvious that the same crew should be continuously and regularly involved in the same practice and application. Command of the situation is the one element of the three that is subject to instruction and that is enhanced by continued efforts to understand its determinants. When competition occurs between skippers whose control of themselves and their boats is appropriate and effective, *the outcome will depend upon the ability of each skipper to evaluate the racing situation, to plan the most logical management of the situation, and to conduct the race in a manner consistent with that initial evaluation and plan, modified as indicated by subsequent evaluation during its conduct.*

The evaluation, the plan, the conduct, and the successful outcome of a race are dependent upon the following factors, which are always operative and must all be continually considered. The perfection of helmsmanship lies in the acquisition of understanding as to the relative significance of each of these factors in the racing situation of the moment and the management of the situation in accordance with the statistical likelihood of that significance as indicated by training and experience. In order of importance in most conditions the factors to be considered are:

1. *Strategy*

   Selection of the fastest course—often but not necessarily the shortest course—chiefly dependent upon wind, current, and sea conditions

2. *Tactics*

   a) Acquisition of the optimal position relative to competitors at the critical points of the race—at the start, turning marks, and finish

   b) Conservation of standing by maintenance of position relative to the majority or the most significant competitors of the fleet

   c) Avoidance of interference with clear air

   d) Control of competitors by interference with their air

3. *Boat speed*

   a) Development of the inherent speed of the boat

   i) Establishment of balance

   ii) Creation of maximal forward thrust from sail construction and trim

   iii) Reduction of wind wave, and water resistance

   b) Development of boat-handling ability, particularly the development of ability in sailing to windward and planing

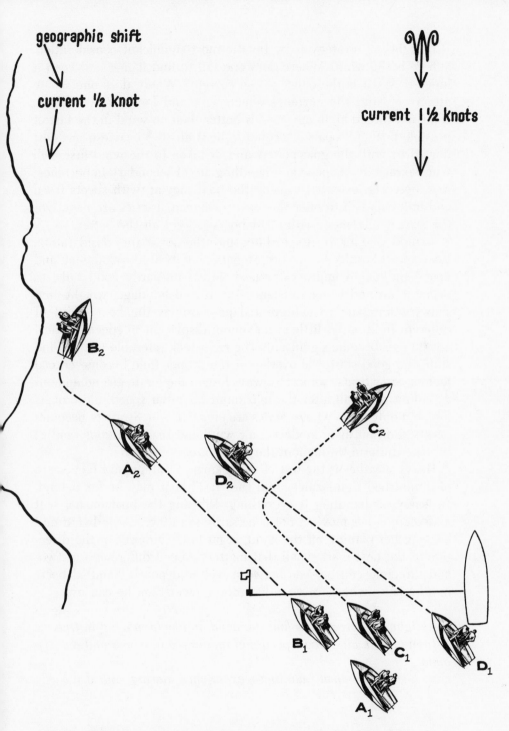

geographic shift

current ½ knot

current 1½ knots

B_2

A_2

C_2

D_2

B_1

C_1

D_1

A_1

To win, **A** must acquire the strategic advantage of the diminished adverse current and the beneficial wind shift to port—even at the expense of a prolonged exposure to the backwind of **B** and **C**.

In light air, strategy is by far the most significant consideration. Where is the wind? Where does one sail to find it first and keep it longest? What is the effect of the current? Where does one sail to attain or avoid the current's effects first and longest? Any wind, from any direction, in any boat is better than no wind in the fastest possible boat. All boats are equal in light air; the heaviest, mossiest dogs drift with the gold platers and, if taken to the wind first, will win the race. Boat speed and handling are of secondary importance; it is, however, essential to keep the boat moving with sheets freed and hull trimmed to offer the least resistance. Tactics are negative: the least involvement with other boats in light air the better.

In moderate air, boat speed becomes the dominant consideration. Boat speed results from a combination of boat development and boat handling to improve forward thrust—primarily good sails; to decrease air and water resistance—decreased windage, weight, and skin friction; and to achieve balance. But as the boat speed of different hulls varies little at maximum displacement speed, tactical advantages become significant. The right tack referable to the wind shift, the good start, the overlap at the proper time become crucial factors. Slow boats (almost) always lose in moderate air; no amount of sailing skill will alter the maximum potential speed. Slow boats lose, but only boats whose tactics are effective win. Strategy becomes least significant as in moderate air wind and sea conditions tend to become uniform throughout the racing area.

Heavy weather is the test of the seaman. Strategy and tactics are of diminished significance. And the "fast" boat may be far behind. In heavy air handling is everything. Keeping the boat on her feet and keeping her moving, not necessarily pointing, to windward and keeping her planing off the wind, regardless (almost) of the direction of the next mark, is all that matters. Speed differences of two- and threefold can be seen between well and poorly handled boats in a breeze—when everyone has more power then he can use.

In light air—strategy—find the wind and keep moving in free air
In moderate air—boat speed and tactics—a fast boat and a sharp mind
In heavy air—boat handling—experience, daring, and drive

B. Handling the Boat

"She had been built for this, my dream ship: to carry sail and to drive hard, to go anywhere in safety and in comfort."

—CARLTON MITCHELL

Tactics are the techniques utilized in dealing with competitors in a race and are thus superimposed upon the basic intent to sail the shortest and fastest possible course. Tactics may thus be considered to be either offensive or defensive, depending upon the intent and/or effect of the action upon the competitor. More appropriately, tactics can be considered to be either controlling techniques or breakaway techniques. Most deliberate tactical maneuvers are breakaway techniques designed to permit one boat to pass or separate from the injurious effects of a neighboring boat. Control techniques are not commonly utilized except as partial covering tactics that insure that competitors do not obtain different or separate strategic advantages. Integral to all tactics and particularly to breakaway maneuvers are boat-handling techniques. Immediate course alterations may be required to take advantage of a tactical opportunity, and the earliest possible application of a breakaway maneuver may be essential to prevent a major loss. Most essential to all tactical maneuvering is certainty; the results of a tack to cover, a port crossing, a luff, or a weather-quarter control position must be accurately predictable.

7

Boat-handling techniques that must be perfected to insure tactical success include slowing procedures, tacking, luffing, bearing away, and jibing. Without effective handling, tactical control is impossible and breakaway maneuvers involve the danger of disqualification. Each skipper must learn the capabilities of his own boat. He should practice sufficiently, preferably under simulated (or actual) racing conditions, so that tactical maneuvers can be accomplished automatically in a regularly reproducible manner. The tack out of the coffin corner across the bows of the entire fleet must be accomplished with the same ease and aplomb with which it is accomplished in the open sea with no competitors in sight. The essential ingredient of good boat handling is a good crew, the same crew, the same determined and enthusiastic crew. Without this ingredient the tactics discussed herein are better disregarded.

Control of speed, *i.e.* chiefly the ability to slow up, is essential to starting technique and to control maneuvers when crossing near the weather mark and in manipulating the overlap at the leeward mark. Now that Manfred Curry's water brake is illegal, slowing must be accomplished by sail manipulation. The headsail is the major determinant of speed so that collapsing the spinnaker or easing the jib is the most effective slowing technique and can usually be achieved without significant effect upon course deviation. Backing the jib before the start can produce marked slowing without the loss of steering control that would occur if a similar degree of slowing were attempted by luffing. The backed jib permits slowing on a close-hauled course with a full main, a position from which forward movement can readily be reinitiated without flailing about with the rudder and bearing away to interfere with boats to leeward. Luffing the main by easing the boom is dangerous because a boat acquiring right of way by overtaking to leeward may run into the outstretched main before it can be retrieved. Excessive trimming of the main or raising the centerboard (as well as backing the jib) result in slowing by converting aerodynamic force entirely to side force at the expense of marked leeway; a fine solution if leeway is desired. Determine a safe and effective slowing technique, perfect it, and insure that you retain steering control with it; there is no worse disaster than to be floundering on the starting line in stays as the fleet disappears over the line.

Presumably a boat is sailed at the highest possible speed continuously. However, total effort cannot be expended throughout an entire race if any strength is to be retained for crucial opportunities; it should be possible to develop just a fraction more speed on the

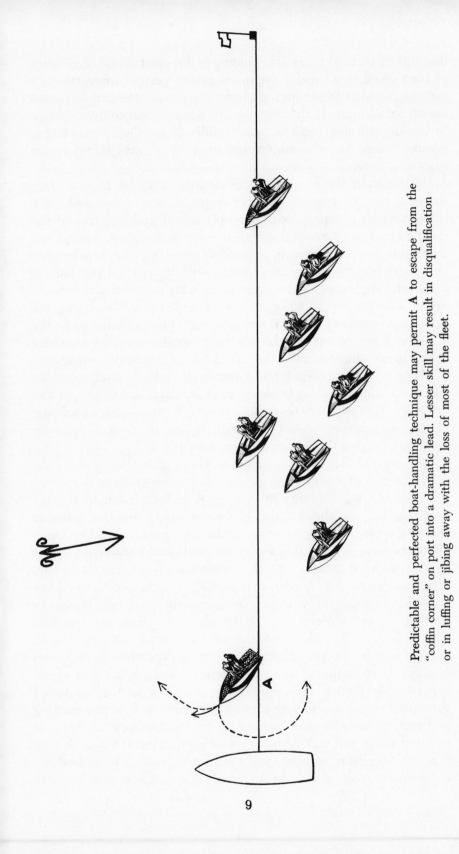

Predictable and perfected boat-handling technique may permit A to escape from the "coffin corner" on port into a dramatic lead. Lesser skill may result in disqualification or in luffing or jibing away with the loss of most of the fleet.

9

demand of tactical necessity. Hiking is the chief modifying factor of boat speed in a breeze; improved hiking permits more effective sail trim without luffing and so allows the development of increased aerodynamic force. It also decreases forward resistance by reduction in heeling, turning moment, and rudder drag, thus permitting a greater dissipation of aerodynamic force in forward thrust rather than in side force.

Utilization of the forward water movement on the face of large waves is the other major additive factor in boat speed and wave riding may be superimposed upon optimal sail and hull trim at the crucial moment of establishing an overlap or finishing. Abrupt sail trim, pumping the mainsail, or sudden trimming of spinnaker guy and sheet simultaneously may permit surfing on the front face of an overtaking wave. Rocking the boat, which utilizes the forward vector inherent in the aerodynamic force produced by arcing the fully eased mainsail across the sky, is, with pumping, illegal in the absence of waves, but may be effectively used to produce a sudden speed burst which permits the utilization of the wave movement.

Jibing may also be useful as a source of sudden, brief speed increase. Continuous jibing becomes an abnormal means of propulsion, but a jibe that is otherwise indicated may, by the sudden trimming of the main acting against the resisting air, produce a perfectly legal surge across the line or into an overlap.

Reduction in the time involved in tacking can materially affect the total duration of the race. Even more important to tactical success, however, is reproducibility in tacking. A realistic estimate of one's boat-handling capabilities should be acquired, and this estimate must be applied with great care to planning tactical tacking. One's ability to tack, develop full way again, and clear a starboard tacker in the windward-quarter control position must be accurately known. Needless extension of a pinned relationship because of uncertainty concerning the ability to clear may forfeit the race; recklessness in tacking without the certainty of the ability to clear may result in disqualification. The determination of the control technique to be applied in a windward-crossing situation is dependent as much on boat-handling ability as upon the tactical need. When well ahead it is possible to chose between tacking ahead or dead to windward for partial cover; when close aboard the choice is between crossing and tacking close abeam, tacking on the competitor's lee bow, or crossing astern and tacking on her weather quarter. If a precise tack is not accomplished not only will the control position be missed but a controlled position may be acquired. When the lee-bow position

10

is sought a sloppy tack may result in a blanketed lee-quarter position!

Bearing away and luffing are simple steering techniques, but they must be applied in a manner that provides maximum effectiveness. Bearing away is resisted by a lowered centerboard, so the centerboard should be raised as the maneuver is initiated. This technique is particularly important in breaking away from the weather-mark turn. The boat with the board coming up may shoot off to leeward, free of interference, while her competitors brake to a wallowing halt with rudders hard over and boards full down.

The use of luffing as a control technique or a breakaway technique necessitates accurate timing. The pass-to-windward maneuver must be accomplished with a puff from a position on the leading boat's leeward quarter, suddenly, up, across, and away. The control luff by the leading boat must be applied with equal accuracy and initiated at the moment that will permit side to side contact, forward of mast abeam, at a 45° angle to the initial course. Again practice is essential as little variation is possible, and downwind the odds are all in favor of the overtaking boat's escape. To windward, luffing is more successful as the course of the following boat is limited by her inability to deviate significantly to windward without marked slowing. The sharp luff is most effectively used to breakaway from a position in which one is pinned by a weather-quarter boat. A slow-up together with a pinch to windward brings the controlling boat within range. A sharp luff may then stop her head to wind or force her about and thus provide the freedom desired. A major limitation on the effectiveness of the sharp luff is heeling. Heeling, particularly to windward at the close of the luff, decreases lateral resistance, increases leeway, and permits the windward boat to escape.

All tactical maneuvers require precise boat-handling techniques. The techniques must be perfected by constant practice with a dependable crew until they are regularly reproducible. Tactical maneuvers provide one of the major opportunities for the demonstration of true seamanship in modern racing.

Effective boat handling is essential to the utilization of tactical control and breakaway techniques.

C. The Psychology of Winning

"No quarter is asked or given. Dinghies are prepared
and raced with meticulous attention to detail. This may not be
the way that everyone wants to sail, but unquestionably it
is the way to win races. There is no better school—and there
is always so much more to learn."

—IAN PROCTOR

It might be said that the prerequisite of winning is the avoidance
of the psychology of losing. Or that the prerequisite is the intention
of winning! A thorough evaluation of one's intentions in advance
and repeated evaluation during the course of the race must combat
any tendency to accept less than victory. In close quarters no emo-
tion should be recognized other than that of the pressure to win.
There should be no compromise with the seeking of the best start,
the best strategy, the best tactical position. Although victory may
not result from its desire, loss will certainly result from any intent
less than aggressive, less than certain.

The offensive role is appropriate at all times during a single race
event but must be tempered in series sailing. In the latter ultimate
victory may require defensive behavior and may more certainly be
achieved by a reduction in the risks inherent in an aggressive offense.
All racing technique is dependent upon continuous estimation of the
risks inherent in action and in inaction; the risks change in series
competition so that the dangers of seeking first may exceed the advantages of reaching first. Defensive techniques are not designed to

substitute for victory but to insure victory, or the maximum score possible, once the best possible position has been achieved. After the start, or after the weather leg when the lead is obtained, or after a position adequate to your requirements (or sufficiently beyond your expectations!) is achieved, the odds may dictate conservation of position. The utilization of defensive tactics should be correlated with the ability of the boat and crew; in conditions or at sailing angles where the capacity for performance is reduced, defensive techniques are reasonable, while on legs and in circumstances of enhanced capacity for performance offensive effort should capitalize upon inherent advantages.

A realistic interpretation of the state of the race is essential to a winning psychology. When the boat seems to be going well and is

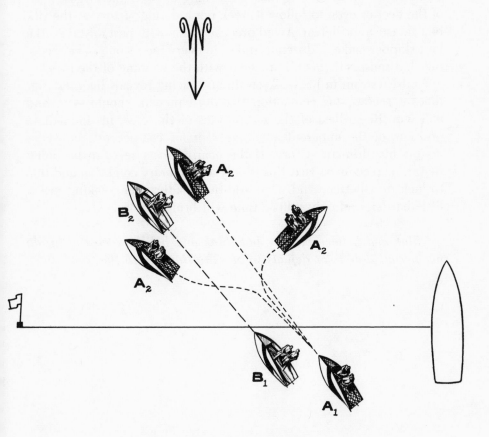

The winning skipper's confidence and determination lead the back-winded boat to a successful attack to windward instead of a surrender to the opposite tack or to leeward.

beating nearby competitors, press on, ignore them; these conditions may not persist; take full advantage of them. If other boats are beating you, dispel the consequent anxiety, analyze the situation carefully, and make the modifications in sail trim or tactics that seem indicated. Determine degree of performance that can be expected from you and from your boat in various circumstances; make such additional efforts and adjustments as are necessary to achieve the standard of performance to be expected, but recognize that you can be beaten. An unwillingness to admit the possibility of defeat, an excessive concern for a perceived reputation in a fixed "pecking order," interferes with a realistic evaluation of one's condition—and effective control over it.

Be willing to admit your errors; tack back as soon as it is evident that you are on the wrong tack. Be willing to cover the largest mass of the fleet or even to follow it; seek not a daring victory at the risk of a catastrophic defeat. Avoid preoccupation with past mistakes; the best skipper makes a dozen mistakes in every race—but, once recognized, dismisses them and proceeds with the winning of the race.

Paul Elvstrom in his book on dinghy racing reveals his most significant secret—his conviction that he can win, should win, and will win. Regardless of the vicissitudes of the race, his immediate position, or the apparent advantages of his competitors, he never doubts his ultimate victory. If the nearby boats seem to be doing better, he recognizes that this is only a temporary condition and due to luck or a better wind. One additional adjustment, hiking just a little harder, and only a little time will bring victory!

Think and believe victory, but think and believe realistically; do not permit doubts or denials to obscure the way to the win.

D. The Psychology of Losing

"Disaster in life is not the consequence of losing but in no longer feeling that winning is worth while, not the consequence of the failure of others to think your accomplishments worthy of approval, but in no longer rejoicing in your accomplishments."
—CHARLIE BROWN

Small-sailboat racing provides a remarkable demonstration of psychology in action—a condition of interest to the psychologist and of great significance to the racing sailor. The skipper's control of his boat, restricted only by the distant authority of the racing and international right-of-way rules, permits maximum opportunity for the intervention of emotional interests. The rapid decisions that are often required in racing afford little time for considered judgment; action is frequently instinctive rather than intellectually determined. Much of tactics, and even strategy, is responsive behavior consequent to the perceived action of competitors and is thus determined as much by emotional reaction to opposing skippers as by the tactical effect of their boats.

Each skipper comes to the race with his own personality, his own character, which is derived largely from his previous experiences and the emotions associated with those experiences. These remembrances are stored in the unconscious where there is little regard for

The skipper who sails off alone on a long tack cannot be beaten. He beats himself, thereby retaining some vestige of power and self-esteem, which he is reluctant to risk in close combat.

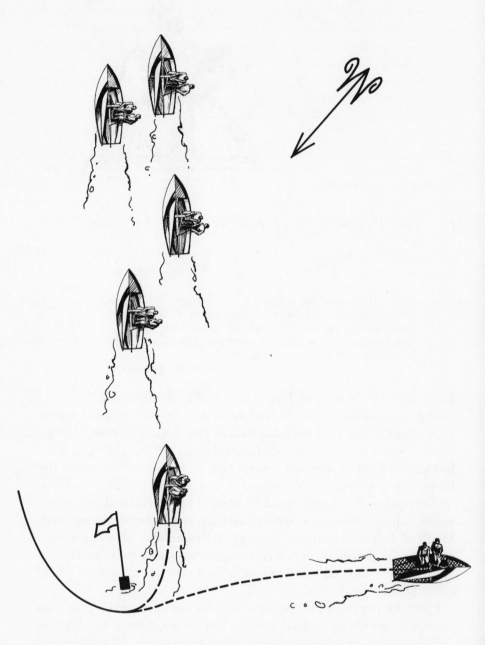

reality, where there is condoning of simultaneous contrary wishes, and a complete repression or disguise of painful or shameful experiences. The energy attached to these irrational memories, however, determines behavior and may arbitrarily compel the individual to react in current situations in a repetitious and irrational way. The skipper may behave in a stereotyped manner whenever the race presents a situation symbolic of a remembered one that was emotionally significant in the past. Consequent to a compulsion of which he is completely unaware, he may behave in a manner completely inconsistent with his conscious intentions. Such behavior patterns can be detected in all individuals to varying degrees; when major elements of behavior are influenced by them, irrational actions directly contrary to apparent intentions may appear.

Racing is always an interpersonal relationship between competing skippers and, depending upon the development of their competitive behavior, may establish a hostile state between them. The sport thus becomes a test of the maturity and stability of interpersonal relationships as well as a test of sailing skill. Those who have had difficulty in competitive interpersonal relationships in the past will probably continue to do so in racing; as racing tends to impair the control of responsive unconscious feelings, any such difficulties may well be exacerbated. In addition to revealing unconscious determinants of behavior, racing is seriously affected by them. In general, a lessened ability to control personal behavior, and thus the boat, by reasoned judgment results in reduced effectiveness, tactical errors, and strategic failures.

In some instances reactions to the competitive situation result in a defiant behavior that expresses fundamental resentment. In other instances, hostility perceived in the race may cause the sailor such concern as to require escape and the avoidance of all close conflicts. At times psychological factors of which the skipper is unaware control him and cause him to lose the race deliberately. We devote much time and thought to our professed intent to win; perhaps we should first consider whether the profession is always valid. It seems likely that many sailors have no intention of winning and in fact have every intention of losing!

Unconscious psychologic factors of which the individual is unaware may substitute decisions and responses determined by unconscious needs for the judgment and action required to sail the race effectively. Such behavior is not unusual; the skilled observer may detect it and detect its influence in almost every race of the season. We have but to look to see, for this substitute behavior is

17

most evident in the very highly competitive skippers, those most likely to win. Indeed, the driving force, the need for victory characteristic of the champions, is often a component of an excessive concern with losing and, at times, a need to lose.

Consider the possibility that losing may be deliberate.

E. Fight or Flee

"Ready about—unzip—ease luff—up plate—shorten traveler—tighten foot—would you please pass the tranquilizers! The tourniquet is not quite tight enough—I am still losing rather a lot of blood. You will find the telephone number of my psychiatrist pencilled on the back of the sailing instructions."

—K. HUMPHREY SHAKEWELL

Have you noticed the skipper, beaten in the preceding race, who dares the port tack start in the next or who, far behind following a wind shift on the first leg, tacks immediately ahead of an approaching starboard tacker at the mark? Or have you observed a skipper who, dropping to last in a team race, planes in to an overlap at the final mark as the leading boat is rounding, forcing his way ahead of his only remaining opponent? In the final race of the 1958 International 14 National Regatta one skipper barged into a two-foot space between the windward starting-line buoy and the boat to leeward, in an obvious, "You can't block me!" gesture. A friend commented later that his intention was obvious 50 feet away and that there was no possibility of his getting away with it. Often stimulated by a prior defeat or a publicly evident error, defiance may be an unconscious response to a perceived threat to personal superiority. As in the cases cited, it substitutes blind instinct for reasoned judgment and usually results in disqualification rather than victory.

19

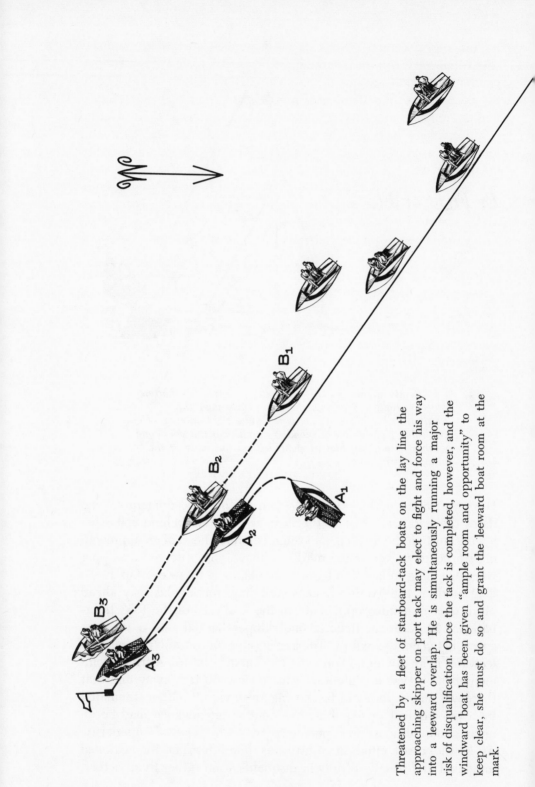

Threatened by a fleet of starboard-tack boats on the lay line the approaching skipper on port tack may elect to fight and force his way into a leeward overlap. He is simultaneously running a major risk of disqualification. Once the tack is completed, however, and the windward boat has been given "ample room and opportunity" to keep clear, she must do so and grant the leeward boat room at the mark.

This angry, defiant pattern is often evident in luffing matches, surely one of the most unprofitable defensive techniques ever invented. Yet again and again one skipper luffs another boat far off the course in a vain demonstration of "You can't pass me!" while half the remainder of the fleet slips by to leeward. To prove the harm of such defiant behavior the occasional exception must be noted: for instance, the meek skipper, who, sufficiently angered, sails far beyond his usual abilities. One of our less avid sailors once objected vehemently to conducting a race in the extreme weather conditions of the day and then, forced to compete, trounced the tormenting expert who had arranged the race!

A more common but less obvious technique for dealing with the hostility perceived in the race is demonstrated by the avoidance of close contacts with competitors. Many losers demonstrate this behavior pattern in their starting technique. They make no attempt to dispute the ideal starting position, avoid all conflict with the experts, and deliberately start well down the line or well behind. If ignorance were the cause of this behavior such skippers would occasionally make good starts by accident; in fact, they never do. Even a usually aggressive sailor may at times demonstrate a need to avoid the fray; one of our better Annapolis 14 sailors capsized in the first race of a winter regatta and then, apparently embarrassed and feeling some need to punish himself for this error, managed to be three minutes late for the second start.

However, it is just after the start that behavior becomes critical and when the outcome of the race is often determined. When a boat to leeward can barely maintain clear air as one to windward drives off on her, the psychological responses of the skippers are often more significant determinants of the outcome than the inherent speed of the boats. Will the leeward boat's skipper give a sharp luff before it's too late, or hike the harder, or just give in and let the weather boat roar over him? Will the windward boat's skipper, in fear of that luff, break away and drop back or drive on relentlessly or tune himself and his boat to that perfection which will eventually, if not immediately, permit him to draw ahead? The typical solution is all or none; one of the two skippers wants no part of this conflict, gives in, and lets the other boat go on—usually to final victory!

Many sailors characteristically take the long chances, split markedly with the mass of the fleet, and win grandly or lose disastrously. These are often the same sailors who keep clear of the melee at the start and once out on the course avoid all close contacts. After a short, port tack from the start, the wind shifts their way. Do they tack to cover, consolidating what they've got? No! This would mean going back into conflict, testing who had the faster boat, who was the better sailor, who the better man. It is psychologically safer to continue on port tack, pleased with the initial conquest, believing in some mysterious additional header which will never appear. Being able to state reassuringly later, "If the further header had only appeared . . .," they need not consider that they were beaten (or could have been beaten), only that the wind didn't come their way.

Deliberate violation of the principles attending covering is another technique that demonstrates fear of conflict and may spell defeat. This is particularly evident when boats are beating in winds of simultaneously differing direction. Rarely does the skipper of the boat ahead and to leeward tack back to cover when her followers are lifting out across her stern nor does he tack when boats on the opposite tack on the other side of the course are being headed. To tack in these circumstances is an admission that they were right and he was wrong, an admission that they evaluated the shifts correctly and that he did not. Unable to reveal to himself that he is less than omniscient, but vaguely perceiving his weakness, the leader becomes even more anxious about the hostile relationship with his competitors and throws away the race, blaming it all on "the winds."

The fundamental principles of avoidance seem to be: take no chances of revealing inferiority by direct conflicts, avoid any admission of fallibility, and tack away or bear away so that the wind, not the competitors, can always be blamed for defeat. This is perhaps most classically demonstrated by the boat on the wrong tack. It may be obvious to everyone else in the fleet that the tack is wrong, but one skipper on that tack sails on and on and on (probably particularly if it is obvious to every one else!). Unable to tack back and thereby admit that he was on the wrong tack, he sails farther and farther down the drain.

It is evident that a good sailor must control rather than be controlled by his psyche, but the hallmark of greatness is the ability to recognize an error as soon as (or sooner than?) anyone else, to be willing to publicly admit the error, and to rectify it immediately after its recognition.

F. Deliberate Defeat

"In the justice of the result and in the healthy life of sailors lie the benefits of yacht racing. Its infallible leveler is that quirk in human nature that makes us all want to sail by our own methods, even when these are manifestly wrong. There is something in the combination of open water, wind and sky that confirms individuality and swells each heart to its largest when it is following its own hopes."
—WILLIAM ALLEN SMITH

When a situation is perceived as too threatening to be defied or overtly avoided, some sailors demonstrate behavior that can only be considered self-destructive. Although fear of victory is usually difficult to detect it may be obvious in the capsize or disqualification of a leader far ahead in a single race. When the perception of winning reflects a remembered danger, the resultant fear may require suicide rather than continuance. Unconscious concerns of which the individual is completely unaware, which he may well completely deny, and which he may be making every effort to control, may be in complete control of him. The apparent fear of being defeated that shatters the skipper's confidence as he sees the fleet inexorably gaining towards the finish may be a disguise for a greater fear, that of winning—and may only be relieved by losing. The rattled nerves that interfere with proper hull and sail trim and produce a major error in the finish-line approach may be serving a determined cause—purposely to produce defeat.

This behavior pattern may be another way of establishing an alibi, "You can't beat me. I beat myself!" In this respect, it may represent a last-ditch effort to control a situation that is becoming uncontrollable—to command and destroy the one thing remaining under control, oneself. After two-thirds of a long race in Annapolis, I planed past the visiting Canadian champion, who had led until this time, and discovered that once I'd passed him, he gave up completely. Unwilling to admit to himself that he was beaten, he sought to defeat himself and to assign the responsibility for defeat to himself—not to me. He had effectively removed any opportunity to be beaten.

On Barnegat Bay when leading the series by a large margin and far ahead in its final race, one of our 14 sailors hit a turning mark, a yellow buoy, almost head on. He pointed out the yellow streak on his topsides for a long time thereafter as a lesson learned. Inasmuch as he has given evidence since of not having learned the lesson, I wonder if he knew then that he was compelled to lose—or that he feared to win. There are many who in sailing (and elsewhere) are reminded of symbolic conflicts with "father" or "brother" and who, in an impasse between a stimulated desire to defeat him and a guilty concern that they might, alternate between pressing on to victory and deliberate self-destruction.

The intention to fail is continuously evident in the skipper who never takes care of his boat or equipment and who acquires his crew on the beach at the last minute, but more often the intention to fail appears periodically and, at times, recurrently when one minor (or major victory) or the sudden awareness of a leading position stimulates the concern that requires a subsequent dramatic defeat. A common illustration of this intention to fail is a willingness to "take turns"; "I won last time, now I'll let you win." The "I'll let you win" preserves a fancied omnipotence while simultaneously avoiding responsibility for conquest. In the 1963 Annapolis Yacht Club Regatta, after the top contender was disqualified in the first race, the series leader, reluctant to accept the easy victory, withdrew readily (in relief?) from the final race consequent to an extremely questionable, but potentially disqualifying, incident. Often a protest against an obvious violation, verbal or formal, is omitted by a series leader, as, already excessively anxious about his conquering state, he wishes to avoid any further appearance of aggression or of victory. These problems are usually more prevalent in the home fleet, when close friends are dealing with one another, as awareness of the personal relationships cannot be avoided. Here, giving the other fellows

24

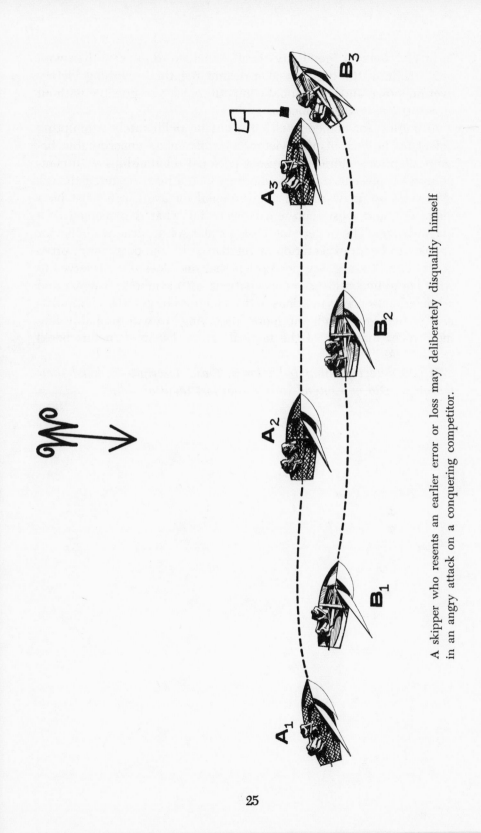

A skipper who resents an earlier error or loss may deliberately disqualify himself in an angry attack on a conquering competitor.

"a break," being a "good guy" is often perceived as safer than winning, while in the big fleet at a distant regatta, a slashing victory over unknown and impersonal competitors may be possible without arousing any evident concern.

Arranging for someone else to win or deliberately attempting defeat in the face of near victory (victory made unacceptable because of prior victories or present personal relationships with competitors) represents a fear of winning. Such a fear, disguised though it may be by unawareness, anger, denial, or avoidance must be a major one and must represent concern for what is perceived as a major danger. The underlying basis for this self-destructive behavior appears to be an expectation of retaliation by the conquered, often accentuated by a guilty perception that one does not "deserve" to win. These unconscious preoccupations with symbolic dangers and semiconscious preoccupations with reductions of guilt by manipulating "justice," to permit the more "deserving" to win, probably lose more races than any of the tactical errors discussed in this book!

If you detect familiar behavior in these descriptions, heed their warnings. Did you intend to lose that last regatta?

G. "Oh Captain, My Captain"

*"I had taken little advice from any one, for I had a right
to my own opinions in matters pertaining to the sea."*
—JOSHUA SLOCUM

Skippers live in the hope of sailing a perfect race—a race without
a single error. Only those with little perception have thought that
they achieved this goal; but only those with perception sufficient to
detect their mistakes will ever do well enough to approach it. It
seems possible—at least as possible as winning a six-horse parlay at
Caliente (more likely in fact as the skipper is riding all six horses!).
Failing to sail to perfection is a standard occurrence and is usually
consequent to an inadequate estimate of the situation, a misjudg-
ment of the risks, or the taking of a long chance against the odds.

Planning is the most important single determinant of success in
racing. All pertinent factors must be considered at all times, in
advance of the race and continuously during its course. The wind
and current and any possible variations in their strength and direction, the effect of shore contours and water depths on wave and
wind formation, and the elements of the race organization must all
be carefully evaluated before the start. Additional knowledge gained
while sailing about in the starting area and on the course necessitates

total re-evaluation of the plans immediately prior to the start and prior to the initiation of each leg. The relative significance of all pertinent factors must be considered prior to each tack (and prior to deciding *not* to tack), in deciding whether the proper side of the course is being approached, whether to cover or retain the offensive, whether to sail high or low on the reach and at a dozen other decisive moments on each leg. The essential principle is complete consideration and consideration prior to, not subsequent to, every maneuver. The final conclusion and the decision must be the result of a calculation of the odds that indicate what action will create the least risk of loss and provide the greatest chance of gain at the moment. The odds are often long; it is essential to know them by knowing everything which affects them.

Many discussions of racing technique recommend taking the long shot when behind, disregarding the odds and risking a probable loss, for an unlikely gain. Although this may be warranted occasionally on the final leg of a single-event race, it is almost never justified in series racing and never until the final moments of the race. It is the skipper who makes the fewest mistakes who wins; let someone else make them (they always will) and stick with the percentages. Clear your wind, if necessary, but don't tack out on a one-leg beat, don't jibe away when everyone else is at hull speed, don't sail on and on when the other side of the course is obviously advantageous, don't tack out into the tide, away from the shift, into the heavier sea in some vain hope that the odds will be different for you.

Keep your mind free to analyze the situation at all times. If you are not making adequate boat speed, determine why you are not, and do something about it. If your strategy doesn't seem to be producing the expected results, reconsider it completely; don't discard it at the slightest loss, but be willing to do so if a new factor appears or is belatedly recognized. Don't allow yourself to become preoccupied with concern over a previous mistake; disregard it, start thinking afresh, and make the best of the position that remains. Expect to make a significant number of mistakes. No race is entirely predictable. (How little fun racing would be if races were predictable!) The effective skipper takes his errors and his losses in stride and does not burden himself with concern over them.

Brainwork wins races—not luck and rarely muscular ability. Planning, calculating, and re-evaluating are the determinants of the results. The tighter the situation, the more desperate the conditions, the more confused the tactical problem, the more significant is this careful consideration. Racing is a matter of command and is deter-

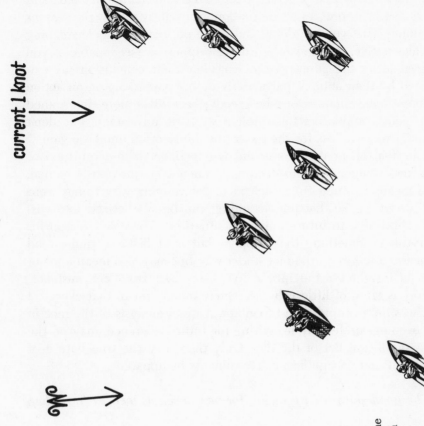

current 1 knot

current 1½ knots

The skipper who is in command of himself and the situation will resist the temptation to tack out of the disturbed air of the fleet and away from an exhibition of impaired performance because he recognizes the greater advantages of lessened adverse current to starboard. Let the opposition make the mistakes!

mined by the skipper who is in command and maintains command of his boat, his crew, and the situation. Constantly review the reasons for doing what you are doing and make no move without weighing the alternative. Recognize that other skippers are as capable as you in evaluating the situation and consider their conclusions as evidenced by their actions, particularly before embarking on an action different from theirs. Don't be greedy; be a little more determined than your competitors to exploit a strategic advantage, but don't risk an excessive loss for the lesser possibility of an immense gain.

The final element of command is experience, the acquisition of new knowledge and the utilization of knowledge previously gained. This means learning from each race, determining why things went well or wrong, so that understanding can be synthesized into wisdom applicable to future unknown situations. There is a reason for everything; something that happens but is at first not understood indicates a failure in the race under way but may also mean a major gain in insight for the future. We learn best from our mistakes; victory is often of little value as it may merely mean that everyone else was more stupid than the victor. A quiet analysis of the race in the evening, preferably in writing for future reference, may be the most significant act of the day. Only then may the true nature of the event and its significant determinants be apparent.

The good skippers are racing for next week as well as for today.

H. The Perfect Race

> "The races start; persist for a course; end; then follows
> a brief period of days or weeks when they provide the
> material for what the cruising people have been known to call
> 'spinnaker-booming in the bar.' Soon that too languishes.
> The races pass into the dustbin of memories, are lost beneath
> the refuse, and are carried out by the final dust cart. They
> have become nothing—nothing at all.
>
> Races may be given if not immortality at least a decent
> lease of life in writing. Many people relive their moments of
> engrossing, and possibly even successful, activity; whilst
> others are enabled to remember during a winter's evening,
> perhaps decades later, what it meant to race a yacht on one
> far-away day."
>
> —ARGUS, *Yachting Monthly*

At the 1964 Prince of Wales Cup presentation ceremony, I said a
few words (and, given the chance, when have I not?) of thanks to
what I thought had brought about the victory—and these words
explain the results as well as any. I thanked the boys at Itchenor for
teaching me what they had about tidal currents (and I should have
thanked Tom Marston and a few others, although I rarely appeared
a particularly apt pupil at Essex). Itchenor had demonstrated again
that, although one might be able to disregard the tide when it was
favorable (sometimes), it became the paramount consideration when
it was against you—and particularly so in light or moderate air. I
thanked *Salute* for being the fastest boat to windward in the fleet—

outstandingly so in light to moderate air and as good as any in a breeze—which she had demonstrated at Itchenor and previously during P.O.W. week.

I thanked my crew for his near-perfect day and his ability to get a 10-foot jib around and drawing as fast or faster than the crews pulling 8 and 9 feet astern. I thanked my wife who had believed me when I said I was going to win that morning. She had accompanied me as I went up on the cliff to look over the water where we would race, as I purchased a new large-scale chart and a protractor to permit laying out the course after it was signaled at sea, and as I spoke to as many old-timers, fishermen, and local racing sailors as I could find to determine what the wind would do that day.

I thanked Bruce Wolfe for demonstrating that good helmsmanship does prevail and that regardless of past defeats today was a new day and all was possible. I also thanked Mike Souter for holding off Stewart Morris. This magnificent accomplishment was performed on one of Stewart's favorite legs, a spinnaker reach, and by means of a luffing match, which Stewart usually has with his morning kippers, and against the wood *Kirby II*, which seemed the fastest reaching boat then devised, and in a P.O.W. which Stewart wanted to win. I should have congratulated Mike rather than thanked him as S.H.M. was never close enough for us to read his numbers. But it was reassuring nevertheless.

The one factor I didn't mention was the wind—and this of course was the determinant of victory. For the first time during our trip to England we had wind and tide together—a beat against the tide—with a fairly steady, moderate northeasterly, ideal conditions for *Salute's* windward ability and the least helpful to her reaching rivals.

I had acquired all the available information concerning the wind, water, and current conditions, had charted the tidal stream, its direction and strength in the racing area for hourly intervals, and had encased this data plus the necessary portion of the large-scale chart in plastic. We were the first afloat, an hour and a half before the start, which gave us time to check the wind, the line and the tacks with the compass, the depth of water at crucial points along the shore, and to chart the course with a marking pencil across the plastic covered chart. The northeasterly winds on the lower forward edge of the high were expected to shift farther east, more perpendicularly to the beach, as the sun rose to the midday start. As the high moved farther in the northeasterly direction it had been traveling, the clockwise revolving winds would become more easterly to the south of its center, and the warming of the north-south coastline on this unusually bright, hot day would add a thermal sea breeze from the same direction. But there had been no change in direction whatsoever during the hour preceding the start according to our compass. We concluded that if the shift occurred it would be delayed until after the first leg was completed. The wind along the shore was at least as strong as it was offshore with no evidence of a significant loss under the cliffs. In the absence of a significant shift or a significant difference in the wind strength, the adverse tide became the dominant strategic consideration.

We elected to start at the inshore end of the line (although the offshore end was slightly farther to weather and most of the pundits were starting there to be inside with the expected shift), tested the lay line for the leeward distance marker, came across behind the committee boat on port with about 1½ minutes to go, tacked in front and to leeward of the fleet approaching down the line, and with the gun were off with clear air to leeward of everyone. *Salute* was pointing higher and with sails trimmed to perfection, was footing faster than any of her competitors. We had a satisfactory lead worked out when we hit the beach and commenced tacking up between the "groynes" (short-piling breakwaters). Except for Andy Green in *Sabre*, who clung enough to keep us pushing on every tack, we were leaving the major portion of the fleet tacking up the shore with us, and those who had elected to stay out in the tide were disappearing in the jib window.

We tacked out into the tide when we thought sufficient allowance had been made for the strong current offshore at a time when a second tack, if necessary, could be made over an offshore shoal. Observation of a range created by the mark with a distant channel buoy then revealed that we were going to lay the mark and that all our near competitors had overstood. We rounded with a two-plus-minute lead, held our position on the reaches, and, except for Stewart Morris's gain on the third windward leg when the shift finally arrived, were never vaguely threatened after that first leg. We pulled away on the other boats, averaging 3½ minutes ahead, which seemed a long way as the follower's came around the weather mark, and finished with that lead to the hoots and screams of the biggest spectator fleet I'd ever seen!

What were the ingredients of success? In this, as in all racing, they were chiefly in the preparation: preparation of the boat so that she was the fastest in the fleet for the conditions to be sailed in; preparation of the crew to insure that they would develop the full po-

The plan's the thing. Successful accomplishment of the pre-race design sometimes results in total victory.

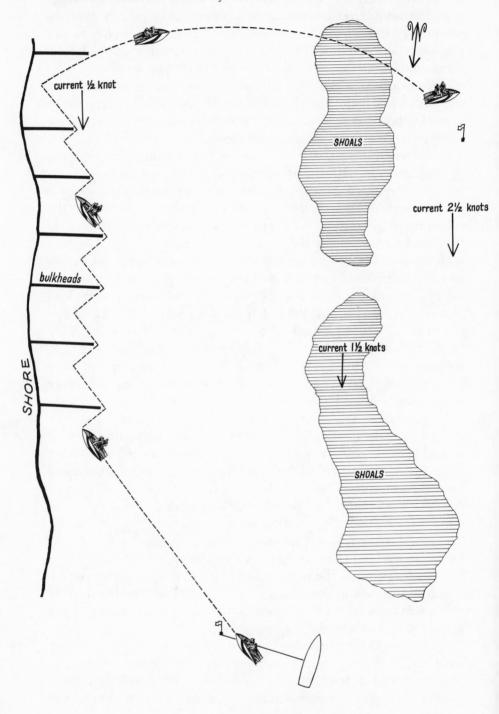

current ½ knot

current 2½ knots

bulkheads

current 1½ knots

SHORE

SHOALS

SHOALS

tential of the boat; and perhaps the most important aspect of preparation—a complete evaluation of all wind and current factors, ashore and afloat, to insure the application of the correct strategy for the racing conditions. Then the final ingredient, once prepared, was the application of appropriate tactics—the start in the right place, with the gun, with clear air, and with no competitors in a position to interfere with a realization of the desired strategy. Thereafter, conservative covering of the opposition behind and maintenance of the desired boat speed in the varying conditions insured victory.

Most significant in this race which comes as near to having been perfectly sailed as I can imagine (we did understand the weather mark on the fourth buck and had to put in an extra tack), is the psychology of the situation.

Belief in the victory not only provides the extra energy and enthusiasm that keeps the boat going at peak performance but makes reasonable the detailed preparation essential to success against top competitors.

I. Slow Up and Win

"We came across for fresh air, to enjoy the deep blue sea, to risk the hazards of a difficult race, and to have a hell of a good time; not to strive for international honors or to test the evolution of rating or yacht measurement rules."
—SHERMAN HOYT

We were pinned on the starboard tack immediately after the start of the long Severn Trophy race after making a good start with clear air at the "favored" leeward end. But to starboard of the fleet was the beneficial offshore shift and less tide. How were we to get there with several boats behind and to windward—and get there before someone else peeled off on port into the shift and a commanding lead? A jibe away is an effective solution particularly if the weather boat is close aboard and there's no one to leeward—but there was a boat to leeward. We couldn't clear the first boat to weather if we tacked, and we couldn't bear away to provide enough room to tack to go astern of her. If we gave her a sharp luff, she would still pin us down as she couldn't tack without risking interference with the boat astern of her. "We'll ease sheets, slow up on our present course, and then, as soon as the first boat goes past to weather, we'll sheet in, pick up a little speed, tack, pull up the board, and slip astern of that second boat—off and in the clear."

The surprising and frequently overlooked advantages of slowing the boat warrant thought and practice. Preoccupation with making the boat "go" prevents most of us from remembering (even after the start) that boats can be beaten and races won by reducing speed.

1. *To windward*
   a) When on port tack in heavy air, luff to slow the boat if you are even or ahead of a starboard tacker rather than bear away excessively to cross his transom far to leeward.
   b) If in a starboard tack header and pinned down by a boat or boats to weather, slow up, drop back, and tack into that lift before they do.
   c) When on port tack approaching a mark to be left to starboard, slow up to allow a starboard tacker to pass ahead (don't let him force you to tack), and bear away between him and the mark as he tacks.
   d) If on starboard tack in the same situation, slow up sufficiently to cause the port tacker to bear away so far that he can't lay the mark!
2. *Rounding marks*
   a) If on the inside approaching a mark downwind, slow up to prevent an outside boat from attempting to pass astern so as to acquire an inside overlap at the last minute.
   b) If on the outside approaching a mark downwind, slow up and luff (or jibe) across the stern of an inside boat (or boats) so as to acquire an inside overlap at the last minute. (Achieving this at the last minute will usually avoid a luffing match!) Remember that an inside overlap doesn't mean a thing if the next leg is a close reach; let the following boat have the overlap, swing wide, retain speed, and kill your opponent with backwind after the rounding!
   c) When clear ahead approaching a mark downwind and the next leg is a beat requiring an immediate tack, slow up so that at two boat's lengths from the mark the overtaking boat will be forced to establish an outside overlap, leaving you clear to tack after rounding.
   d) After a downwind start slow up and wait for a mass of boats to reach and round the first mark so as to avoid being entrapped in the mass, unable to round inside, and prevented from tacking in the clear.
3. *Downwind*
   a) When passing to windward, slow down before blanketing to insure that the blanket will be applied at the crucial time—just before the finish or just before reaching the mark—otherwise you may find yourself blanketed in turn and at the crucial time!
   b) Would it be a good idea to slow up and wait for that mass

If the port-tack boat slows sufficiently, she can slip in behind the starboard tacker who cannot tack dead ahead. If the starboard-tack boat also slows, she may force the port tacker below the mark and subsequently be free to tack ahead in the clear.

of boats that always comes down the run in a private breeze to pass the leaders on both sides? (Sometimes it is better to be behind and to let someone else do the experimenting!)

We once started downwind in a race of the Warner Trophy Series at Fenwick on the Sound and arrived at the leeward mark in a mass of multicolored nylon and mahogany. From all sides and in some instances without a clear idea of where the mark was or on which side it was to be rounded, the unprepared fleet was swept down sooner than anticipated by the strong favorable current. I noted a group of boats coming across our bow towards the wrong side of the mark; we were about to be caught in their sweep. I ordered the crew to collapse the spinnaker and then to get it down so as to slow the boat, free ourselves from the confusion and await our opportunity. Some boats were swept the wrong side and had to claw their way back uptide, and others were swept wide as they rounded. We moved from tenth to first as we sliced through a big hole inside and went on to win.

Uffa Fox describes a similar situation in the 1929 P.O.W. Conditions were ideal for his new boat *Daring*, but the race was started under spinnaker, and he feared a foul in the expected confusion at the first mark. Although *Daring* arrived at the mark sixth, Uffa luffed her head to wind until the entire fleet had rounded, cut across their sterns in free air, passed forty-odd boats on the first beat, and won the Cup going away.

Don't rush ahead blindly without considering the advantages of holding back. Slow up and win!

J. Look over Your Shoulder

"The art of racing is not in winning, but in winning so that the rest of the fleet are pleased you have won, and the only way they can be pleased is for you to have shown better helmsmanship than they and also shown perfect sportsmanship."

—UFFA FOX

In the fourth race of the 1964 Regional Regatta we were barely able to tack clear ahead of Sam Merrick as he approached the weather mark on the starboard-tack lay line. Walt Lawson, initially just to leeward of us, had to pass astern of Sam and tack. We rounded to port, bore off dead downwind, and jibed. I "urged" the crew to get the spinnaker up and drawing as soon as possible. While I sorted out the spinnaker sheets, eased the main all the way, cleared the jib sheets so the jib could be furled, and raised the board (while continuing my urging), Sam jibed astern and worked out on our weather quarter and Walt bore away wide on starboard without jibing. When the chute was up and drawing (at last!), I looked around. Sam had our wind, and Walt was scooting off to leeward. Bob Reeves was now coming up fast with a puff to windward of Sam. We wallowed. By the time I sorted things out I had lost Walt for good, had to fall astern of Sam in order to get clear air across his stern, and, while passing Sam, lost Bob.

Excessive concentration on hoisting the spinnaker, making the boat go, accomplishing a particular tactical or strategic maneuver, or beating the next boat may sacrifice the race for the pleasure (or confusion) of the moment. Racing is always a matter of coming in ahead of the others—how far ahead or how accomplished the coming in is immaterial. Thus it pays to keep an eye on the others; not only to stay ahead, but to profit by the discoveries and accomplishments of the opposition. Sometimes the boys in the other boats are pretty clever!

At the start a glance astern may often reveal the presence of a horde of windward boats that are about to produce a complete blanket or a boat rapidly overtaking to leeward that will steal the very hole you have been working towards. A look in time may permit an immediate preventive bearing away. On the beat a look behind and to weather may reveal that boats on the other tack are being headed—sailing at an angle greater than 90° to your course—or that boats on the same tack are lifting out across your quarter—sailing at an angle less than yours to your apparent wind. Either observation indicates an immediate tack, and every moment's delay may be costly. On the reach a glance astern may reveal better wind to weather (or to leeward), gains made by boats tacking downwind (or sailing the rhumb line), or boats about to take your wind (or break through to leeward). No advance planning can be completely adequate; constant readjustment in course as indicated by the evidence produced by the experimentation of others is essential.

A few other characteristic situations brought this theme to mind during recent racing. In the 1963 Mallory (I was chairman of the Race Committee) Bill Cox lost a ¼ mile lead, the fourth race, and perhaps the series by failing to look over his shoulder to note the boats working uptide and upwind behind him. He went for the finish line out from a protective shore in a dying wind across a 1.2 knot tidal current and never gained the 200 feet uptide he needed until three boats had passed him. In the third Emerson Team Match (U.S. vs. Canada) at Toronto in 1963, I went from fourth to first (and won the race) by reaching directly for the mark while the leaders mistakenly sailed off to leeward—never looking behind to note that my course was 30° above theirs. The following day in the Lipton Trophy Race I rounded the final mark, fifth, for a dead reach to the finish. As the first boat had retained her spinnaker (successfully I thought), though the others had not, I carried on with mine. John Clarke had been 300 feet astern, but one-third the way down the leg he suddenly appeared, planing past to weather— under jib! If I had only taken that "look over my shoulder" a little sooner, the spinnaker would have been long since stowed!

One should take that look astern particularly while planing. This

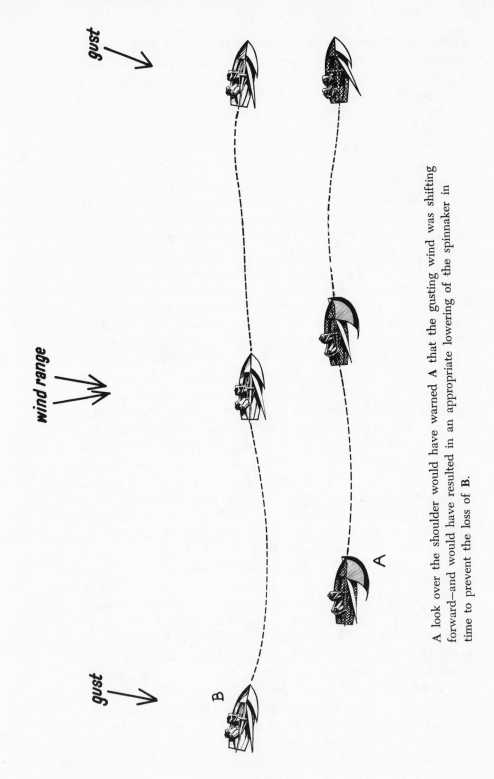

A look over the shoulder would have warned **A** that the gusting wind was shifting forward—and would have resulted in an appropriate lowering of the spinnaker in time to prevent the loss of **B**.

is the leg upon which so much distance is gained and lost; Paul Elvstrom claims that this is when distance behind is made up (when *he* gains his needed places). Sailing rapidly on the reaches is chiefly technique, and some skippers have it and others don't—but only by watching can the technique be discovered, if not for this race, at least for subsequent ones. There's something quite threatening about a boat with spray flying, booming across the waves at you. Often the instinctive response is to duck and let her roar by. But with adequate warning, a look astern in time, the puff the follower is riding can be utilized by you as well. Knowing that the puff is coming, with its opportunity for you to bear away drastically at full speed later, permits a much higher course while awaiting it. The higher course, by providing more speed, permits intercepting the attacker, driving her up into the wind or forcing her to bear away to leeward. The prolonged slowing consequent to being blanketed while planing must be avoided; passage to leeward may be tolerated but passage to windward may not. Recognition of the puff by the altered behavior of the boats astern permits the utilization of its benefits before it arrives.

Competitors are thinking and experimenting, too; utilize their discoveries as well as your own. Look over your shoulder!

K. Steering Technique

"He explained that to win this race had been almost the be-all and end-all of his life for four summers. He had been trying desperately to win and had been failing, and this tremendously heightened the triumph of victory when it came."

—RICHARD HECKSTALL-SMITH *of* PETER SCOTT

One of the most valuable racing tactics is to sail a fast boat fast. Thus, it is justifiable to discuss steering techniques that improve boat speed as an element of racing tactics. Steering is usually accomplished by manipulation of the rudder, which whenever it is turned to an angle of greater than 4° to the centerline of the boat causes more drag than lift and slows the boat. Whenever possible steering should be accomplished by other means. Familiarity with handling the boat without the use of the rudder is invaluable in racing. The techniques available include adjustment of the sails, variation in the immersion of the hull, and alteration of the position of the centerboard.

To windward the boat should be so well balanced that little or no displacement of the rudder is necessary to keep her on course. Sufficient adjustment of the sails should be achieved to provide such balance. Once well balanced by sail trim, variations in hull immersion can be utilized to steer without excessive rudder action. Heeling causes lee-bow immersion, which deflects the bow to windward; hiking causes weather-bow immersion, which deflects the bow to leeward. Crew weight shifted forward increases lateral resistance

44

forward and deflects the bow to windward (increases weather helm); crew weight shifted aft increases lateral resistance aft and deflects the bow to leeward. The major trick in sailing a small boat to windward in a breeze is to distribute crew weight and to apply hiking power so as to eliminate rudder drag. With every puff the boat tends to heel and to deviate to windward; with every let-up she tends to straighten and to deviate to leeward; with every wave she buries her bow and deviates to windward; in every trough she frees her bow and deviates to leeward. Constant adjustment of crew weight compensates for these deviations, keeps the sails consistently oriented to the wind, and maintains maximum boat speed. With crew and skipper working synchronously to adjust hull immersion with every puff and every wave, the boat races to weather undetained by rudder drag.

Off the wind, frequent variations in hull immersion for steering purposes should usually be avoided inasmuch as they are dangerous in a breeze and slowing in light air. However, on a light- to moderate-air run heeling to windward frees the weather helm consequent to the eased boom and permits desirable elevation of the sail plan. The centerboard should always be as far up as possible on a reach to avoid the drag of a weather helm, but should be lowered moderately on a run to prevent oscillation and enhance rudder steering (thereby preventing excessive drag).

To initiate and maintain planing, sail adjustment and hull immersion variation (with the centerboard well up) are essential as they provide steering control without the slowing effects of rudder drag. The boat won't plane with the centerboard down, but, without the centerboard to lever against, rudder steering results in severe drag. Hiking to produce bearing off is essential not only to the initiation of planing in a puff but to maintain planing and obviate weather deviation in each subsequent puff thereafter. Hiking and movement aft are essential to steering against the weather deviation of each wave and movement inboard and forward essential to counteract the leeward deviation of each trough. Sails should be trimmed simultaneously to aid the steering. The main may be eased as she rounds to windward and tightened as she bears away. Even more effective is the trim of the headsail, jib, or spinnaker. The danger of slowing and even a capsize can often only be avoided by the crew's control of the headsail sheet. A quick pull on the sheet will drive her head off far more effectively than a prolonged drag on the tiller.

Manipulation of the centerboard is often essential to facilitate an abrupt maneuver. By providing a major element of lateral resistance

45

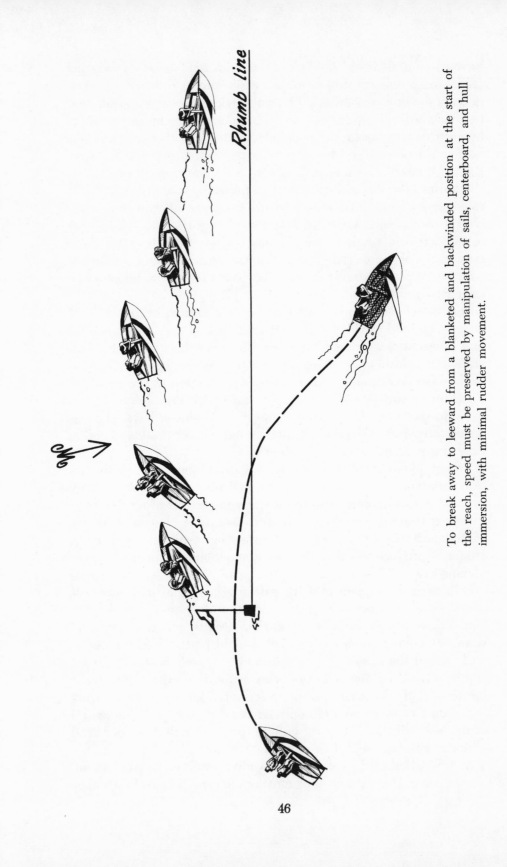

Rhumb line

To break away to leeward from a blanketed and backwinded position at the start of the reach, speed must be preserved by manipulation of sails, centerboard, and hull immersion, with minimal rudder movement.

forward of the rudder it tends to produce deviation to windward and resists an attempted deviation of the boat to leeward. When sailing to windward, the centerboard should be so positioned that it beneficially deviates the boat to windward whenever rudder pressure is eased. Its resistance to leeward deviation produces major interference with the rudder action necessary to bearing away and results in slowing of the boat and impairment of the turning maneuver. The board should always be raised to facilitate bearing away. This is essential when rounding the weather mark and when attempting to bear away from a close-hauled course to avoid the control effects of a competitor. When tacking to port, as in a breakaway after the start, it may be essential to bear away abruptly after completing the tack to pass astern of a starboard-tack competitor. This maneuver can only be successful at close quarters if the board is raised as the tack is completed. The greater the side force, as in very light and in very heavy air, the greater the resistance of the centerboard to bearing away and thus the more essential its elevation.

Tacking, particularly in light air, may be successfully accomplished by alteration in hull immersion and a consequent marked reduction in the slowing effects of rudder deviation. Allowing the boat to heel to leeward produces a deviation of the bow to windward due to the resistance to the arched, immersed bow. Thus, tacking may be achieved by the crew leaning inboard or to leeward to create heeling and by their remaining in this position until the tack is nearly completed. Once the sails fill on the new tack the boat will begin to heel in the opposite direction. The crew must then move to a position producing neutral heel and a cessation of the turn. Practice in this technique may provide a rapid, smooth tack in calm water completely unimpeded by rudder deviation.

Whenever an adjustment in course is required, remember that an alteration in sail trim, centerboard position, or hull immersion is far more effective and less slowing than a movement of the rudder.

L. Know Your Race Committee

*"There is a factor, affecting to a greater or lesser extent
the outcome of every yacht race, that is unknown to many
skippers and disregarded by most of the rest of them. This
factor is the difference between the way the participating
sailors see their race and the view taken by the race
committee. You would hardly believe they were dealing with
the same sport."*

—C. STANLEY OGILVY

Stan Ogilvy has said "expect the unexpected" and has recommended
a tour of duty aboard the committee boat for all racing sailors to
find out how race committees think. The implication is "know your
enemy," and the recommendation is to attempt to analyze in advance
how the committee will handle their problems. For their problems
are your problems, and how they administer the race may well
determine its outcome. In planning your tactics and strategy, one of
the most important considerations is whether the race committee
will behave competently or incompetently, whether they think like
racing sailors or bingo players!

The conditions and the race instructions should be thoroughly
analyzed before the race, and if any ambiguities exist, the committee
should be questioned at the skipper's meeting or before going afloat.
It is essential to understand fully how the course will be signaled,

what marks will be used, whether any similar marks exist that might be confusing, and how the course will be established. Will the marks be fixed for all races and the committee boat moved to establish a good weather leg, or will the committee boat remain fixed and the marks laid according to the wind direction? Can the committee boat or the mark-boat operator be expected to lay out a first leg with the mark dead to windward and of an adequate length as indicated in the instructions? Many such questions can only be answered by local sailors familiar with the committee personnel. Ask them!

While rigging ashore, the first question to ask is, will they start on time, as indicated in the instructions, or will they wait for a settled wind or for all the boats to reach the starting area? The excuse of missing the start because "most of the fleet were still ashore" or because the wind was insufficient to make the line in time will not influence a determined race committee. Starting tactics depend upon the length of the line and upon which end of the line is farthest upwind; if there is doubt or little time to attempt an evaluation, prior knowledge of the committee's usual habits may permit a correct decision. Particularly important is an understanding of the committee's habits regarding adjustment to wind shifts before the start. Will they postpone and reset the line; will they let the race go as is; will they sneak an adjustment of the flag mark after the ten minute gun (or maybe just "a little" easing of the committee boat anchor line!)? A carefully planned start to hit the favored end with the gun may be catastrophic if the favored end is no longer favored!

Where is the line watcher? Is he really at the white flag or does he wander about the afterdeck behind a cloud of pipe smoke? More important, how will he react to a few boats over the line—or half the fleet? A start made on time immediately to leeward of a boat a half length over the line at the gun is fine—if they call him back! If they don't intend to do so, you'd better drive along with him and have clear air to leeward when the gun goes, disregarding the line. And if it is obvious that half the fleet is swinging up across the line five seconds early, you'd better go with them—if you know the committee is reluctant to call back that many. Even if you expect a general recall, go with them, keep your wind clear, your bow even with the nearest boat to weather (don't overdo it!), and drive her until you're certain they have made the recall signal. After five general recalls at the start of the 1959 Governor's General race at Montreal, one of the seventy-seven International 14's sat out the sixth recall, luffing, 50 feet to weather of the line to await the seventh and actual start! Perhaps such confidence in the stability

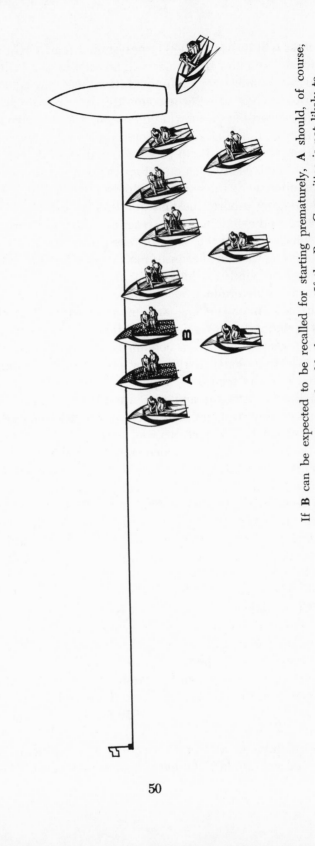

If **B** can be expected to be recalled for starting prematurely, **A** should, of course, make a proper start in her blanket zone. If the Race Committee is not likely to recall **B**, however, **A**'s only recourse is to continue along with **B**, keeping her air clear to leeward.

of the race committee's behavior is unwarranted, but it is exceedingly illustrative.

If in doubt about the position of the weather mark, prior knowledge that the managing race committee usually sets short weather legs or is never able to set the mark dead to windward may be extremely helpful. If this committee always sets a beam reach for the second leg, the spinnaker may be safely rigged for the third, while if that committee always attempts an equilateral triangle, the spinnaker will have to be suitably arranged for hoisting on either side. Most important of all is an understanding of what to expect at the finish line; if the wind dies or blows up, will they shorten the course or let the race and the time run out? If the finish is to be in the planned location, will the finish line be the starting line as initially established, will the committee boat be moved to the opposite side of the mark, will the mark be adjusted to make the line perpendicular to the last leg, or, if the final leg is to windward, will the line be established at right angles to the wind direction? Although the latter solution is recommended as the fairest solution, it is neither commendable nor fair, if the sailors do not expect it—nor (particularly) if you don't plan on it!

Although it may be impossible to obtain all these answers from the committee in advance or from "friendly" competitors, remembering to ask the questions of your crew, if no one with any knowledge is available, will at least force you to consider the various and frequently amazing solutions that the committee may attempt!

Consider the Race Committee's solution to race management problems; they may not resemble your own!

M. Slow Boat? Fast Boat?

"One of the real lessons to be learned was the need as a skipper to be able to switch to passive sailing at will; to concentrate on getting to the next mark as quickly as possible more or less regardless of one's opponent ahead."
—JOHN ILLINGWORTH

Some boats are slow, and some boats are fast, and the greatest speed differentials are often seen in the most "one-design" classes—where options for adjustment of critical factors may be most restricted. Much can and should be done to improve performance—and this improvement can be most successfully accomplished where windward performance is defective by adjustment of balance. But there are conditions in which each boat will have distinctive abilities or inabilities, sails that provide varying performance, and financial or emotional (I'd never sell old *Maybell III*) reasons why an outmoded boat is retained. Each season, in each regatta, and on each leg of the course an analysis of expected performance should be attempted so that tactical intentions can be realistically correlated with expected attainments. Although "nothing makes a helmsman look so good as a fast boat" (Shorty Trimingham), fast boats do not always win. Strategic and tactical considerations are *usually* far more significant than boat speed, but slow boats must be sailed appropriately to their capabilities—not in the same manner as fast boats.

At the start the essential is clear air, for slow boats or fast boats. If the leeward end is favored, only one boat with the perfect start at the buoy has clear air; the slow boat had better be there. For the fast boat a more conservative start, back on the line, pinching up under the close competitors and tacking away if necessary, is a safer solution—but an impossible one for the slow boat. If the weather end is favored, the slow boat must be at the mark with the gun, while the fast boat may more reasonably start with clear air down the line and subsequently work her way to the lead. Just before or after the start when two boats are close aboard attempting to pass one another, the skipper of the fast boat should push on with determination to break clear. The slower, *as soon as she recognizes* that she is losing, should tack away or bear off to leeward. Pressing on in the backwind of another boat just to demonstrate determination serves no useful purpose and results in progressively increasing losses relative to the fleet in general. Winning rarely results from beating one other boat (or all other boats) singly, but from regularly beating all other boats collectively.

On the windward leg the fast boat protects her position and capabilities by remaining with or ahead of the main body of the fleet. From whatever advantage she has achieved, she covers and relentlessly forges farther ahead to pass her remaining close competitors. The slow boat looks for and plays the shifts, recognizes the varying effects of current and seeks the area of maximum benefit, calculates the variations in wind and wave and seeks the location of maximum advantage, and disregards the remainder of the fleet. In close quarters, the slow boat continues on her strategic way, only tacking to clear her air, while the fast boat seeks the lee bow of her nearest competitor and forces her to tack away. The fast boat tacks up the middle of the leg, avoiding the dangerous lay lines where so much can be lost; the slow boat approaches the desired lay line, risking the loss to obtain the major gain, if the shift comes her way. The fast boat settles into the train of starboard tackers on the lay line knowing that she can pass them later; the slow boat, if strategy so demands, approaches on port, hoping for a chance to dart in between the elements of the approaching train.

Reaching is usually the weakest point of sailing for the slow boat. Here is where defects in hull form, sail construction, air or water resistance, and excess weight become most evident. A basically slow boat can be made to go well to windward where balance and pointing are the determinants of performance, but on the reach the truth will out. In a slow boat the race will be won or lost to windward, and she must daringly do or die on that leg. On the reach, however, the slow boat must become conservative to preserve her position for the beat or finish to come. She should avoid tactical conflicts, seek clear air as close to the direct course to the mark as possible, and hang on. For the slow boat strategic loss here will destroy any hope of ultimate victory; only the fast boat can afford a major strategic risk on the reach, and even she should only attempt such a risk if her position is poor. Of course, if the reach is the final leg and loss of position seems inevitable, a marked deviation to leeward or to windward in a varying wind or current will be justified. The fast boat should concentrate on strategic position, giving up speed and progress, initially, to achieve the best sailing angle at the termination of the leg.

On the run differences in basic boat speed are usually least significant. Beyond the stall, sail shape means little, but hull weight and skin resistance may be extremely important. Clear air and sailing angle are of equal importance to slow and fast boats; the fast boat, however, can accept the disadvantages of maneuvering near competitors in order to insure position and tactical control. The slow boat must jibe away or tack downwind to insure free air, avoid sailing by the lee regardless of tactical control, and place herself in a position so that her final approach to the mark provides both right of way and speed.

When approaching the finish, the slow boat must disregard the boats ahead and concentrate on conserving whatever position she has achieved. She must carefully cover her nearest competitors, keeping them in her interference zone if possible. Only if the final leg is her best point of sailing can she afford to take any chances. The fast boat on the other hand, if she is not in the lead, can and should avoid excessive concern with covering and strike out for victory. Finishing tactics are, of course, always determined by series position; if position is already as desired, nothing but careful covering is in order regardless of boat ability.

John Illingworth speaks of "passive sailing," and, except in the final race of a series, this technique should be constantly remembered. When defeat is recognized, it is far more sensible to conserve the position attained than to take a major strategic risk in a forlorn gamble for victory. The usually disastrous result of the gamble puts the skipper in such a depressed state that his performance in subsequent races is adversely affected. Even more significant is the need to maintain relative position for future advantage in the same race. If at a particular time or on a particular leg position is poor and

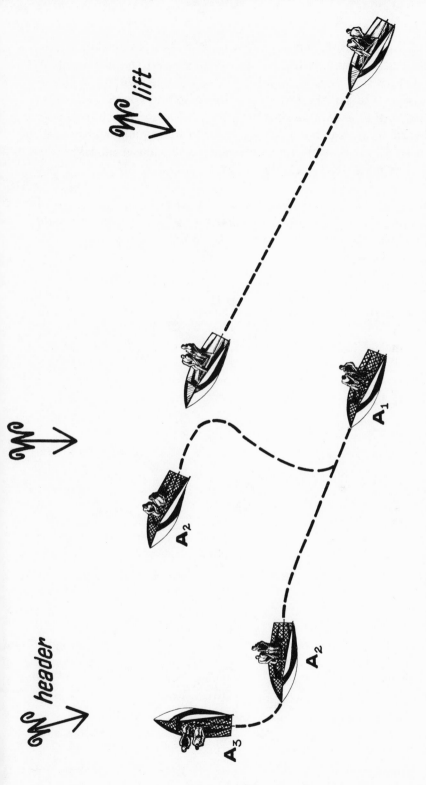

lift

header

A, to leeward and ahead, threatened by a competitor lifting out on her weather quarter, should tack to cover if she is fast enough to stay with the opposition, but if slow had better gamble on a subsequent header to restore her lead.

55

boat ability is insufficient to recover, it is best to resort to conservative sailing until a later opportunity permits the needed gain. If the boat is slow on the reach but extremely effective to windward, it is essential to sail the fastest possible reaching course, remaining as close to the leaders as possible, so as to be in a position where windward ability can be meaningful on the subsequent weather leg. And it is always possible that the leader will make a mistake; stay close so as to be able to capitalize on it.

Though there are ways for the slow boat to win, the fast boat always has the advantage. Once slowness is recognized it should be corrected. Go home and correct the impaired balance, the poor sail trim, the excess weight, the surface resistance, and return to victory!

N. Don't Be Greedy, or, How to Lose a Race

"For Daring *often finished second in light and moderate winds whereas* Avenger *would have finished first and she brought home to me the fact that for racing one really needs a vessel that is fast under all conditions of wind and sea, and that speed in hard weather can be bought by too great a sacrifice."*

—UFFA FOX

The ten best ways to lose a race are:
1. Failure to read the instructions
2. Forgetting the current
3. Not starting in clear air
4. Tacking away from the fleet
5. Sailing to the lay line early
6. Overstanding the weather mark
7. Working to windward on the reach
8. Entering a luffing match
9. Failing to check the position of the finish line
10. Being greedy

Of these ten, being greedy is the most common and the most deceptive. Greediness becomes evident even in the service of conservatism, common sense, and covering. It is difficult to draw the line between reasonable control and unreasonable avarice—to decide how far a tack should be continued to insure the advantage of the shift ahead or how soon deserted to insure coverage of the boats behind. It is the wise skipper who is able to give up 100 yards to insure 10, who will cross behind to insure coming out ahead, who will stay with the group when he *knows* the new wind is coming to starboard. Few can control their greed to win big, to demonstrate their brilliance, to hide their mistakes—and few win, these few.

I've seen Glen Foster, ahead and to leeward in a lift, tack and come right back to the fleet, sailing 160° to their course, to insure his lead, and I've seen myself carrying on in the same situation looking for the return of the header that never came. In the 1960 Princess Elizabeth Series when ahead and to leeward of the fleet, a header arrived that would have permitted me to cross the lot. I held on as another 100 yards would permit me to lay the mark; when that time came the wind shifted back, the fleet lifted up inside me, and I rounded fifth. How much more sensible to be satisfied with what's at hand instead of pushing on in vain expectation of greater advantage to come.

One of the major risks is being pleased with oneself. Smugly knowing that only you have correctly calculated the strategy essential to victory, you throw away the race and the series to prove that you are right. In the 1964 Warner Trophy Series, I calculated the course down the line against the tide so well as to be the only starboard tacker who cleared the committee boat and was off and alone in free air. I was so pleased with myself that I failed to notice that the windward mark could be laid from the other end of the line—and lost the series. How many times does a boat tack to port early or hold on starboard, her skipper certain that to that side of the course the expected header, the reduced current, the smaller waves will insure a dramatic victory, when in reality the advantages are with the opposite tack? Instead of carrying on and on, greedily seeking the maximum expected advantage, how much wiser these skippers would be to tack back, just a little closer to the side of their expected advantage than their competitors. In a Miles River Yacht Club Regatta I sailed on and on into a beautiful lead, seeking a header to port of the fleet; when it arrived, just as I had predicted, I discovered that I was overstanding the weather mark by a ¼ mile and dropped to fifth! The same thing happens downwind to the boat determined to make the big killing. Sailing farther to leeward, higher to windward, farther out of the tide, farther on each tack downwind, she more often finishes farther out of the race!

It doesn't pay to be too smart. To the skipper who has figured it all out there often seems but one solution—often the wrong one (inasmuch as it is never possible to figure it *all* out). Nothing is more irritating than being beaten by a skipper who has no idea what he is doing or why he does it, who believes that "it's all luck

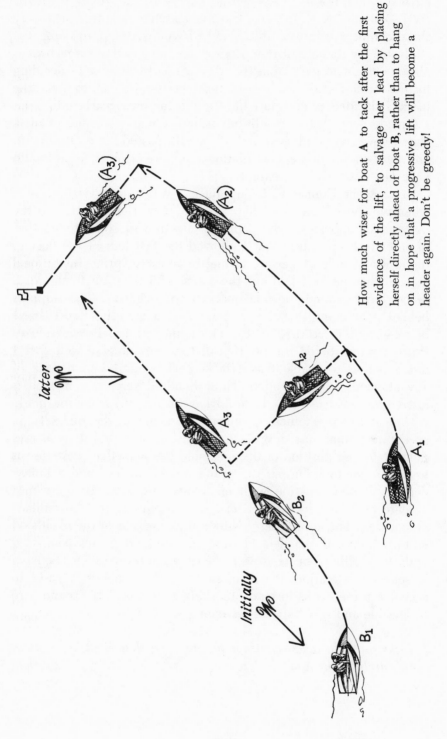

How much wiser for boat **A** to tack after the first evidence of the lift, to salvage her lead by placing herself directly ahead of boat **B**, rather than to hang on in hope that a progressive lift will become a header again. Don't be greedy!

anyway." The lesson to learn from him is a little humility. In the 1964 Douglas Cup (U.S. vs. Canada match race) against a very sharp competitor, I was ahead and to windward approaching the starboard lay line a half mile from the mark. The following boat is almost certain to gain from this position as the leader in deciding his tack from this distance will either overstand or fail to make the mark. I decided to outsmart him by tacking away early into what I thought were better conditions near the mark. He picked up a shift I never received, cut my lead in half, passed me on the reach, and went on to win. Less calculation and more common sense would have been extremely valuable.

In a recent Connecticut Cup Race I was amongst the leaders when we started the third leg. No one knew the direction to the next mark 4 miles away, but I didn't have to work so far to weather in order to keep uptide that I allowed the first half of the fleet to round it a ½ mile to leeward of me! In an early Spring Invitational on the Chesapeake I laid out the course and then, far in the lead, proceeded to round the final mark the wrong way. The skippers behind called out that I was rounding incorrectly, but I *knew* better—until I returned to the finish line. At the Buzzard's Bay Bowl, I remembered the position of the finish line so well that I didn't bother to check it as I tacked off on port into a zone of advantageous wind direction. Three hundred yards and five boats lost later, I realized that it could have been laid from the mark.

One of the preeminent problems in racing is the difficulty in accepting a small loss in order to avoid a greater one. It is always difficult to lose position or distance, and the immediate response is usually a combination of "they can't do this to me" and a guilty, depressed preoccupation with one's own stupidity. Such feelings obscure rational solution and tend to urge one on to "show them" and oneself. The appropriate solution is an analysis of the likelihood of further loss if the deteriorating situation progresses compared with the likelihood of recovery if the situation reverses. On the basis of such consideration, it will often be evident that it is wiser to accept a present loss instead of risking a greater. This is the core of sensible and successful series racing.

Risks must be taken continually and, in a slow boat, more than are desirable, but don't be greedy.

O. Disqualification

*"Disqualification is somewhat of a paradoxical penalty.
It seems to be always the same, but actually it varies
greatly being of different severity for each yacht in the race."*
—GREGG BEMIS

The guillotine of disqualification hangs over every race and threatens every competitor. The recognized need to play the game properly and to take no unfair advantage of the competitor is reinforced by the continual presence of the swift sword of justice. The awareness of this presence should become inherent in the planning and practice of every skipper. Innate to every maneuver involving a mark or a second boat is the possible commission of a foul. The acquisition of strategic advantage, the employment of tactical control, the escape from interference, all require maneuvers that when applied at the earliest possible moment, balance the risk of disqualification against the risk of loss.

The leeward end of the line was favored as we started down Annapolis Harbor in a moderate southeasterly, and I was off in the lead at the gun. *Goose*, the most dangerous competitor, started in the middle of the line, tacked to port, sailed up under the southern shore, and then tacked back in a geographic starboard tack lift. I could see *Goose* lifting out on my quarter progressively, and I wanted to get over there in the worst way. But *Bacalao X* was astern and a half boat length to weather. I couldn't clear her if I tacked, didn't have room to tack and bear away astern, and couldn't bring myself to drop back three boat lengths to fall astern or jibe away. I gradually pulled away from *Bacalao* and finally tacked, squeaking across her bow with but a few feet to spare. But *Goose* was gone.

61

The entire race was defined by those limits. I had risked the advantage of initial position farther to windward against the danger of being pinned to the initial tack with the expectation that superior boat speed would permit escape. *Goose* had risked the disadvantage of a late start in an area of major wind interference for freedom to tack so as to be first to acquire the advantages of the geographic shift. The limitation on my tacking was as essential to *Goose*'s victory as her recognition of the overwhelming importance of the geographic shift. I had gambled that my initial gain would more than compensate for my delayed entrance into the shift area; I had gambled, gambled high, and lost.

Take away that tacking limitation, and you take away the gamble, the excitement, and the challenge. Any fool could tack to cover *Goose* once she had revealed the shift. Take away the risk of disqualification, replace it with a 30% penalty, a slap on the wrist, or a polite ignoring of the incident, and you take away the race; you change it from an all-demanding, head-on, toe-to-toe, no-quarter-given-or-asked battle to victory or defeat into a dull, compromising, parody of "after you, Pierre." If the rules are to be wielded as a weapon to disarm the enemy, they must occasionally, in a competitor's hands, be expected to annihilate the unwary.

Some American comments have been to the effect that as the penalty for overparking is not the same as for murder, disqualification is an excessive punishment for minor (and unintended?) breaches of the rules. Elsewhere, particularly in continental Europe (see Paul Elvstrom's "The Spirit of Racing" in his new book and the reports of various North American competitors in recent major European regattas), the practice of ignoring "minor" and "unintended" rules violations has already been established. Bumps and bangs before the start or while rounding marks or slight interference with starboard-tack boats on the windward leg are ignored, and protests are considered to be unsporting. Of course, *deliberate* interference with right-of-way yachts is condemned!

The 1965 rules, on the other hand (**14. Award of Prizes**), recommend "that the sailing instructions require the member in charge of each yacht to submit within a stated time after she has **finished** a race a signed declaration to the effect that 'all the rules and sailing instructions were obeyed in the race (or races) on (date or dates of race or races).'" Although this technique is in regular use in England, it has not been applied even to prize-winning yachts elsewhere as presently recommended. Does Rule 14 imply that the conditions above alluded to as common in Europe are to be expected and that a declaration of this nature will correct the problem? Or does it imply that yachtsmen are a dishonest and irresponsible lot who need a police system to insure their compliance with the rules? Either implication is a poor commentary on the state of yachting. And if either is true, what reason is there to believe that such a declaration ashore will produce a more responsible response than the demands of competitive interplay afloat? If the "spirit" of racing can justify a behavior in the boat that modifies itself to the occasion, how will a declaration alter the justification?

The traditions of yachting have distinguished the sport as self-disciplined, responsible, and scrupulously honest. One of my most memorable sailing experiences occurred during my first C.D.A. regatta when on the final weather leg of the final race one of the series leaders crossed me on port (I stood about thirty-fifth). He called back to ask if I had had to alter course. Reluctantly I admitted that I had—ever so slightly, at the last moment. He waved, bore away, and headed for the beach. I wished that I had said nothing—but felt so proud then and ever since to have been a part of a sport in which this could happen. Should we demean this act or this helmsman by asking that he sign a declaration ashore? Should we belittle the nobility of the sport and deny the spontaneous repetition of this gesture which gladly announces faith in one's fellow sailors, pride in one's class, and determination to defend the traditions of yachting? How much more was added to the stature of this man and to all his fellow sailors that day than that which would have attended a mere victory.

The concern over the inequity of equal penalties for all offenses is accentuated by the differentiation made in the wordings of Rules 33 and 52. Rule 33 states that when a yacht recognizes that she has violated the rules or sailing instructions she "should retire"; when she hits a starboard-tack yacht amidships, the port-tack yacht "should retire." But if a yacht should wrongfully touch a mark, she "shall withdraw" (Rule 52)! For deliberately interfering with and/or seriously impeding a right-of-way yacht, she is encouraged to retire, but for merely touching a mark, she is commanded to withdraw!

No compromise in penalty for varying degrees of interference with competitors seems reasonable; a non-right-of-way yacht cannot be permitted to interfere with a right-of-way yacht. Period. Deliberately, slightly, significantly aside—she does or she doesn't. Not only is it completely impracticable to determine deliberacy or any other variation of intent or degree that might be proposed, but the entire exciting system of racing tactics would be jeopardized by any

63

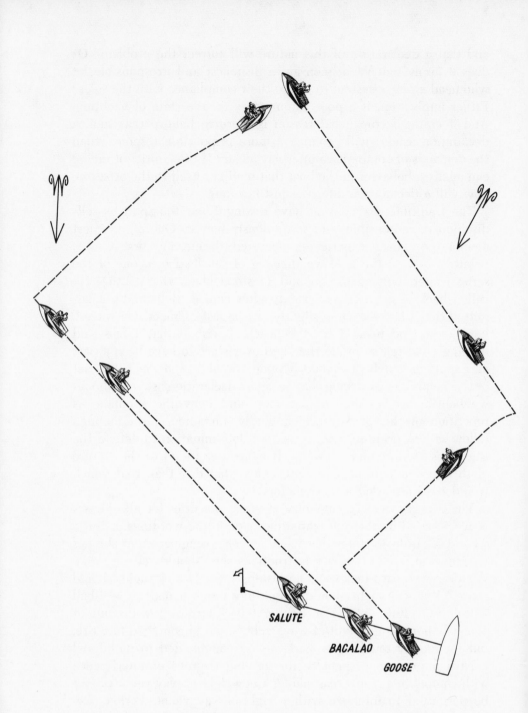

Salute starts in the most upwind position on the line but, pinned down by *Bacalao* close astern, is unable to counter *Goose's* early acquisition of a lift to starboard.

system of graded penalties. In this sport there can be no compromises; all maneuvers must be susceptible of determination as either right or wrong.

Finally, the world is a confused mass of gray shades between right and wrong. Only on the water can we escape into absolutes. We fly from the dull repetitiveness of daily life to an all-out assault on the sea and our competitors, seeking the risk of victory or disqualification—all or none! Our rules should not destroy this pearl of great price.

P. Hailing

"A racing sailor must expect to be wrong a fixed percentage of the time."

—THOMAS MARSTON

At the start of one of the races of a Harry Hall Regatta on the river at Essex, the wind lifted radically a minute before the gun. We bore away to avoid a barging approach and suddenly were hailed by a boat approaching on the new lay line about two boat lengths to leeward. "You can't come in there!" We rounded up as rapidly as possible and had achieved a position ahead, parallel, and slightly to windward of her course when the hailing boat was still almost a boat length away. She held her speed and course and moments later established an overlap to leeward by colliding with our boom (the aftermost point on *Daring*) as it was being frantically trimmed. I was momentarily sufficiently intimidated by the determined hail and my vulnerable barging position to presume that I had fouled the leeward yacht. Seconds later I realized that I had been given *no* room or opportunity (not ample!) to keep clear after the leeward overlap was established—and so informed the irate helmsman to leeward. Shouting on the water, righteous and presumed appropriate as in the instance recounted or deliberate and without justification, has become increasingly prevalent. Except in situations specified by the rules it is meaningless in the ultimate determination of right or wrong, and too often has an intimidating and for the hailer unjustifiably advantageous effect.

There are reports of aggressive helmsman who roar into the starting melee on a full plane shouting "Watch out!", expecting the sheep to scatter from their path. And others who come up to a favored starting position scream "Protest!" to clear their way. A few still find that, despite the antibarging rule, if they yell "Let me in" loudly enough, room will be provided for them to leeward of the mark. In Bermuda recently one helmsman on port tack called "Hold your course" to a converging starboard tacker and then complained that the opponent tacked beneath him. In a similar manner a skipper tacking to starboard may call "I'm tacking—watch out" and expect the continuing boat to avoid a collision. None of these hails has any binding effect; no direction from one helmsman to another can require any behavior not inherent in the rules. A non-right-of-way yacht can never direct the course of a right-of-way yacht. The yacht on a tack need make no effort to keep clear until the tacking yacht completes her tack, and the starboard-tack yacht may vary her course, occasioning the disqualification of the port tacker, if she feels it necessary and regardless of any hail to the contrary.

There are specific circumstances when a hail is required by the rules and a number of others in which courtesy strongly indicates its use, however. Rule 35 states "A right-of-way yacht, except when **luffing** under rule 38.1, Luffing after Starting, should hail before or when making an alteration of course which may not be foreseen by the other yacht or when claiming room at a **mark** or **obstruction**." The hail is not required in these circumstances (the auxiliary verb is *should*), but the traditions of the sport demand sufficient consideration of the opponent to provide fair warning. This recommendation becomes particularly important at marks now that the two-boat-length rule permits a clear ahead yacht to maneuver at will once she is within the two-boat-length circle.

The rules *require* that a hail be given in the following circumstances:

1. By a windward yacht when the mast abeam position is reached.
2. By a leeward yacht intending to luff a windward yacht to windward of a mark (required to be passed to leeward).
3. By a leeward yacht requiring room to tack at an obstruction.
4. By a yacht anchored or aground when another yacht may be in danger of fouling her.

There probably is never a justifiable reason to disqualify an op-

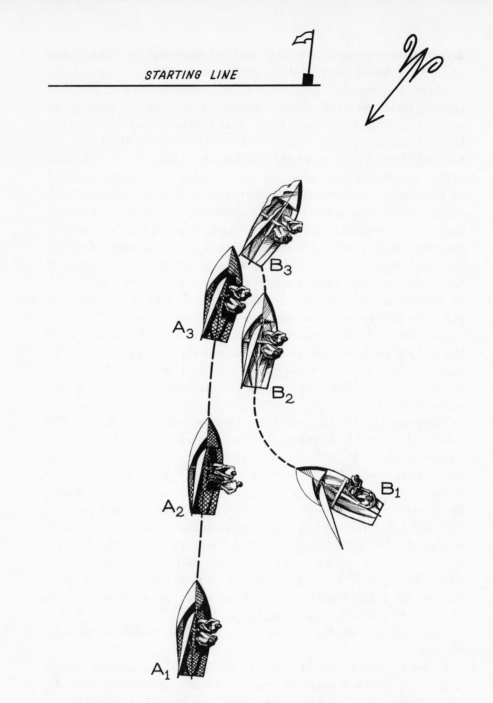

B, to windward, takes evasive action when hailed by **A** at position **1**. At position **2** she is on a parallel course but making leeway after her rapid turn. **A** establishes a new overlap to leeward at position **3** without providing **B** ample room and opportunity to keep clear. If a collision occurs, **A** is the burdened boat.

ponent deliberately (except in team racing). The race is composed of the victor and the defeated; the continued presence of the opponent is an essential element of the game! Whenever a danger of disqualification exists it is thus reasonable that the competitor be warned. The converging port tacker should be hailed "Starboard!"; the windward boat about to be luffed told "Coming Up!"; and the windward boat being passed to leeward on a downwind leg warned "Don't bear away." Some means of notifying a boat that is to be protested is required (usually the display of a flag); courtesy demands that a hail be included. A decision to protest after consideration of the resultant effect on the standings is to be condemned. The immediate hail states that we are comrades in art, not cutthroats in crime. (At the same time it should be noted that a protest is not required by the rules. There may be occasions when the offending yacht has done all in its power to avoid a foul and been unable to keep clear.) Strict adherence to the spirit of the rules includes tempering justice with mercy. It has been said that any helmsman determined to disqualify an opponent could do so in every race he entered.

The hail is an emblem of our fellowship in a sport; it should not be misused to obtain unjustified advantage.

II. *Starting—*

The Maneuvering for Tactical Position

A. The Principles of Starting

The start is the one element of the race that requires the successful application of tactics. To windward—strategy on the reach-boat speed, on the run-free air and the better sailing angle, but at the start it is tactics that determine the result. Strategy determines the plan, determines the utilization of the preferred location on the line, and determines the acquisition of the tack that permits reaching the advantageous side of the course. But the presence of competitors will almost certainly prevent the accomplishment of the strategic plan unless tactical control is achieved. Starting tactics include both the application of techniques that permit arriving at the line with free air at the gun and techniques that permit breakaway to the desired side of the course unobstructed by neighboring competitors. To achieve both goals the strategic plan must include a decision to seek either the preferred lee-bow position on starboard tack or the freedom to breakaway on port. Appropriate tactics must be applied to achieve one or the other of these solutions in the presence of varied wind strength, varying wind direction, current, or waves, and the interference of the competition. Nowhere else on the course is the fleet so densely packed, does boat speed, dependent upon clear

73

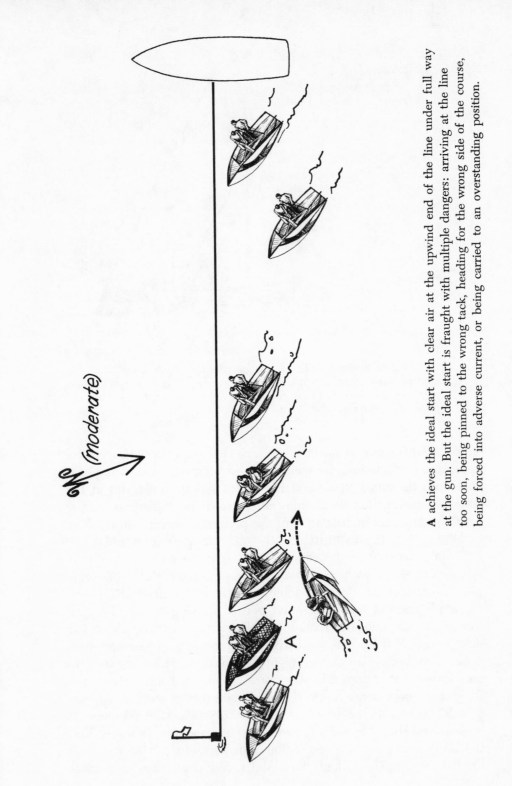

(moderate)

A achieves the ideal start with clear air at the upwind end of the line under full way at the gun. But the ideal start is fraught with multiple dangers: arriving at the line too soon, being pinned to the wrong tack, heading for the wrong side of the course, being forced into adverse current, or being carried to an overstanding position.

air, vary so greatly, and can the proper application of tactics provide such large gains.

1. The primary consideration in starting is to reach the favored side of the weather leg, first.
2. For clear air and full speed at the gun, a controlling position relative to the competition must be acquired and maintained.
3. Being trapped in the control of a competitor must be avoided; acquire clear air *and* freedom to reach the desired side of the course.
4. Keep clear of yachts on the lee bow. Acquire right of way, use it, and move out at maximum speed.
5. Work into the first row of boats approaching the line, keep close under boats to windward and break away from those to leeward.
6. In light air, stay in the middle of the line until last minute changes in wind strength and direction can be determined.
7. In heavy air, avoid slowing, side force, and leeway.
8. Find a location and approach that permits extrication with clear air from the confusion of a start against the tide.
9. Keep well to leeward and below the lay line to the favored point on the line when starting in favorable tide.
10. In small fleets preoccupation with specific competitors must be avoided; stick to the plan.
11. A match-race opponent should be controlled from close astern or on the opposite tack.
12. The port-tack start should be utilized—carefully—in situations where tacking from starboard to port is hazardous and to facilitate obtaining the preferred side of the course, clear air, and/or the lifted tack.

B. The Strategy of the Start

"Efficiency of a practically flawless kind may be reached naturally in the struggle for bread. But there is something beyond, a higher point, a subtle and unmistakable touch of love and pride beyond mere skill; almost an inspiration which gives to all work that finish which is almost art—which is art. And—the sailing of yachts is a fine art."

—JOSEPH CONRAD

Most sailors know how to determine and to take advantage of the upwind end of the starting line. Fewer coordinate this knowledge with the strategy of the first leg.

George O'Day has won at least two Buzzard's Bay Bowl Regattas (premiere East Coast International 14 event) by simply accepting a late start at the weather end of the line to insure being the first boat on the port tack and thus the first boat to reach the expected header along the starboard Converse Point shore.

The first consideration at the start must be the tack of the course favored for the weather leg. Secondly, the upwind end of the line must be determined and a decision made as to whether use of its advantage is consistent with the strategy of the first leg. Thirdly, a method of reaching the favored location on the line at the gun, with clear air, must be developed.

In any competitive fleet many boats should have sufficient boat speed to maintain readily any position achieved at the start, but the actual determinant of position at the weather mark is not starting position but subsequent weather-leg position. The weather-leg position that will permit entering into an oscillating wind-shift system from the proper location (avoiding deleterious wave or wind conditions on one side of the course) or that will permit being the first to reach a geographic shift will result in a major gain in contrast to the slight advantage associated with better positioning on the starting line.

In a recent Ulmer Bowl Series in Annapolis we attempted to start at the leeward end of the line in a heading shift in each of the last two races. In the first of these we recognized, just before the gun, that we would be unable to clear the leeward starting-line buoy on starboard, would be unable to tack to port in the clear, and so jibed away from the line to come back through the fleet on port, the lifted tack. In the next race we were able to tack to port early from the leeward end and then duck behind three successive starboard tackers into clear air on the lifted tack. In both instances, being amongst the first boats to tack to port, we were amongst those farthest to the starboard side of the course when the next port tack-heading shift appeared. Tacking to starboard in each instance, we were then far ahead of the mass of the fleet, a position we held or bettered thereafter. There was little change in boat positions for the remainder of the legs, each boat entering properly into the shift sequence thereafter, their ultimate positions determined by their relative locations at the time of appearance of the shift. We were able to capitalize on a proper strategic move which provided major advantage ultimately almost without regard to defective positioning on the starting line; indeed, the sacrifice of many boat positions at the start was essential to the ultimate acquisition of the lead.

In open water and steady wind (how rare!) the upwind end of the starting line is closer to the weather mark and may be selected as the preferred starting location without concern. (On any beat, regardless of the location of the mark, providing that no boat has reached the lay line, the boat farthest upwind is ahead and closer to the mark.) To find the upwind end, luff head-to-wind on the line. It will be readily evident whether the wind is blowing perpendicularly to the line or at some lesser or greater angle to it. No matter how good the race committee, no line is ever square to the wind. *One end is always favored* by virtue of being farther upwind. In case of any doubt, the leeward end is favored initially as the backwind of a leeward boat is far more deleterious and covers a far larger zone than the blanket zone of a windward boat.

If the wind is oscillating (particularly in an off-shore "north-wester"), the upwind end may not be the "favored" end. If the wind heads the starboard-tack boats at the start, the leeward end of the line becomes the upwind end, but the *port tack becomes the lifted, "favored" tack.* The ideal start must permit assuming the port tack as soon as possible—not necessarily at the upwind end where assumption of the port tack may be difficult, if not impossible. If a favoring lift, a decrease in tide, a decrease in sea, or an increase in wind strength to starboard of the rhumb line is anticipated, early assumption of the port tack may be essential again regardless of which end of the line is farther upwind.

When the upwind end is the starboard or windward end (for the starboard tack), this is the favored end of the line almost regardless of the strategy of the first leg. However, when the upwind end is the port or leeward end (for the starboard tack), this end is the favored end only if the port tack or the starboard side of the course is not favored for the first leg.

Once the desired starting location on the line is determined on the basis of these considerations, a plan must be created that will bring the boat to this point with the gun and with right of way adequate to acquire clear air. This is the art of starting and in general requires (1) starboard tack, (2) lee-bowing of neighboring boats to windward (controlling them by luffing), (3) freedom from the backwind of neighboring boats to leeward, and (4) sufficient time for a controlled approach.

Start so as to facilitate reaching the favored side of the weather leg first.

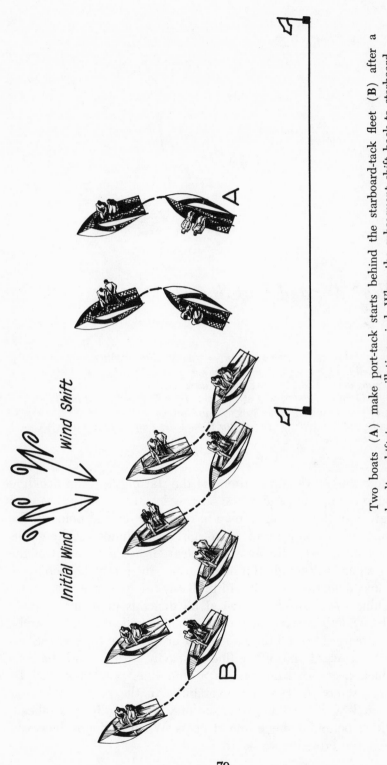

Two boats (**A**) make port-tack starts behind the starboard-tack fleet (**B**) after a heading shift in an oscillating wind. When the subsequent shift back to starboard occurs, the port-tack boats assume the lead by virtue of having sailed the lifted tack initially towards the direction of the "next expected shift."

C. Clear Air and Full Speed

"For those afloat and those ashore, this racing has a
wealth of the joys of life, reaching their climax in the close
proximity of fast-moving boats, all striving within the rules
to be in the same place at the same time. The sweeping hand
of the stopwatch gives full measure to every second until
the call to action, 'Let's go for it' and the puff of blue smoke
—the gun."

—KEITH SHACKLETON

After determining the upwind end of the starting line and deciding
if utilizing the upwind end as the starting location is consistent with
the strategy of the first leg, a plan to reach the desired point on the
line must be developed. An ideal start necessitates reaching this
desired point under full way and in clear air at the moment of the
starting signal. Although this ideal may only rarely be achieved,
any serious deviation from it will probably lose the race.

Reaching the desired location at all depends upon maintaining
right of way. Other boats will interfere, incidentally and deliberately,
as they attempt to reach the same point at the same time. Occasionally if the leeward end of the line is heavily favored and the starboard-tack fleet is strung out in a thin line, port tack may be
attempted safely. As the maneuverability of the port-tack boat is
unrestricted by the balking rule, she may successfully cross ahead,
through, or behind a single line of boats. When in doubt, however,
approach and cross on starboard.

In addition to obtaining the right of way relative to boats on the opposite tack, it is essential to be to leeward, or sufficiently clear of boats farther to leeward, so as to have right of way over boats on the same tack. Failure to assume this position will permit leeward boats to interfere by luffing and, consequently, to prevent reaching the desired location on the line in time. Assumption of the leeward position, on the other hand, will permit the maintenance of clear air by luffing boats to weather and working upwind of boats to leeward, as well as permit sufficient speed variation to reach the line with the starting signal.

Arrival at the desired point on the line, under full way, at the moment of the starting signal requires a controlled approach. The length of the approach run should be determined well in advance. The stronger the breeze, the more time should be allowed for the run. In small boats a 2 minute run is maximum, and in light air it should be 30 seconds or less. The length of the approach should usually be about one half the distance that could be traveled at top speed in the time available. This provides sufficient time to make course and protective adjustments relative to other boats at a controlled half-speed. An International 14 averages 5 knots to windward, approximately 500 feet per minute or 8 feet per second. Thus, an average one-minute approach run for moderate air should be less than 250 feet. The approach should be made on a course slightly to leeward of the lay line to the desired location so as to provide right-of-way for deviations to windward.

In moderate air a position slightly to leeward of the lay line to the desired point on the line and 200 to 250 feet behind that point should be sought one minute before the gun. In light air, at a speed of 2½ knots, a one-minute approach run would be 125 feet in length. In very light air, a 30-second approach from only 60 feet or less behind the line may obviate loss due to variation in wind strength or direction.

To arrive at the line under full way with wind clear necessitates periodic luffing of boats to windward and separation from boats to leeward. It is essential to be free of the backwind of boats to leeward and of the blanket of boats to windward as the gun goes. Protection against blanketing requires control of boats to windward by allowing them to sail clear ahead, by luffing across their sterns if excess time remains, or by luffing up under their lee bow to stop them if time is short. Each luff will permit further separation from boats to leeward. If there is danger of reaching a barging position by excessive luffing, or if leeward boats cling on the lee bow, it may be necessary to bear away suddenly across their sterns to assume a safe lee-bow position farther down the line. Full way, that should be acquired in the last few seconds of the approach, provides, in moderate air, a speed of 8 feet per second, and a maximum of 40 feet which could be covered in the last 5 seconds. It is better, however, to be closer to the line than this at minus 5 seconds, delaying windward boats by luffing and allowing leeward boats to sail farther down the line until the last crucial seconds.

Acquiring a position (10 to 20 feet behind the line) from which the desired point on the line can be reached at maximum speed in the last few seconds is the major element of the battle, but inappropriate utilization of this position may still lose the war. A boat close on the lee bow may interfere with progress far out on the leg; it is better to luff up above her at the last moment than to follow closely in her wake. Boats may come barging down from above to blanket; it is better to let them pass rather than to continue speed at the risk of continued blanketing or collision. Collision should be avoided at all costs; no matter which boat is in the right, both lose. Reaching the line with clear air is the determinant of success; a few seconds may well be sacrificed to rid the waters ahead of interference. Hold back till the ideal opening appears, slightly farther to weather, ahead, or to leeward, and then bear off, trim sheets, hike, and go!

For clear air and full speed at the gun, a controlling position relative to the competition must be acquired and maintained.

Position 1 is untenable for A. She must determine immediately which of the three possible solutions is most desirable and aggressively break away into clear air to leeward, to windward, or by tacking.

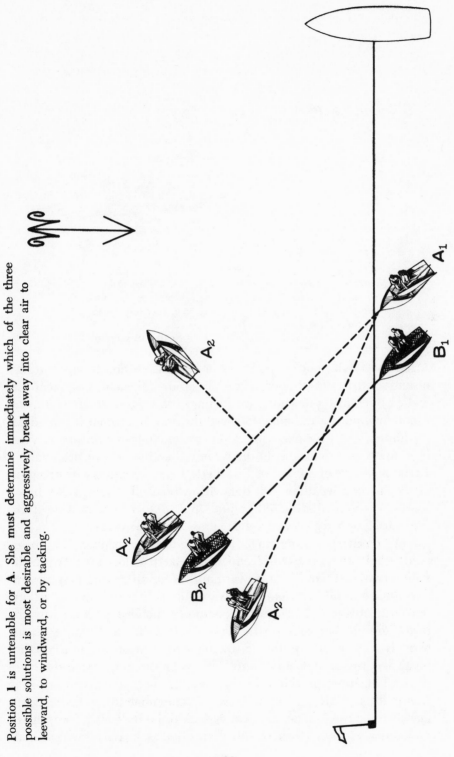

D. Breakaway

> *"Never forget the overall object of the race and never waste time dueling with one other competitor. Often you see two boats fighting together and forgetting the race as a whole, so that by going the wrong way they are losing several places."*
>
> —PAUL ELVSTROM

After a week of poor starts, I was in a good position to analyze the essential attributes of good ones. These are (1) achieving clear air and (2) achieving it while proceeding in the right direction. In the usual upwind start, being farthest upwind is ordinarily an ideal attribute, but if this does not result in the continued availability of clear air or if it takes one in the wrong direction, it is of little value. In the final race of a Princess Elizabeth Series, I started with the gun at the favored weather end, but with a boat close on my lee bow. I was soon backwinded, fell behind, and, forced to tack away from the subsequent major wind shift, finished disastrously.

In the heat of starting it is often difficult to remember the power and extent of the backwind effect of a boat to leeward. Any boat within two boat lengths to leeward and as far aft as the mast abeam position, certainly any boat to leeward that is bow to bow, as well as any boat ahead and leeward, is seriously hindering the windward boat. The blanket zone of the windward yacht on the other hand extends only as a rapidly narrowing cone, never wider than the boat's length, aft and to leeward. There can be no question that the leeward boat is far safer herself and far more dangerous to her competitors. Thus, we should always remember to avoid boats to leeward like the plague and always seek to be to leeward ourselves.

Even when the weather end of the line is heavily favored and boats are crossing the line perpendicularly, a leeward boat has clear air herself and is seriously backwinding her neighbors to windward. Although this advantage is usually recognized in leeward end favored starts, when only the single boat at the leeward end buoy will have clear air, it is commonly overlooked by the barging fleet approaching the weather mark when this end is farthest upwind.

In many circumstances it may be sufficient to approach the line slowly, with time to spare, periodically luffing the boats to weather so as to keep the lee side free. Often, however, competitors will shoot across one's stern at the last moment to establish a protected position to leeward. For this reason it is wise to hang back a bit so as to retain initiative and then, with but seconds to go, to bear away at high speed and shoot into a lee-bow position oneself. In order to be able to achieve this, of course, it is essential not to be caught barging by a gang of leeward boats, and it is preferable to be far enough down from a favored weather end to find maneuvering room.

As the starting gun sounds, positions become fixed, every boat concentrating on obtaining clear air and maximum speed. The strategic plan to proceed to the advantageous side of the windward leg must take precedence, however. If tacking away from the fleet is the plan, then tack. If not, but tacking seems the only way to obtain clear air, tack and then tack back again to the preferred tack as soon as clear air is obtained. *The worst possible mistake in any race is the continuance of the wrong tack immediately after the start.* If the initially assumed tack is preferred and clear air is not immediately available, tacking away may result in a greater ultimate loss than hanging on in the disturbed air. Determination to succeed often brings its own solution as other boats tack away and boats ahead and to leeward fall away or drop back. If pointing ability is available, keep high; if not, bear off and break through to leeward; in either instance retain the preferred tack. There will always be believers and disbelievers, the confident and the diffident; the most successful boat is the one that gives in last, the one that breaks clear, above or below, to clear air and the lead. And if clear air *is* unobtainable, second or third place in the right strategic location is still more desirable than tenth place with clear air in the wrong location.

Once the choice is made every effort in hiking and sail trimming must be expended to insure not only the acquisition or maintenance of a safe position but freedom from boats farther to leeward. If it has been possible to find the ideal opening from which no boat farther to leeward can produce a significant backwind effect, one can afford to ease sheets, bear off a bit, and drive her out of the mob.

If, as more frequently happens, there are one or more boats at various distances to leeward, which are producing a harmful back-wind effect, it becomes necessary to develop every inch of possible lift to windward with maximum forward drive, keeping "her right on edge," every muscle and every perceptive brain cell tuned to the utmost effectiveness. This is no time for planning the approach to the mark, let alone for worrying that the spinnaker pole is adrift, no time for the crew to adjust the board or discuss the next expected shift. These are the seconds that try men's souls—and backs—and those in the fleet that make the effort and sail their boats emerge with the lead and the race, as their less determined competitors flounder helplessly in the backwind.

Avoid being trapped; acquire clear air and freedom to reach the desired side of the course.

The lee-bow position provides control of boats astern and to windward as the backwind zone is large and powerful, but it may be a dangerous handicap if breakaway to the opposite tack is strategically desirable.

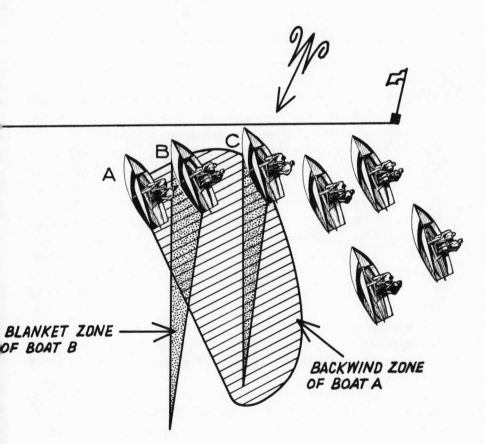

BLANKET ZONE OF BOAT B

BACKWIND ZONE OF BOAT A

E. Over or Under?

"*To continue sailing in the company of people who are killing their boats with pinching reduces one's own speed to that of theirs and the longer you stay with them the longer you sail slowly.*"

—ROBIN STEAVENSON

Although the permutations of the results of two (or more) boats meeting just before the start seem countless, there are in reality only a few basic situations and a few basic solutions. The successful solution for each boat is to emerge at the line (presumably somewhere near the desired point on the line) on time with clear air. Clear air in general is consequent to separation from boats on the lee bow. If the absolute ends of the line are avoided, there should be sufficient room to solve successfully any problem resulting from two boats meeting. (And the converse is also true; only when a start precisely at the mark—windward or leeward—is attempted may an ideal start occasionally be impossible. When caught barging or reaching the leeward buoy with five seconds to go, there is *no* successful solution.)

Elsewhere on the line the following options exist: (1) slow up, (2) speed up, (3) bear away, (4) head up. The option selected will, of course, depend upon the time remaining and the character of the opposing helmsman. In general, if sufficient time remains, it is better to slow up and let him by and not to become committed to an argument with a single competitor at this crucial time. The only exception to this dictum occurs when the leeward end is heavily favored and letting a competitor by means being stuck in his backwind thereafter. Under these circumstances it may be wiser to luff sharply if the competitor is to weather, bear off, and come up under him if he tacks ahead or outrun him down the line if he is to leeward. The latter maneuver is dangerous, however, and should only be attempted if two prerequisites are met: (1) the time remaining is insufficient to reach the leeward mark, and (2) he does not have luffing rights (or cannot retain them). Otherwise he may force you past the mark too soon or luff you over the line. Discretion thus becomes the better part of valor; luff up, separate from his lee-bow position and settle for partially clear air astern.

If you have approached, luffing, with adequate time to reach the line, the boats ahead will have to either luff or peel away and in the final moments will be either stopped to weather or sailing free and away from you to leeward. It is the boats behind and alongside that are the dangerous ones. If, with little time remaining, another boat approaches from astern (and the leeward end of the line is not favored), it becomes necessary to protect the lee bow. If possible keep her on your windward quarter. Bear away in front of her before she comes too close. Once she is overlapped to weather, she is under control; a sharp luff at your convenience will keep her in her place. If she seems determined to break through to leeward (and it is impossible to cross ahead so as to trap her to windward), then a choice must be made between luffing sharply and letting her go (so as to be as far to weather of her as possible after the gun) and driving ahead with her thereby preventing her from acquiring luffing rights (so as to keep your lee bow clear). The former is usually the better technique until the final few seconds. Then it is essential to drive ahead and to reach the line as the gun goes in order to maintain clear air above and below. Usually a sharp (but not too sharp!) luff and then a bearing away to pick up full speed just as the gun goes provides clear air above and usually takes one far enough to weather to be free of boats to leeward.

The major danger and the one most misunderstood is involved in bearing away in front of a boat approaching from astern or to leeward in order to trap him on the weather quarter. There is no proper course before the start and no prohibition to bearing away to prevent an overtaking boat from passing to leeward. Indeed an overtaking boat is required to keep clear of any gyrations that the boat clear ahead may undertake—until—until that critical moment when the gyrations of the leading boat's transom suddenly permit a perpendicular extension to pass behind the bow of the follower. Then, abruptly, the following boat becomes the right-of-way-yacht,

A luffs **C** to hold her to windward and astern, then bears away across **B's** bow to prevent her from establishing a lee-bow position. Meanwhile **D**, who has arrived at the line early, is forced to bear away down the line clear of **A**.

and it is the leader who must keep clear. The latter is left with two recourses: (1) to continue on, bearing across the bow of the follower, recognizing that she is "at risk," but far enough ahead to get away with it, or (2) to luff thus breaking the overlap, but leaving the follower the option of breaking through to leeward. If the follower is forced to alter course or a collision occurs in instance (1) the leader is disqualified. If, however, the overlap is broken as in (2) the follower must keep clear, and if a collision occurs, prior to giving the windward yacht "ample room and opportunity to keep clear," the follower is disqualified. If an overlap is established, and not broken, the leeward (overtaking) boat may hold her initial course (or bear away) so long as she gives "ample room and opportunity" and may disqualify the windward boat by subsequently running into her boom. She may *not*, however, luff—which means *she may not alter course towards the wind* at all—until she reaches the mast-abeam position. This means that the windward boat may hold the leeward boat off down the line on whatever course the leeward boat was maintaining at the time the overlap was established—and that no amount of shouting "get up" need have any effect until, of course, the gun goes. (After which the leeward yacht may assume her suddenly acquired "proper course.") If, with two boats sailing parallel and side by side before the start and with the leeward one behind the mast-abeam position or in the process of establishing an overlap, it can be demonstrated that the leeward boat subsequently luffed so as to cause the windward to alter course the former would be disqualified.

Keep ahead and to leeward; don't luff until you have acquired luffing rights, and then use them to manipulate the situation your way! Also remember that if there is any doubt as to whether the following boat was luffing across your stern or you were bearing away across her bow, the doubt will usually be resolved in the leeward boat's favor—particularly if she had an overlap for any significant time before a collision.

Keep clear of yachts on the lee bow; acquire right of way; use it, and move out.

F. Starting at the Leeward End

"Starting a boat in a large fleet is like playing Russian roulette with five bullets instead of one. One mistake and the finish is very quick!"

—GEORGE O'DAY

When the leeward end of the starting line is favored, several tactical plans may provide a successful start, on the line, under full way, and with a clear wind. If the favoring of the leeward end is consequent to a temporally oscillating wind shift, it is essential to achieve the port, lifted tack immediately after the gun. This necessity may demand a port-tack start or a start near the middle or even the windward end of the line that will permit an immediate tack to port. Unless the port tack is lifted or the starboard side of the course is definitely favored, however, it is better (and safer) in moderate air to develop a plan to start on starboard tack at or near the leeward mark.

If the leeward end of the line is upwind and therefore favored, all boats starting on starboard, except the leader, are to varying degrees in each other's backwind. Backwind is the most disastrous form of interference, and, therefore, starting lines that favor the leeward end seriously handicap all boats except the single boat nearest the leeward mark. Starting tactics must be developed so as to obviate this interference.

In a small fleet or an inexperienced fleet, it may be sensible to dare the ultimate and seek that one ideal location nearest the mark. It is usually possible to time a run down the line from about 20 to 30 feet below the windward mark, keeping on the lee bow of boats behind, so as to control the fleet, and to arrive at the leeward mark under full way, with the gun. In larger fleets the danger of being pushed over (or under the mark) early or of being jammed into a foul at this sought-after spot must be weighed against its obvious advantages. Even in large experienced fleets, however, most skippers will utilize this basic technique. About 1 or 2 minutes before the gun the main fleet organizes near or beyond the windward mark, and most boats align themselves on starboard tack, luffing slowly down the line at varying intervals.

This mass can be joined from above the line in order to insure clear wind, from beyond the weather mark, or by approaching on port and tacking into position, ahead and to leeward. Joining from above the line is extremely hazardous as leeward boats may block all openings. Early joining from beyond the windward mark grants control of timing and position to right-of-way boats ahead and to leeward. Approaching the mass on port tack from the leeward end is usually the preferable technique, as clear wind and opportunity to maneuver are retained until the ideal location is acquired. The port-tack boat, unrestricted by balking regulations, can luff along against the stream, finally tacking ahead and to leeward of a group of starboard tackers whenever a likely opening appears.

If the mass is late, it may be wise to "go for broke" by tacking ahead and beneath the leading starboard tacker, retaining sufficient free air to luff her and the fleet, if necessary, for control. This tack should be made not more than 30 seconds before the gun, allowing sufficient but not extra time to reach the leeward mark with the fleet stalled, behind and to windward.

If a large portion of the mass can be expected to reach the leeward end on time, it is better to allow the leaders to pass and to tack ahead of a later group whenever a significant gap appears. Clear air, free of backwind, on the lee bow of nearby boats is the *sine qua non* of leeward-end starting and the ideal location at the mark may better be relinquished to insure these advantages. After tacking ahead and to leeward of a second or third group, the group leaders should be luffed to slow them and, in turn, the other members of the group. This allows the earlier groups to move farther ahead along the line and provides increased freedom from their backwind.

Luffing and stalling close to the line to prevent blanketing by a windward competitor should be continued until within 3 to 5 seconds of the gun. Keeping slightly ahead and close beneath windward boats will allow leeward boats to sail clear ahead. Windward boats should be luffed higher and higher, as necessary, without quite going over. the line—and boats on the lee bow avoided like the plague. If a sufficient gap to leeward has been produced by these means, it will be possible to bear off and go after the gun, while the remainder of the fleet flounders in each other's backwind.

Keep close under boats to windward and avoid those to leeward.

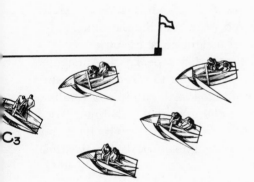

C₃

Boat **A** makes a successful start when the port ("leeward") end of the line is upwind by approaching the fleet on port and tacking ahead and to leeward of an approaching group of starboard tackers. Thereafter, she preserves her freedom from boats on her lee bow by luffing up and slowing the boats astern and to windward.

G. The Light and Fluky

"Stay really near to the starting line for the last minute. Anyone who is more than fifteen seconds late for a start, provided there is any wind at all, should feel themselves utterly disgraced. Most of us are, half the time."
—CHARLES CURRY

The requirement of starting in the light and fluky is simple: maintenance of maximum speed with clear air at a location that will permit unimpeded movement towards the area of greatest wind strength. The prerequisites of this accomplishment are the preservation of clear air and full speed for the final minute (or two) before the gun while heading in the favored direction. Simple, but in the confused and uncertain conditions of a light-air start, how?

We once started in a race in the open Chesapeake off Annapolis in a light easterly which was varying 30° to 45° in direction and from 1 to 5 knots in strength. We remained in the middle of the line until approximately a minute before the gun at which time it became evident that the weather end was favored by greater wind strength. On port tack we sailed up the line towards the weather mark. As we met the oncoming starboard tackers, they were headed; we crossed behind the first few, continued on port till close to the mark, tacked above the fleet where none could reach us, and crossed the line with the gun clear to weather of all competitors. From this point with free air we were able to move rapidly away from the mass of the fleet, tacking at will in the subsequent shifts.

The reasonable place to find clear air before the start in light air is on the line (or ahead of it), between the fleet and the wind. In as much as the favored end may not be determinable until just before the start, it is reasonable to remain in the center of the line (or ahead of it) until the last minute. At this moment with the least possible chance for a subsequent shift the move towards the favored end can be made. If the wind completely disintegrates at least clear air on the line has been preserved, and when the new wind arrives it will only be half the length of the line away. This is a far better position than being down in the pack at the wrong end or even in a similar blocked position at the right end. In light air it is better to be behind but moving in clear air than to be motionless and blanketed 100 yards ahead.

If at one minute to the start the windward end is favored, *i.e.* a starboard-tack lift has appeared, one should move back up the line on port and tack beneath the oncoming starboard tackers. In a lift it is essential to tack beneath the lay line to the mark, however. There is a real danger of being caught barging in light air if the lift increases as this allows the leeward boats to sail up to the weather end in a long slow curve. What may seem a perfectly safe position at 30 seconds to go may be a desperate one at 10 seconds when the leeward boats close what seemed like a large hole beneath the mark. Being forced the wrong side of the weather mark in these conditions may be disastrous if it requires a long slow return with a tack and a jibe, awaiting the passage of the entire fleet and followed by a longer and slower trailing in disturbed air and water. If caught barging, a better solution is to luff sharply or back the jib so as to stop before the mark is reached and then to dip in behind the leeward boat or boats after they pass. It is frequently possible to salvage a second or third position across the line by this technique retaining clear air to windward, backwinded but not blanketed. Be careful not to stop completely or the dip back may not be effectively achieved. Once out on the course in this backwinded condition consider carefully before tacking to clear air; never tack out of a lift unless certain of significant advantage, and if tacking is necessary, make it short, quick, and back to starboard.

Even if a starboard-tack header appears before the start it may be preferable to move up to the weather end of the line so as to retain freedom to tack to weather of the fleet. In this instance (as in the Chesapeake race mentioned above) it is often possible to cross the approaching starboard tackers on port to reach an invulnerable position above them, but still below the line. In a more extreme starboard-tack header, it is more reasonable to head down the line for the leeward end remembering, however, that the port tack is then lifted and that freedom to tack to port immediately after the gun is the key to ultimate success. In light air this freedom may only be available to a boat on or above the line just prior to the start. Boats starting conventionally from below the line in light air may be unable to point high enough to threaten the weather quarter of a boat ahead (or may not even be able to lay the leeward end of the line!). It is best not to move down the line until there is insufficient time remaining to reach the leeward end and only at a time when a sizeable hole appears. One must be moving at maximum speed when the gun sounds so as to surge over the boats to leeward and so as to have momentum to tack in the clear. Killing way just before the gun at the leeward end will result in one's being trapped in a leeward boat's backwind, unable to tack, and may even make clearing the leeward mark impossible. The only solution to this situation is to jibe away and return on port looking for a reasonable gap in the line of backwinded starboard tackers.

As port is the lifted tack when the starboard tack is headed, it may be desirable to start on port. Tacking to port is dangerous in light air so that the boat already under way on port is under better control. The port-tack boat is usually unimpeded by the backwind of other boats ahead on her tack and if the starboard header is marked, only has to break through a single file of slowly moving starboard tackers to cross the line. In addition the port-tack yacht is unencumbered by right-of-way restrictions whereas the starboard-tack yacht must hold her course when approaching another yacht. In light air, therefore, the port tack is often less hazardous than the starboard as greater speed is possible when reaching alone against the traffic (greater speed, better control) and is certainly less hazardous than tacking to port, which may result in the boat coming to a complete stop. If a port-tack start is elected, movement towards the leeward end from the center of the line should be undertaken sufficiently early to permit reaching the leeward mark and initiating the return before the gun.

The other major consideration of a light-air start is the current. If it is unfavorable, staying above the line until the last second is essential, and the techniques described are suitable. If it is favorable, however, staying near the line and utilizing techniques along the line are hazardous. In this circumstance all pre-start maneuvering must be displaced an appropriate distance behind the line.

Except in favorable tide, stay on the line near its center between the fleet and the wind until the last minute, poised to move towards the preferable end in clear air and under full way. With these advantages speed in excess of that available to the remainder of the fleet should permit last second-course adjustment to take maximum advantage of the continually changing circumstances.

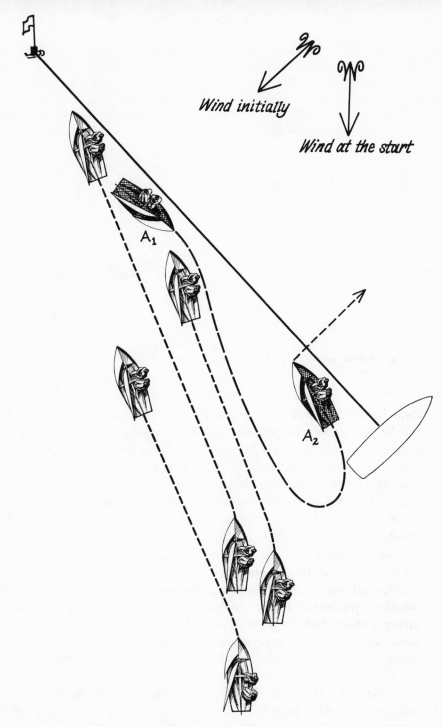

Wind initially

Wind at the start

A₁

A₂

A hovers near the middle of the line until the wind settles—with one minute to go—as a header for the starboard tack with stronger air to starboard. A then reaches across the headed fleet, tacks in the clear, crosses the line, and is free to continue or to tack towards the stronger air to starboard.

H. When It's Blowing

"There are still too many skippers who don't look in the mirror when they are looking for reasons for not winning races."

—TED WELLS

One fall in Annapolis we enjoyed a day of racing in a cold gusty northwester that capsized one and then another of the fleet until in the final race but three boats remained. I commented to my crew that the series should now be "easy pickings," as we had already won the earlier races, and prepared for the start. In a start in which only a few boats compete one easily becomes preoccupied with the individual competitors, whereas in a large fleet attention is usually concentrated on the start per se, and the competition is perceived only as an amorphous mass. I became concerned to reach the line ahead of my two rivals, and constantly looked astern to insure that I remained ahead and to leeward. In this manner I arrived at the weather (preferred) end of the line about 10 seconds early, necessitating a sharp luff to prevent a premature start. I could not bear away again until the gun was about to fire, and, as it did, one boat swept through to leeward on a semiplane, and the other, coming from well astern with full way on, marched over me to windward. I wallowed in their disturbed air until I had cleared the committee boat and was able to tack.

It is self-evident that excessive preoccupation with one's position relative to other competitors can detract from the effectiveness of the starting plan. Awareness of immediate neighbors is essential in the last seconds to insure separation from boats on the lee bow but (except in a match-race situation) serves no purpose in the starting pattern. I routinely make better starts in large fleets than I do in small ones; my personal involvement with and awareness of individual competitors in small fleets undoubtedly accounts for my behavior. A more subtle but equally significant lesson provided by this start is the recognition of the harmful effects of loss of way at the start in heavy air.

Stalling at the last instant before the gun is damaging in any condition. The necessity of maintaining maximum forward motion in a light-air start has been repeatedly emphasized. It is equally evident, however, that in moderate air luffing up to the line with almost no forward movement and bearing away in the final seconds is an extremely effective technique. This effectiveness is dependent upon the ability of the boat (some better than others!) to pick up way rapidly from a stalled position. In light air this ability is impaired and *in heavy air it is even more impaired*—and the explanation is essentially the same in each circumstance. Both very low and very high wind velocity result in a major increase in side force. In very light air the increased side force is consequent to the minimal forward movement when skin friction alone matches thrust. In heavy air increased side force is created when the aerodynamic force produced is in excess of that expendable in forward movement. In either instance side force is inversely proportional to the rate of forward movement produced by thrust, *i.e.* side force plus forward thrust equal aerodynamic force. Thus, until a major portion of the force produced is expended in overcoming forward resistance, *i.e.* until significant forward movement has been initiated, side force is extremely high and results in major leeway effects. Unless the boat's designed lateral planes adequately resist this leeway making force, the boat "crabs" at an angle in excess of 4° resulting in critical increases in forward resistance. A vicious cycle which results in progressive slowing is thus created in heavy air. The marked side force created when the sails are trimmed in initially results in a degree of leeway that prevents dissipating the excessive aerodynamic force in forward movement. The sails are trimmed in, and the boat stops! In contrast, in moderate air the total aerodynamic force produced does not exceed the designed lateral resistance provided by the hull and fins; the boat takes off immediately as the sails are trimmed. Large waves produced in heavy air and the loss of balance consequent to the lee-bow resistance of leeway, of course, further increase the resistance to forward movement, cause further slowing, and consequently further increase side force and leeway.

As the main is trimmed on the halted yacht, side force is increased, the boat skids laterally, markedly increasing forward resistance, and forward progress is inhibited until a reduction in side force permits its development.

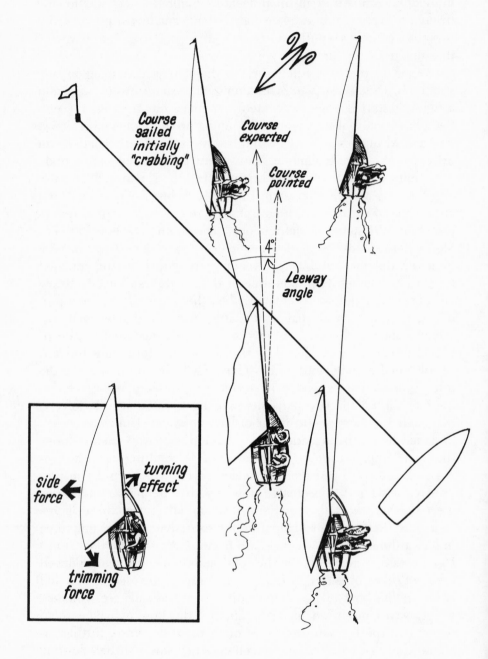

The basic lesson: avoid the stopping and slowing in heavy air that permit critical increases in side force, leeway, and forward resistance. Avoid bashing into waves, tacking frequently, pinching. Trim sails gradually so that forward movement increases synchronously with side force. Trim the boom and the jib at low angles of attack, as far outboard as possible, so that aerodynamic force is reduced and the maximum percentage of created force is acting forward instead of laterally. Move crew weight and centerboard aft to restore balance. Keep the boat moving at all times; sail her as freely as possible without heeling, play the waves, and bear away after feathering in a puff before she slows excessively. Thus, the major concern in sailing to windward in a breeze is to avoid the bugaboo of side force; tactics are much less important.

But, at the start don't stop! If you do, they'll be sailing by on both sides as you wallow with your side force, trimming and fuming. Come in late if necessary, come in farther down the line if necessary, but come in moving. Any boat ahead stalling and luffing will still be stalled and sliding off to leeward as you roar by! If you do find yourself stopped, trim slowly, and drive off—keep loose!

Avoid slowing, side force, and leeway—keep her moving!

I. Starting with the Current

*"When getting ready for the start, picture in your mind
what is likely to happen when all the boats in your race
approach the starting line at the same moment. What happens
then is always so different."*

—JOHN FISHER

Sixty-eight International 14's started the 1964 Itchenor Gallon in the
narrow upper reach of England's Chichester Harbor. We were
started at the beginning of the ebb when the harbor was about twice
the width that it would be six hours later. The line was set to favor
the leeward end at an angle across the harbor, shore to shore, to
provide the maximum possible length. By the time the warning
signal was displayed, the tide was rushing across the line, upwind,
at nearly 3 knots. We attempted a reach on starboard down the line
sufficiently far below it to prevent being swept across early. And so,
of course, did everyone else except a dozen port tackers who
smashed into the oncoming fleet head-on with the gun. In the confused melee half the fleet was over early—fortunately, as we were
dead in the water after being hit amidships by a port tacker. The
starboard tackers were being set laterally across the line and had
no place to go but across; they were unable to bear away because of
the mass of boats farther to leeward, unable to continue down the
line as they had reached the committee boat, and in the current
unable to stop and wait. The port tackers had even less option; they
aimed and were shot across the line willy-nilly at 3 knots plus boat
speed. After three false starts and their certain smashes, shouts, and

confusion, the line was reset and, at last, in one final Donnybrook, the fleet swept down the harbor.

In a narrow harbor with insufficient room for the fleet to cross and less room to arrange for an adjustable approach, no entirely safe and effective solution is possible. Indeed the only solution is to avoid a "good" start; only the late starters at the wrong end can reasonably expect to cross the line after the gun without a collision. Someone may and someone will break through the melee at the ideal location, will be just far enough to leeward to be behind the line when the gun goes, will have all the boats to windward called back, will not collide with the port tacker who can find no hole to sink in, and will suddenly be out in the clear, free, in a start that won't be recalled! Someone may and someone will, but only one will. Why back a 64-to-1 shot?

In the open North Sea a few weeks later, we started in the practice race for the P.O.W. across a perfectly laid starting line in a similar two-plus knot favorable current. On this line and with all this room we expected to be able to achieve the start we desired: clear air at the leeward end heading for the increased current off shore. We now had 84 other boats with the same intention so that accurate planning would be essential. While awaiting the warning signal we timed the sweep to the line at its leeward end from varying points to leeward. It was soon evident that an initial position anywhere near the line required a continual fight to work to leeward while reaching down the line. This would obviously be much too dangerous when the fleet joined us in the final pattern. We would have to approach from a position well to leeward so as to come up under the mass of starboard tackers and to break into the clear only at the gun. The remainder of the fleet approaching from nearer the line would have to bear away and slow by easing sheets as they fought to prevent being swept over early. We would be able to increase speed at will thereby constantly improving our position and maintaining a course of our choosing along the lay line to the leeward mark.

We decided upon a two minute run on the final approach, an unusually long one for the light to moderate air that prevailed. Inasmuch as testing revealed that we could sweep over the line almost head to wind with all sails luffing, we selected our initial position below the lay line to the leeward end. From this position we would have freedom to escape from boats farther to leeward and would be able to luff to achieve slowing without crossing to windward of the lay line. We worked downwind and uptide from the line for about six minutes before we reached the desired initial position. Here we merely stemmed the tide until but two minutes remained till the gun. From this position we could not reach the line by current alone before the gun—but all our competitors to windward could and would. We turned close-hauled for the line (which seemed a half mile away!) and luffed along adjusting our speed to the time remaining. The gathering fleet began to press close astern and to windward, and as we closed the line a few shot through to leeward. With little available space to leeward remaining we bore away to protect our lee bow and trimmed in for the final rush to the line. We were now in free air with no one to leeward, timed to cross the line right at the committee boat with the gun. However, we had had to work so far to leeward that we were luffing almost head to wind as we neared the line. The gun fired just as we reached the mast of the committee boat, and we were off to a perfect start with the entire fleet in a confused melee behind us. Off and clear—until suddenly we slammed to a stop and were flung about on the port tack in the direct path of the fleet!

In the strong current the committee had been unable to set their distance mark for the leeward end of the line and instead had hauled the mark aboard leaving its anchor line extending perpendicularly from its side just beneath the water. We had caught this line on our rudder—and were now disqualified.

As I waited out the race making plans (successful) for the Prince of Wales Cup on the morrow, I also had time to review the start in favorable current. This seemed the most difficult starting situation, and it was obvious from a quarter (or more) mile away that a fractional miscalculation would spell disaster. We had retained the dominant uptide position by working far enough to leeward to be under the entire fleet throughout the approach. From this conservative position with right of way over all our competitors, we had been able to adjust a course to leeward of the actual lay line so as to arrive on the line exactly at the gun with free air. We had had to modify the plan and to cut our reserve space to zero so as to avoid any boat rounding up from astern to our lee bow in the final seconds. But we had done it and the plan had worked—only to be ambushed by an enemy we hadn't realized existed!

In favorable current initiate the approach from a position that will not permit reaching the line by the effects of current alone, farther uptide than any of the competitors, to leeward of the lay line to the preferred site on the line, and luff along the approach so as to maintain control of speed and competitors throughout.

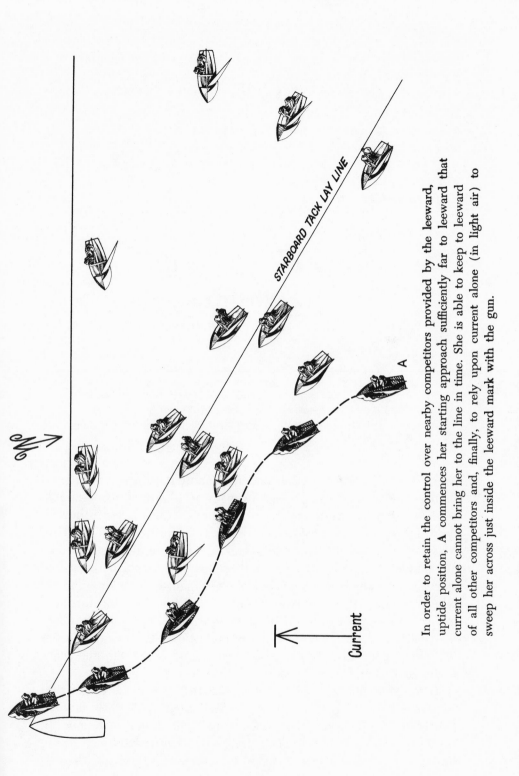

STARBOARD TACK LAY LINE

Current

In order to retain the control over nearby competitors provided by the leeward, uptide position, A commences her starting approach sufficiently far to leeward that current alone cannot bring her to the line in time. She is able to keep to leeward of all other competitors and, finally, to rely upon current alone (in light air) to sweep her across just inside the leeward mark with the gun.

J. Starting against the Current

"The importance of a good start, regardless of the strength of the wind or the size of the fleet, cannot be exaggerated. The good helmsman after a bad start can catch up to the inexperienced and less able helmsmen he would have beaten in any event, but he will never catch up to the other top helmsmen in the race."

—LIVIUS SHERWOOD

Mass confusion, shouts, collisions, no one at the line on time, and finally one or two boats break away to an almost insurmountable lead—usually by accident rather than design. But there can be successful design in a start against the current and successful solution. Most essential usually is maneuverability and an alertness to take advantage of the situation as it develops. The usual conservative starboard-tack approach may be hopeless against a two-knot current when the entire fleet wallows in dirty air. Unless the windward end is favored it may be difficult to lay the line on starboard and impossible to lay the leeward end from any point down the line. And even if the weather end is favored the accentuated crowding, and blanketing at this end prevent an easy solution.

At the start of the 1964 Connecticut Cup Race a moderate wind shift plus the committee's attempt to lay a line that slightly favored the leeward end actually produced a line that could not be laid on starboard against the 2½ knot tide. The fleet attempted to run the line on starboard and met the few port tackers head on at the leeward end committee boat. As the leading starboard-tack boats came about on port to clear this mark, they met the remainder of the fleet coming down to windward still on starboard. After multiple tacks, near misses, and a few collisions the fleet desperately broke away on port, blanketed, and backwinded. The boats on top included one who wove his way through the fleet on port and a few who tacked early to port from the downwind "weather" end, boats that managed to find the momentary holes they needed to break away across the bows of starboard tackers.

The ideal, most upwind point, on the line thus becomes of secondary significance compared with finding a location and an approach that will permit extrication with a clear wind. If the weather end is favored it may be possible to come in barging with the gun, or at least late, as the mass of the fleet is swept off to leeward by the current. Or a more conventional start ahead and to leeward of the mass, being careful to work up close to the line early, may provide clear air as the remainder wallow about in their own blanket and backwind. Such simple solutions are obviously ineffectual for the more common, leeward-end favored starting lines, however. With leeward-end favored starting lines clear air may only be acquired by approaching from above the line or on port tack or from a starboard-tack position that permits an immediate tack.

Dipping down from above the line is rarely safe except in the presence of an adverse current when it is unlikely that many boats will be able to crowd up to leeward of the line. A hole to dip into at the last moment is usually available, but the danger of dipping in so far down the line that the leeward mark cannot be cleared must be remembered. In a race on the river at Essex, I hovered above the middle of the line barely stemming the tide as I awaited the gun, and the fleet bore down from the weather end. When I bore away with the current at the last moment I shot across the line but found that I was unable to clear the leeward mark, which, in the extremely light air, apparently could only be laid from the weather end! It is often impossible in very light air to test the approach before the start so that a conservative dip well back on the line may be the only safe solution. If a large weather-end committee boat prevents the normally starting boats from reaching the adjacent segment of the line at the weather end, a start from above the line may permit a safe entry into this protected zone and a start to windward of the fleet.

The port-tack approach seems the most radical technique, but in practice it may be the safest. In a strong adverse tide few boats

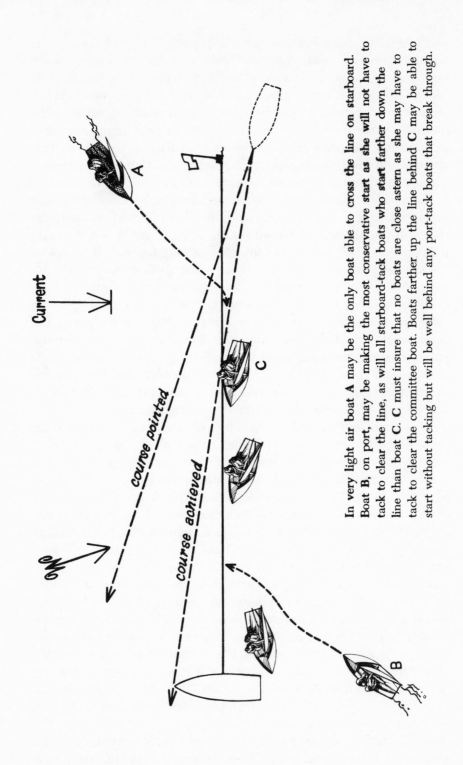

Current

course pointed

course achieved

A

C

B

In very light air boat **A** may be the only boat able to cross the line on starboard. Boat **B**, on port, may be making the most conservative start as **she will not have to tack to clear the line, as will all starboard-tack boats who start farther down the line than boat C.** C must insure that no boats are close astern as she may have to tack to clear the committee boat. Boats farther up the line behind C may be able to start without tacking but will be well behind any port-tack boats that break through.

110

(with clear air), if any, will be able to cross the line without tacking, when the leeward end is favored. Tacking is a dangerous maneuver on the starting line in the best of conditions and when tacking is to port it results in a prolonged period of vulnerability. The boat approaching on port, under no proper course restrictions, however, may weave along to leeward of the fleet, under good way, until the ideal opening appears and then shoot through. Once free on port, she should have clear air and be working steadily into a commanding uptide position while her competitors flounder about, tacking, back winding, and blanketing. Although it is rarely possible to break through precisely at the leeward end, it is almost always possible to find a hole someplace back along the line and in any case usually no farther back than the position of the first starboard tacker who is able to tack.

By a judicious combination of an approach from above the line or directly along the line, carefully observing the range of the line to prevent being swept below it, a boat may with even greater safety start on starboard in these conditions. The essential feature of the standard starboard start along the line is the avoidance of boats close astern. Controlling boats astern is difficult but can be accomplished in two ways: by holding back luffing and allowing overtaking boats to pass to leeward or by starting well back on the line so that few competitors will be astern. The usual precept, instinctively followed, is to keep boats off one's lee bow and to catch and hold them astern and to windward. This technique must be assiduously avoided in these conditions, stepping aside gracefully in an "after you, Pierre" fashion, to clear the water astern for a quick tack at the most opportune moment. Although such freedom requires careful prestart positioning, it provides not only the opportunity to break away on port uptide but control of the entire fleet downtide and to leeward. Port-tack boats will have limited chance to cross ahead and all starboard-tack boats must reckon with the presence of the most windward starboard tacker when they dare to come about ahead and are slowed by the reduced apparent wind on the up-current course. It may be appropriate to sail on just beyond the leeward mark, shaving off the close starboard competitors, who, in your backwind, will be unable to lay the mark, and to tack beyond it, protected from the close port tackers.

If you are unable to tack clear ahead or when approaching on port must bear away rapidly to go astern, have your rig adjusted to permit such maneuverability. Many a small sailboat with the board full down and the main strapped in just will not bear off. Have your board up a bit (or ready to come up) and the mainsheet in your hand, ready for easing, as soon as you complete your tack and until you are clear away.

Only a few successful gambits are available, and most of the fleet will miss them. Alertness to the last-minute conditions of the fleet and the variations of the wind will indicate which technique will be most successful. Stay close to the line near its center while deciding your approach.

Arrange for the speed and the control of the opposition necessary to place you either on port at the favored leeward end or above the line on starboard for the necessary breakaway in clear air—but look before you leap! Gambling is only successful when you control the deck!

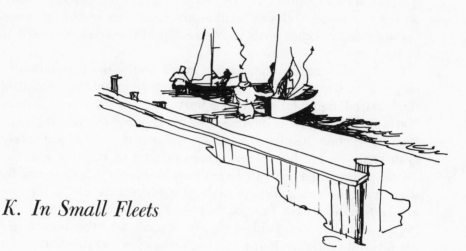

K. In Small Fleets

"I maintain that a skipper who is familiar with the racing regulations and well routined could get rid of half of his competitors in a race simply by protests, if he directed his efforts strictly to that effect."

—MANFRED CURRY

There are problems in starting in large fleets, and these are disturbing to the inexperienced. The problems of starting in small fleets are sometimes greater, however, and usually more dangerous. Perhaps it is because the large fleets demand planning and caution, qualities often lacking in small fleet starts. Failure to adhere to a plan and/or preoccupation with specific competitors is often the downfall of the start in a small fleet. It might almost be said that the successful start in a small fleet requires the assumption that the fleet is large.

In one of our winter regattas only two other boats besides mine appeared for the final races. Preoccupied with keeping between my two competitors and the favored weather end of the line, I sailed along ahead of them on the lay line approach and suddenly found myself at the line too soon. As I luffed to a halt, my rivals roared by on each side. I was soon backwinded 30 feet astern.

When the termination of the approach is close, keeping ahead of the competitors on the lay line to the weather end or racing them down the line to the leeward end becomes a dangerous game. Far better to utilize the big fleet technique, luff up to the weather end

113

or hold up on the way down the line to break away from competitors on the lee bow. A studied unawareness of one's competition and a determination to follow a reasonable plan to reach the desired point on the line under full way at the gun regardless of the presence (or absence) of other boats is as essential in the small fleet as it is in the large.

Perhaps the greatest danger in a small fleet is the temptation to barge. In a large fleet the risk of barging is so evident that it is rarely dared. Being caught by one boat is as disastrous as by a fleet, however. If one boat is interested in the capture, the barging position leaves one helpless. A major risk exists in not accurately evaluating the lay line to the windward end of the line and the course of boats along it. In large fleets the general flow is readily detectable and recognition of one's position relative to the lay line is ascertainable at the time of tacking into the final approach run even from a hundred yards away. In a small fleet the open water permits wide variation in the approach course so that the other boats become poor indicators of the safe course below the lay line. Frequently the leeward boats may sail a circular course, heading low of the lay line initially, which may lead the unwary weather boat into a trap when she attempts to slip between them and the weather mark.

Several tactical control techniques can be applied in small fleet starts that facilitate a successful start but that would be untenable in large fleets. The smaller the fleet the closer it simulates the match start in which success is determined by holding the competitor to a less advantageous start. I once watched a Snipe Class start in which the entire barging fleet (of about six boats) was trapped by a boat ahead and to leeward at the weather end. The leader luffed almost head to wind with each competitor overlapping her neighbor to leeward forced to luff responsively. When the gun went the leader bore away to clear the weather mark while each of her competitors was forced to fight her way around to leeward of her and the mark. This technique can be successful against a major portion of a group of barging boats and is most effectively applied by approaching the weather-end lay line from down the line on port, then tacking ahead and to leeward of the approaching bargers.

A modification of this same technique can be applied at any location along the line to permit tacking just ahead and to leeward of the approaching starboard tackers. When this technique is applied just before the gun and just below the line it can insure reaching the starting position ahead of the competition. The technique is

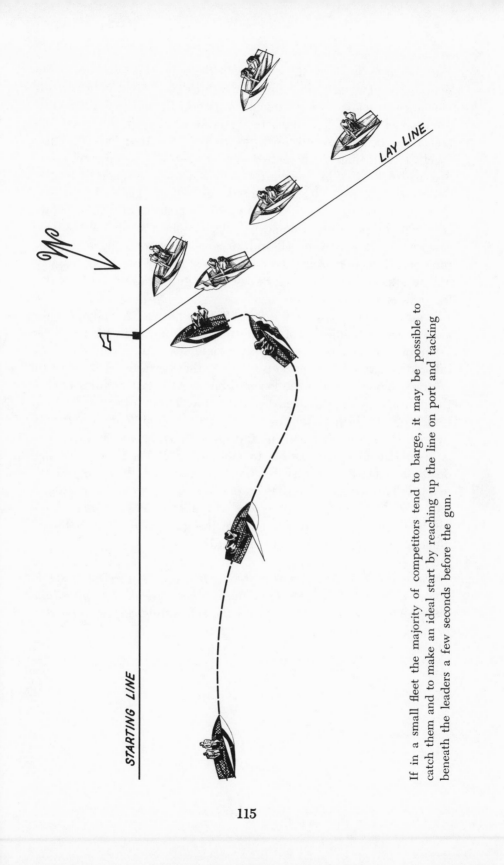

STARTING LINE

LAY LINE

If in a small fleet the majority of competitors tend to barge, it may be possible to catch them and to make an ideal start by reaching up the line on port and tacking beneath the leaders a few seconds before the gun.

115

risky in large fleets or at times when the small fleet is excessively scattered, but even then, if properly timed in a hole between advancing starboard tackers, can be successfully accomplished. The duration of a 180° tack must be accurately recognized so that the tack may be completed, forward way reinitiated, and the line reached immediately thereafter with the gun. This technique is extremely effective in a leeward-end start when the reach down the line to the favored start at the mark can not be readily timed and is fraught with the risk of a competitor appearing on the lee bow. It should be possible to come in from beyond and below the leeward mark with between 10 and 20 seconds to go, to tack beneath the nearest approaching starboard tacker, to luff her as necessary, and to slip across at the mark with the gun, leading and on the lee bow of the entire fleet.

It may also be possible in a small fleet to mislead the competition (if you are considered of sufficient competence to attract their attention!) into making an inappropriate start. If the port tack is favored but the line is cocked to place the leeward end farther to weather, hanging about the leeward end for the last minutes before the gun may bring the fleet down the line. Then in the last minute it may be possible to reach below the approaching fleet on port and to cross their sterns for a clear start on port. When the weather end is favored it may be possible to tack ahead of the fleet gathering on the lay line and to rush for the line as if but a few seconds remained. This may induce the competition to come rushing in astern and, while you luff to a halt, to roar past, above and below, on down the line. Twenty seconds later when the gun goes you may be all alone in the ideal position, crossing at the mark.

Planned, conservative starting techniques are as essential in small fleets as in large, but control techniques that mislead the opposition and provide additional freedom for the calculating skipper may also be successfully applied.

L. Starting on Port

"So much for experts! It's good to listen to them. It's good of them to advise, but don't allow yourself to be misled."
—BEECHER MOORE

It has been said that any line that can be laid on starboard should be crossed on starboard. Although the converse does not deserve equal status, there are many lines that can be laid on port that are better crossed on port. This is largely consequent to the general acceptance of the first statement with the result that, except for the few fortunate leaders, most of those starting on starboard are unable to secure the essential requisites of a good start—clear air and freedom to maneuver. The following selected circumstances indicate the opportunities (and dangers) for clear air and freedom to maneuver inherent in the port-tack start.

1. The second race of the annual U.S.–Canada Team Match for the Emerson Trophy was started on a line that heavily favored the leeward end. As my teammates held back the Canadian defenders, I slipped across on port at the leeward end and went on to win with ease. This is the classical port-tack start that we all dream about but which is actually more fantasy than fact. Without the support of my teammates and in a larger fleet this gambit would have been impossible—and more to the point it was unnecessary. The port-tack start in this instance provided nothing more than that available from a well-timed start on starboard at the leeward end.

2. I was over early at the weather end of the line in a Penguin race in Annapolis Harbor. After circling the huge committee boat I started in the same spot—now last instead of first. But as soon as I had cleared the committee boat, I was able to tack to port towards the north shore of the river where a more perpendicular, off-shore wind provided a significant starboard-tack lift. I rounded the weather mark first having passed all 30 of my competitors. This opportunity to reach the preferred side of the beat is the most significant element of any start. If starting on port best provides this opportunity, the port tack start should be utilized.

3. Ben Minor sets a line off a pier or a barge in the Washington Channel when we race in the Washington's Birthday Regatta, readjusts it the following day (whether it needs to be or not), and in the interim sits back to howl at our antics as we attempt to negotiate it. Once when the line could barely be laid on starboard, we swept down on starboard cutting off the port tackers one after the other. Exhilarated by having caught everyone, we sought to tack so as to cover the fleet only to find that we were pinned down by a boat astern and that the fleet had already left. They picked up the Hanes Point shift ahead and to leeward and disappeared. When the weather end of the line is favored, starting on starboard at the extreme weather end provides freedom to tack to port after clearing the line. When the leeward end is favored only the port tack provides freedom to assume the port tack immediately after the start.

4. At the start of The Bucket in 1960 a dramatic heading shift pinned us into a chain of starboard tackers as the gun sounded. We jibed away, sliced behind the entire fleet, and were away in the port-tack lift as the remainder of the fleet squirmed anxiously past the committee boat's anchor line. Here the port tack was essential to obtain the advantages of the port-tack lift and the breakaway into clear air from the mass of the fleet all pinned to starboard tack, none daring to tack, and all barely able to clear the leeward end of the line.

5. At Kingston in 1959 it seemed almost impossible to get clear from a starboard-tack start at the heavily favored leeward end in the 60 boat C.D.A. fleet. We started on port in the fourth race weaving our way through the starboard-tack mass, slipping behind this boat, ahead of that one, until at last we broke through the most windward line. Suddenly we were all alone

in clear air, no backwind, no blanket, no wake, and we were moving. The same attempt at the start of the Ice Bowl in 1960 met with near disaster. I attempted to cut through early and only by a violent bearing away and a subsequent tack back did I avoid disqualification and then ended up exactly where I'd hoped not to be—pinned down on starboard. It is thus essential to be conservative (on port?) in reaching down the line close under the starboard-tack fleet and to await a truly adequate clearing before attempting to slip through. It always comes, and the advantages gained by the port tacker in clear air once he is through will more than compensate for distance lost to windward while awaiting the appearance of the clearing.

6. It is particularly dangerous to attempt a port-tack start in very heavy air or in very light air—say the books. If your competitors have read these books your port-tack start will undoubtedly be safer. It is when several competitors wish to join you that the port-tack start becomes dangerous. It is the freedom to maneuver that provides its advantage and its safety; if adjustment to the course of starboard-tack yachts is impaired by the presence of other port-tack yachts the danger of disqualification becomes extreme. At Rochester in 1959 in a 30 knot westerly that decimated the fleet, Paul Henderson crossed the entire fleet on port from the leeward end. He was able to bear away and drive across while the rest of us bobbed up and down pinching to clear the committee boat anchor line. We hadn't dared to press down close to the "coffin corner" before the gun and after the gun did not dare to tack with the danger of stopping in those seas. At Miles River in '64 Bob Reeves swept across immediately behind me on port as I squeezed past the leeward-end flag in little wind and much adverse tide. I couldn't tack because of the other pinchers behind me until after I'd cleared the buoy, borne away, and picked up sufficient speed. By that time Bob was long gone. It is exactly in these very light and very heavy conditions when tacking becomes most dangerous, leaving the tacker barely moving and vulnerable in the path of another starboard starter, that the port-tack start becomes most advantageous.

Thus, the port tack may be the essential means of (1) reaching the preferred side of the beat, (2) obtaining the advantage of a port-tack lift, and (3) obtaining clear air. When it is dangerous to tack from starboard to port immediately after the start in order to achieve these advantages, as in large fleets, when the port end of the line is farther upwind, in adverse tide, in very light air, and in very heavy air, it may be reasonable to cross the line on port tack. Port tack provides the advantage of speed on the approach, which is the essential element of freedom to maneuver, permitting a breakaway in clear air and in the desired direction. It should be avoided, however, when freedom to maneuver is impaired by several boats starting together on port (unless the line cannot be laid on starboard), and the break through the starboard-tack fleet should only be attempted when a sufficient clearing in the mass of starboard tackers appears. Two elements of the freedom to maneuver should be utilized at all times while on port tack: (1) speed—keep her moving; and (2) steering control—have the board part way up to facilitate bearing away and the sails well controlled by immediate sheet adjustments to course changes.

The port-tack start should be utilized—carefully—in situations where tacking from starboard to port is hazardous and to facilitate obtaining the preferred side of the course, clear air, and/or the lifted tack.

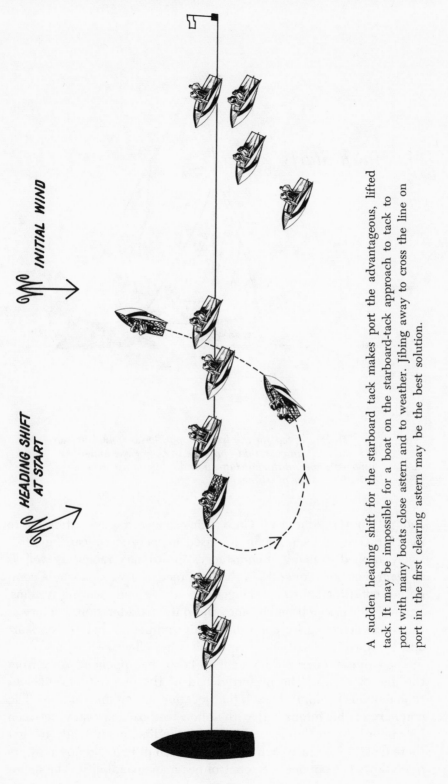

INITIAL WIND

HEADING SHIFT
AT START

A sudden heading shift for the starboard tack makes port the advantageous, lifted tack. It may be impossible for a boat on the starboard-tack approach to tack to port with many boats close astern and to weather. Jibing away to cross the line on port in the first clearing astern may be the best solution.

M. Match Starts

> *"Having opted for the leeward position or found herself
> in it she must do everything possible to keep close under her
> opponent; even at the last luff up under him at the expense
> of half a length of distance."*
>
> —JOHN ILLINGWORTH

Interest in the America's Cup racing has attracted attention to
match-race starts. The technique used in these starts can be effectively applied to many circumstances in ordinary racing as well as
in team racing. Frequently in the final race of a series a single competitor constitutes the only danger and, under many scoring systems,
beating this competitor becomes the only consideration. Victory is
then best achieved by controlling this competitor before the start
and by starting ahead and free of his wind effects.

The primary offensive intent is to keep the opponent away from
the line or at least the preferred end of the line until insufficient
time remains for him to reach that location on the line on time. The
corollary of this intent is that the offensive boat must stay between
his opponent and the desired point on the line, every ready to "get
there first." In defense each boat must attempt to avoid any position
that allows her opponent to control her maneuverability. The major

premises of defense are thus to prevent the opponent from achieving a controlling position close astern and, whenever closing the opponent, to be moving in the opposite direction.

If the opponent is not aggressive, *i.e.* makes no attempt to achieve control, and intends a conventional start, the port-tack approach is advantageous. Port tack is unrestricted by balking limitations and therefore permits greater freedom of maneuver. When the leeward end of the line is favored, a reaching approach permits crossing ahead of the major opponent, if an opening appears, or if not, crossing his transom with clear air on the lifted tack. When either end is favored, the port-tack approach permits tacking beneath the opponent and starting on his lee bow. The port-tack start not only eliminates the balking restrictions of the starboard-tack while maneuvering before the start but provides the right-of-way advantages of the starboard-tack boat at the time of the first meeting of the boats after the start.

When the opponent is aggressive, a more forceful technique may be required. If he voluntarily sails away from the line so that a relatively high-speed return will be required, tacking ahead and blanketing or back-winding will provide the desired starting advantage. Riding the opponent's transom after the 5 minute gun (or sooner if necessary) will often insure this type of control. From behind, the opponent's movements can be countered and he can be continually forced ahead, preferably to a position beyond the range of his ability to return with the gun. As soon as an overlap to leeward is established, the trailing boat acquires right of way, and the leading boat must speed up to keep clear. Once the boat ahead is forced too far from the line in either direction, the trailing boat can tack away and reach the line in the lead.

The control-from-astern technique can be useful on the approach to the line as the leading boat may be forced ahead from the leeward overlap position, possibly to cross the line early, and provides the option of reaching off below to start on the leader's lee bow in the final seconds. The achievement of the control-from-astern position is best accomplished from upwind as the opponent sails by below or by tacking or jibing behind after a crossing. If the position can be achieved when the opponent is sailing away from the line (or well before the gun when he is sailing towards the line) it may be impossible for him to break away to cross the line until permitted. Tacking is impossible as the prolonged maneuver without right of way cannot be completed in the path of a following boat a few feet astern. Jibing, being a more rapid maneuver, may be more reason-

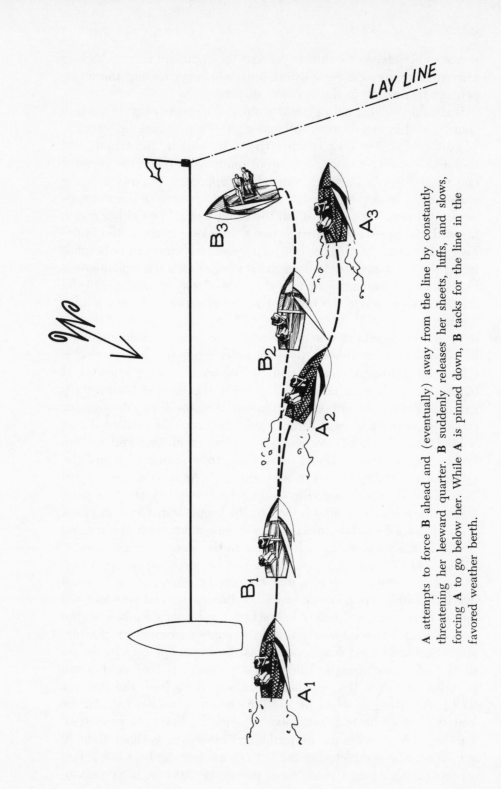

LAY LINE

A attempts to force B ahead and (eventually) away from the line by constantly threatening her leeward quarter. B suddenly releases her sheets, luffs, and slows, forcing A to go below her. While A is pinned down, B tacks for the line in the favored weather berth.

able but, if the following boat alertly bears away close on the leader's leeward quarter, is usually preventable. When the leader is being forced away on the starboard tack she is completely trapped as even after completion of any attempted tack or jibe she will be caught on port tack. When forced away on port tack, there may be some hope of completing a sudden jibe to starboard and, in return, trapping the follower on port. If the control-from-astern position has not been achieved until shortly before the gun and the opponent is approaching the line it may be possible to turn her by tacking into, or reaching down into, a lee-bow position. We were able to achieve this position at the start of the second Douglas Trophy Race (U.S. vs. Canada annual match series) in 1964 and succeeded in scraping the Canadian defender off on the committee boat, thereby forcing her to tack back. We then tacked immediately behind her to create the force-away pattern.

The defense, of course, becomes, with perfection, more effective than the offense. The intention of the leading boat's skipper is to return before being forced too far from the line and to time his break-away maneuver for an ideal return run. Even if the leading boat is able to jibe away, however, the following boat can continue the controlled follow or, if late, can tack inside to reach the line ahead. If the following boat is slightly to weather, intending to prevent a tack to return to the line, a sudden slow-up can catch him unaware, permit a luff head to wind and force him about before he desires. If the following boat is slightly to leeward, prodding the leading boat ahead, a sudden slow-up can catch him pinned to leeward, permit a tack away, and a return to the line in the covering position, to windward. *Gretel's* unique technique, displayed in her first America's Cup Race with *Weatherly* riding her transom, was to luff suddenly head to wind from a fast reach. *Weatherly* had to avoid hitting her transom, was in danger of fouling out if she shot past to weather, and thus had to shoot by to leeward. Once she had swept past, *Gretel* fell away on *Weatherly's* transom and, later, was able to tack for the line in the lead!

Unless match-race conditions exist and all depends upon beating a single competitor, forget the above and concentrate on a good start with clear air.

But if there's only one boat to beat, jump on him early, push him away from the line, and keep him there! (And hope that he hasn't learned a little defensive match racing himself!)

III. *Beating —*

The Accomplishment of Strategic Advantage

A. The Principles of Beating

"For while the tired waves, vainly breaking
  Seem here no painful inch to gain,
Far back, through creeks and inlets making,
  Comes silent, flooding in, the main."

*"For knowledge and wisdom come to us gradually and
silently, and just as we must live long to have either, so we
must sail long to become past masters in the arts of sailing
and seamanship."*

—UFFA FOX

The windward leg is universally considered to be the major determinant of racing success. The helmsman who is first at the weather
mark is often conceded the victory and granted magical ability in
his fingertips. Magic or not, the first position at the weather mark
is a most enviable condition as it provides not only the lead but the
indispensable asset of clear air on the reach.

Although success to windward is in part determined by boat-
handling techniques, the major factor is strategy. The considerations
that determine the proper side of the course, the area of advantageous wind, wave, and current conditions, are the usual determinants
of success to windward. Tactical considerations are concerned with
reaching the area of strategic advantage first and remaining therein
more continuously than any other competitor. Boats become more
widely spread and experience more varied conditions on the beat
than they do at any other time. The acquisition of a beneficial wind
shift, a less disadvantageous current effect, a greater wind strength,
or a lessened exposure to large waves creates the sometimes immense
difference between the position of the leading boat and the losing

129

boat at the termination of the windward leg.

1. The new wind must be planned for and sought after.
2. The preferrable tack for the second beat must be determined in advance and acquired.
3. The windward leg must be sailed as if in the lead, conservatively, covering the Frenchmen.
4. In light air the middle must be avoided; keep to the side of the course.
5. In oscillating winds the lay line must be avoided; the boat on the lay line loses with any subsequent wind shift.
6. A controlling relationship to the massed competitors on the lay line must be insured for the approach to the mark.
7. The inevitability of loss due to adverse wind shifts must be accepted; confine its degree, once recognized, by immediate compensating action.
8. Plan for wind shifts; the resultant wind at any time is a combination of a prevailing wind, a weather system wind, and a local thermal wind modified by the vertical stability of the air and the local geography.
9. The compass is essential in determining the favored tack in an oscillating wind by indicating the degree and direction of variation of any shift from the median wind direction.
10. Following compass indications blindly must be avoided on a short beat or in the presence of thermal, geographic, or weather-system shifts.
11. When beating against the tide one should sail directly to the area of the beat with the least unfavorable current and short tack in this area until a sufficient distance beyond the lay line is reached to permit recrossing the current and rounding the mark.
12. When beating along the shore against the tide one should tack as infrequently as possible consistent with keeping farther into the slack water than the competition.
13. One must keep to the side of the river from which channeled wind will next emerge and be on the inside of the fleet when rounding all major bends in a river.
14. Areas of large waves must be avoided; one should sail through them with proper respect for their damaging effects.
15. The luff is the most effective means of breaking away from the lee-bow controlled position.
16. Tactical control must be attained at the weather mark and the lay lines.

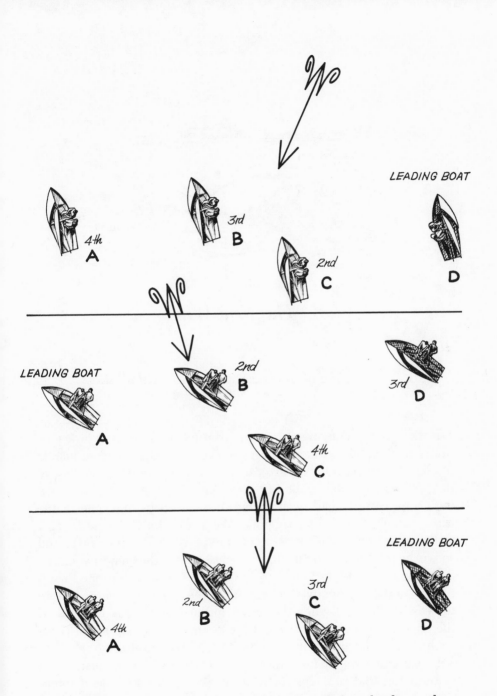

Major changes in relative position to windward result from heading and lifting wind shifts. The strategy of position is the determinant of success on the windward leg.

B. The New Wind

*"I was born in the breezes, and I had studied the sea
as perhaps few men have studied it, neglecting all else."*
—JOSHUA SLOCUM

We tried to break away on to port from the weather end in a race in the 1962 National Regatta but, stopped in a flat spot, were unable to clear a starboard tacker astern. After a few minutes of luffing in determined anguish, we set off to test our intended plan. The morning's northeasterly had been dying all day and by the time of the three o'clock start was nearly gone. We looked for the wind to shift farther east as the high-pressure system moved on to the north, and so we headed out into the Bay on port while the majority of the fleet took the starboard tack up the shore. The wind dropped completely and then finally filled in from the east; we were well to the east of the fleet when the new wind arrived and as they sailed the great circle, we went straight for the mark to round a 100 yards in the lead—but, unfortunately, no longer in the race.

In every race the major determinant of success is an understanding of the wind that provides for it, its vagaries, variations, and intentions. Long before the start, weather reports, past experience, and the knowledge of local sailors must be utilized to determine the origin of the wind observed and the possible variations that may be expected. All wind is due to a combination of a prevailing wind, a weather system wind, a wind due to local thermal influences, and variations in these winds due to local terrain features. These combinations may be additive or interfering. A northeasterly due to the presence of a high-pressure system center to the northwest during the summer in the Chesapeake is a light wind because its direction opposes the thermal sea breeze that comes up the Bay from the southeast. As the high moves past to the north the weather system wind swings around to the east and still later comes in strong from the southeast as the sea breeze and the weather system wind reinforce each other. It was reasonable to have expected this new wind from the east.

Consideration of the factors producing the wind present at the start of the race and of possible changes in it due to changing wind factors should permit the development of a strategic plan for each leg of the course. If the wind is at least moderately strong and steady at the start of the race it is unlikely that major directional changes will occur during the first round. Although the northeast wind at the start of the 1964 Prince of Wales Cup was expected to shift offshore as the easterly sea breeze came in with the rising sun, we could detect no trace of such variation in the hour before the start. We went inshore out of the tide disregarding the expected shift—which didn't arrive until the second round when we were already far ahead. When the air is light and varying at the start, however, particularly in a morning start before the full effects of a thermal wind appear, look for a new wind early. Beware the anxious race committee that sends the fleet off before the wind has settled. In Annapolis we often start in the remains of yesterday's northwester at ten or eleven in the morning to be met on the run by the noon southeasterly. A dramatic zone of chaotic calm then separates the portion of the fleet still sailing in the northwester upriver from those in the lively southeaster at the mouth of the harbor.

The time of the day during which the race is conducted and the presence or absence of sunlight is thus of critical importance in determining any wind changes that may occur. If the sun is out and the day is young, expect the thermal wind to become increasingly significant with a sudden shift to the sea breeze if a light weather-system wind opposes it, or a gradual shift if the weather-system wind more nearly parallels it. If it is late in the day expect the thermal effect to become less significant as time goes on and the wind to shift back in the direction of the weather system effect. In Toronto's horrible Humber Bay the summer thermal is a southeasterly on-shore breeze which lifts above the offshore northerlies due to weather-system winds, leaving a zone of calm and reversed wind within ¼ to ½ mile of shore. In the Baker Trophy Race off Toronto's Boulevard Yacht Club we once took off in the early afternoon in a twenty-knot southeasterly to a 100 yard lead at the weather mark and improved it for two laps only to have the roof fall in as we *planed* under spinnaker into a zone of flat calm just short of the near-shore finish line. The effects of the midday thermal had faded with the falling sun, and the fitful northerly was back along the shore. We were barely able to salvage second as the entire fleet slatted all around us, dropping spinnakers for the 100 foot beat to the finish. In the 1964 Ice Bowl we rounded the last leeward mark of the five laps a close second and held southwest in the dying westerly expecting that the high pressure weather system would have moved far enough east during the long day to have converted the dying westerly into a southwesterly. It had, but too late. Its effects were not detectable until we were on the port-tack lay line, sailing away from the shift.

The location of the weather mark to the shoreline will also determine the possible appearance of variations in the starting wind consequent to terrain features. A new wind direction consequent to deviation around a bend in a river or to deviation more perpendicularly, close to a windward shore, must be considered together with the variations in the weather-system position or thermal influences. At the Barnegat Bay Bowl we once worked to the south of the beat as we expected the sea breeze to bring in the afternoon southerly, but the weather mark at the mouth of the Tom's River was actually in a zone of more westerly wind emanating from the east-west channel. At Buzzard's Bay we expect the sea breeze to turn any westerly (prevailing or weather-system wind) more to the southwest as the sun rises and for the wind to swing back in line with its basic direction aloft as the sun goes down. But we keep in mind the more westerly deviation of any southwesterly at anytime of the day close to the western shore of the Bay.

Consider the possibilities for new wind before the race, and then be continuously alert to indications of the appearance of such expected (or unexpected) new winds during the race. Both skipper and crew should watch for that telltale dark line on the water as the sea breeze or the new northwesterly comes in. Check boats in other classes, flags on marks, or smoke ashore repeatedly so as to be the first to detect the shift. We once saw a hard line of northwesterly wind race across Round Bay, capsizing the tail enders before it, as we beat to windward in a light southerly and were sufficiently forewarned to plane away in it without a capsize. Watch your com-

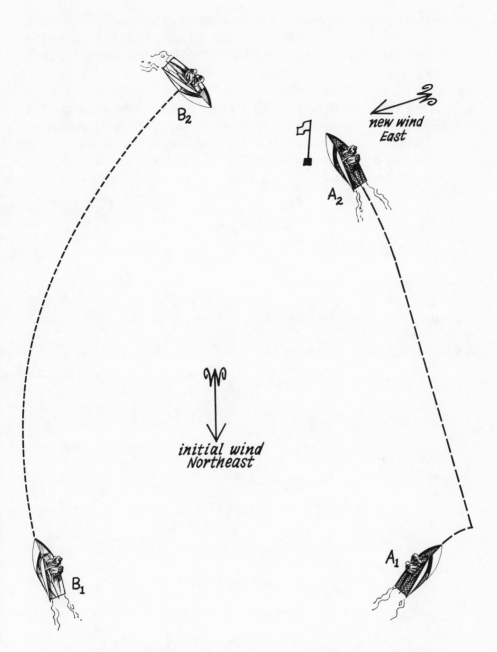

A sails towards the expected "new wind," a movement of the weather-system high farther north and east. The "new wind" from the east provides A with a direct course to the mark and increased wind velocity (nearer to the wind source) and causes B to sail a great circle course around the mark.

petitors on the beat; stay a little closer to the area of a possible new wind than they. If one boat sails off on a long tack far to the side of the course, keep an eye on her. If she does receive the shift first, be in a position to receive it second.

New wind must be planned for and sought after. Consider the movement of the weather system and the possible effects of thermal influences in relation to the strength and direction of the present wind, the presence of sunlight, the time of the day, and the proximity of the shore.

C. Starting the Second Beat

"It may be that good windward work is the main criterion of good helmsmanship. But successful yacht racing depends on a host of other things besides helmsmanship."
—C. STANLEY OGILVY

We rounded the weather mark overlapped by *Glastrocity*, and she worked to leeward and ahead as we moved down the run. During the early part of the leg the varying northwesterly shifted more to the west requiring a jibe, but as we approached the leeward mark the wind shifted back to the north and we jibed back to port. *Glastrocity* rounded the leeward mark and took off to windward on the headed port tack for the north shore of the harbor. We tacked immediately to the lifted starboard tack and continued till the wind oscillated back to the west again. We then tacked back to port well to windward of *Glastrocity* who seemed to be behind in the progressive lift. Our jubilation was short lived, however, as *Glastrocity* began to be headed as she entered the main outflow tract of the river on the far side of the harbor. Here the wind, funneled down between the steep banks of the Severn, was permanently shifted north to a greater extent than had been produced by even the most northerly oscillation in the remainder of the harbor. *Glastrocity* tacked early in the header and crossed us with ease. Fortunately this permitted us to continue on to the starboard-tack lay line where the greatest effect of the northerly shift could be expected. We tacked for the mark and were just able to cross *Glastrocity*.

The second (or subsequent) beat often determines the race. Even if this leg is not the last, it is reached after the fleet is already spread out, so that a lead acquired here is usually permanent. The plan's the thing; once entered into the leg it is usually too late to retrieve the desired position. The initial tack seems of even greater significance on the second beat than it does at the start, perhaps because each boat is able to make an immediate selection—right or wrong— and thus commit herself more totally to that selection. After the start the slowing, confusion, and breakaway difficulty prevent a gain comparable to the rapid and immediate progress of the yacht selecting the right tack after rounding the leeward mark. Nothing is worse than the realization, half way up the buck, that you have tacked the wrong way.

Tactical and strategical considerations at the commencement of the leg depend upon the tactical condition: defensive or offensive? If in the lead or in a position that needs only to be preserved (or cannot be improved), covering is essential. The standard technique is to remain on the initial tack until equidistant from the mark with the second approaching boat, then to tack so as to be dead to windward as the competitor rounds. From this position a second tack or a continuance will maintain control. The exceptions to this rule are two: (1) if the next mark or the finish can be fetched (or almost) on a single tack, assume that tack immediately and continue it— *never tack out on a one-leg beat* (the boat ahead and to leeward gains with any shift) and (2) if the second boat is so close behind that coverage will be lost by tacking, the best tack must be selected in advance and assumed regardless of the follower. In the latter case if the initial tack is to be continued a brief luff will induce the competitor to seek to break through to leeward and will provide freedom to tack at will thereafter. If the opposite tack is desired, an immediate luff is essential, a strong one (tacking while rounding is subject to the tacking rule), followed by the tack when the competitor bears away to pass to leeward.

If the situation requires offensive tactics, the best tack and the best side of the beat must be selected and acquired. One or the other side of the beat may be favored because of geographical differences in wind direction, wind strength, current, or wave patterns.

138

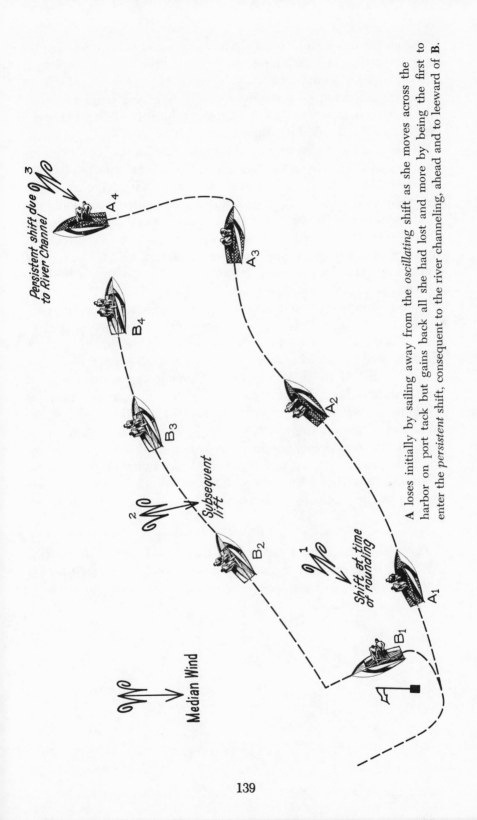

Persistent shift due
to River Channel

Subsequent
lift

Shift at time
of rounding

Median Wind

A loses initially by sailing away from the *oscillating* shift as she moves across the harbor on port tack but gains back all she had lost and more by being the first to enter the *persistent* shift, consequent to the river channeling, ahead and to leeward of **B**.

139

When an immediate tack is the desired maneuver every effort should be made to threaten the leader's weather and the tack accomplished as soon as possible after rounding. This will represent the only hope if the leg is a fetch or a one-leg beat. If a varying wind has been evident, the compass will be extremely helpful in determining the lifted tack that should be assumed immediately—unless a persistent shift from a new or distant source is expected. Thereafter a continuing attempt to remain on the tack towards the next expected header, to leeward of the leader, will provide additional advantage with each recurrent shift. If specific boat ability is recognized, it should be capitalized upon. In general if the boat has speed advantages one should stay to leeward and move rapidly towards expected advantages consequent to geography or oscillating shifts. If the boat points high, stay to windward, retain clear air, and seek a position between the leader and the mark.

If no geographic or oscillating shift advantages are apparent, control of the boat ahead must be attempted by tactical means. If close aboard, work to windward and try to pin the leader in the lee-bow position until the lay line is reached. (The defense here is, of course, a quick luff.) If the beat is short, achieving a position that will permit approaching the mark on the starboard tack or the finish on the most perpendicular tack may be essential. If the leader is too far ahead to permit the effective use of these techniques, he must be induced to err. A tacking duel is only helpful if your own tacking ability is superior. A false tack or several tacks, however, may induce the leader to settle for the wrong tack as he either wearies of covering or can be made to feel foolish in responding to your every maneuver.

The second beat often determines the race. The tack towards a persistent shift, current, or wave advantage must be selected immediately while retaining or gaining control over nearby competitors.

D. Fifty Million Frenchmen
Can't Be Wrong

"You must under no circumstances get flustered or take a chance or make a hundred short tacks in order to try to gain a small amount—never do the opposite of what the leading boats are doing in the hope that you might pick up a little distance."
—PAUL ELVSTROM

One of the nation's top Snipe sailors, Stovy Brown, delights in pointing out, "Fifty million Frenchmen can't be wrong." The man who disagrees with this dictum may win races but rarely series. As Stovy knows, I tend to be a race winner not a series winner, but I am hoping that eventually his conservative approach will sink in.

Stovy uses his dictum particularly in regard to crossing many boats on the opposite tack. The dictum can equally be applied to the straight-line course to the reaching mark, the start at the weather end of the line, or the avoidance of the wide tack downwind. Perhaps it is most significantly applied in deciding on which side of the course the beat should be sailed. With Stovy as crew, I won two races at the 1962 Canadian Dinghy Association Regatta partly because of making this decision correctly and lost (really lost!) at least three others because of making it incorrectly! When a single major shift or an unequal number of shifts or a shift that affects different boats for different lengths of time affects the fleet on a beat, position to the side of the course is the major determinant of the outcome of the race. The conservative tactic is to cover or follow the fifty million Frenchmen. Even if they *are* wrong, the conservative boat will retain his position relative to the majority of the fleet!

The compass often seems to conflict with this conservative approach and may, if followed blindly, often lead to disaster. Many damn the compass as dangerous, but damning merely shows an inability to be independent of its dictates. If the compass indicates a lift, the lifted tack may be advantageous if a return shift can be expected but may represent the outside of a great circle if the lift persists. Aside from the compass data which can only indicate the relationship of present wind direction to previously established medians, a decision must be made regarding the possibility of a significant deviation in the median wind itself. If a significant permanent shift can be reasonably expected, the lifted tack indicated by the compass is the tack away from the shift and should be avoided. Even when a significant permanent shift is not expected, the use of the compass must be limited by the dictates of the fifty million Frenchmen. When starting or rounding the leeward mark for a subsequent beat, the lifted tack should be pursued if the compass indicates a clear-cut (5° or greater) lift—until it is evident that the majority of the fleet are on the other tack. Then a tack even into a header may be justified—if the lift is only a slight one, is diminishing or if the smart, the top, the series-leading Frenchmen are on the other tack! If initially the compass does not indicate a clear-cut lift, it is best to tack to cover early, to stay on the major tack, and in no case to sail outside the sixty degree midzone to the weather mark.

In one Severn Trophy Regatta we broke away from the starting melee, after a heading shift, on port tack towards the distant shore. We expected a geographic shift to starboard (a port-tack header) due to the more perpendicular deviation of the wind coming off that shore, which would become progressively more significant as we approached that shore. When we had reached a position approximately ¼ mile out on the port tack, but still approximately one mile off shore, we encountered a significant header. We presumed that this was probably an oscillating shift. The question then became whether to take what we had, to tack and cover the fleet, now all to port, or to continue on to the ultimate advantage of the geographic shift. We tacked and carried on in the temporary starboard lift. The fleet now began to move across beneath us on port and several worked out considerably to windward astern of us. As they came about on starboard, we worried that they might have entered into the geographic shift area. As we debated tacking against our lift,

A tacks to cover the "Frenchmen" when a heading shift appears rather than continuing towards the expected geographic shift near shore. She consolidates her lead in a subsequent oscillating wind shift in the opposite direction and continues towards the geographic shift.

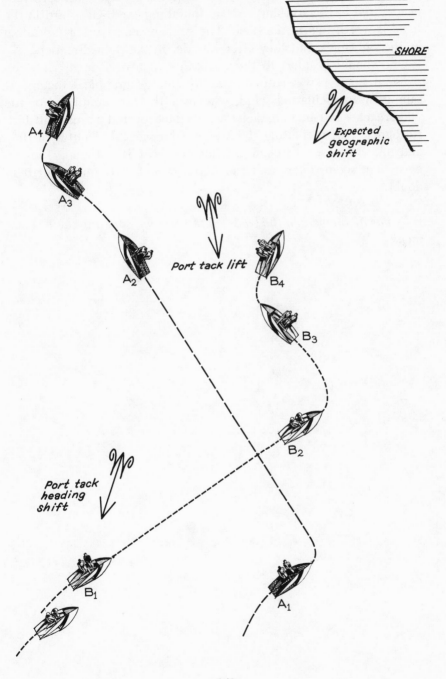

the oscillating wind shifted back, the followers were headed down into our wake, and we were able to tack into the port-tack lift again towards the shore. Had we carried on farther towards the shore on our initial port tack we would have met the same starboard-tack header and lost everything we had initially gained. Or a bird in the hand is worth two in the bush! The Frenchmen may not be sailing on the right tack, but they often blunder in the right direction!

One should be alert to the possibility of a permanent shift dependent upon new weather conditions or geographical factors. If sailing in an oscillating wind, whenever the lift diminishes or the wind reaches the median, tack towards the expected permanent shift. Recognize that oscillating shifts persist for variable lengths of time and may be about to change when the beat is initiated. Tack to cover if it seems likely that the shift is about to terminate or if in doubt.

Sail as if you were in the lead, conservatively, covering the Frenchmen!

E. Avoid the Middle!

"It is best to stay where you are, relying on the law of averages to bring the next break your way. A boat that spends all afternoon chasing the advantages of others is never in a position to get any of her own."
—ROBERT N. BAVIER, JR.

Conservatism (cover the Frenchmen!) is fine for racing in a breeze —as was preached in the previous chapter. But in light air, in the usual sense of covering the competition (taking the compromise course, the middle road), conservatism is hazardous. Then the results regularly demonstrate that the boats that take the single long tack farthest to the side of the course come out ahead. And it often seems to matter little which side of the course is selected!

This is a surprising situation, but consistently demonstrable, and deserves analysis. Success consequent to assuming the preferred side of the course is, of course, understandable. If a single major shift or an unequal number of shifts occur, then the boat farthest to the side of the course from which the major shift or the final shift appears, gains the most and emerges victorious. If there is a variation in the wind strength, the current strength or direction, or the size of the waves, the advantage of the preferred side may be significant. These circumstances may justify adhering to a radical course of one long tack far to the preferred side of the course, but doubt as to the side that is preferred and to its significance usually prevents the utilization of such extreme strategy in a decent breeze

—better to compromise! In light air, however, the advantages of the radical course are apparently increased; indeed, the advantages of the radical course may be so greatly increased that even the wrong side is preferrable to the conservative middle route!

In a recent invitation team race in Gannets at the Naval Academy in extremely light and fluky air, I took an early lead and then tacked up the middle, keeping between the mark and the major group of the opposing team. Meanwhile light-air, Penguin-Thistle-14-Mobjack ace, Walt Lawson, took one long tack out of the adverse tide down the starboard shore, while other members of our Severn Sailing Association team tacked far out into the tide and benefited from a new wind that appeared to port. Walt was a quarter-mile ahead at the weather mark! I still covered three opposing team members, but they were breathing down my neck at the mark, and everyone else had passed me—on both sides! Fine for team racing but catastrophic for ordinary open racing.

The defects of my course, of the course of the conservative boat in light air, include staying with the fleet and tacking frequently. Wind is always disturbed by a fleet of boats, but particularly so in light air, so that a boat staying with the fleet is sailing slower than a boat to either side of the course. Making the boat go to windward in light air depends upon full sails, slack sheets, sailing free (well off the "pinching" course), and the avoidance of movements and maneuvers, which initially slow the boat and require additional energy to overcome inertia in reestablishing speed. Obviously, the worst possible violation of all these principles is tacking; frequent tacking up the middle may lose hundreds of feet to the boat that keeps going continuously and settles for but one tack.

Finally, and perhaps most important, the conservative boat tacking up the middle is confronted with every shift with the apparent gain of each boat dead to leeward. A boat dead to leeward *is* aided by *every* shift regardless of direction; with a heading shift the distance between the two boats along the sailing axis is shortened; with a lifting shift the distance between the two boats to windward is shortened. The corollary of the gain of a boat ahead and to leeward in a header and the gain of a boat behind and to windward in a lift is that a boat dead to leeward, being at the precise mid-position, gains with a shift in either direction. For the following boat, being covered by a competitor dead to windward is ideal; she need only to relax and to enjoy it and cannot help but gain. The leader, watching the inexorable gain of the follower, frantically tacks

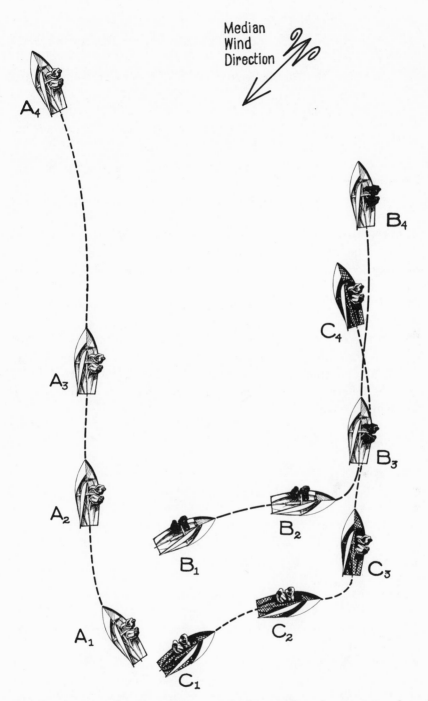

Median
Wind
Direction

B, attempting to cover **C**, tacks frequently, loses with each covering tack, and sails in the disturbed air of the main fleet. **A** maintains clear air and continuous forward speed to the side of the fleet and emerges ahead.

again and again to cover but until she gives up the cover cannot do other than lose.

In addition to the vain hope to cover, the desire to take advantage of every small shift (which seems to be a corollary of wanting to be in the middle anyway) results in frequent tacks. Frequent tacking in fluky winds, the variations of which may or may not be major, *i.e.* may or may not be followed by subsequent shifts in the opposite direction, results in frequent assumption of the wrong tack, *i.e.* sailing away from the next expected shift. It has been well demonstrated that such inappropriate tacking (out of phase) results in far greater losses than failure to tack appropriately (as merely waiting for the next shift brings the boat back into phase even farther to the advantageous side of the course). Obviously then, the boat in the middle places herself in the worst possible position relative to the boats she is covering, as they gain on her with every shift in either direction, and to all boats, when she periodically sails out of phase by tacking on minor headers.

When these defects in positional progress relative to the other boats are combined with decreased boat speed consequent to disturbed air and frequent tacking and the lost opportunity for the big gains inherent in being far to the preferred side of the course, conservative covering tactics become hopeless.

In light air, avoid the middle.

F. The Post-Mortem

*"It is very important to train yourself to recognize the
difference between good and bad luck, and also skill and
good fortune. If competitors in front of you have been lucky,
for instance, with favorable windshifts, you must be very
careful not to allow this to influence you in future races."*
—PAUL ELVSTROM

There is always an explanation for losing a race, although it is
difficult at times to determine. Winning may be doing (almost)
everything right, and an analysis of victory may be dull, but the
why of defeat is intriguing—and we do learn from our mistakes.
More specifically we learn by analyzing them in writing or in a
diagram. My victorious competitors commented after a recent race
in a strong, varying northwesterly that they just "responded"—
tacked when headed—and that was all the explanation they needed.
The opiates of success! I, meanwhile, considerably less at ease in
defeat, was determined to find a more complete explanation—and a
mode of preventing another defeat for me in the future.

It could have been luck—different winds for different boats at the
same time—and this happens in varying northwesters. If you end
up with more lifts than headers on the port side of the course and
your competitor to starboard receives the opposite treatment, you've
had your day and you might as well get back to the bar. But a
good long beat—and we'd had two that day—should have evened
things out, and while my competitors could have been expected to

149

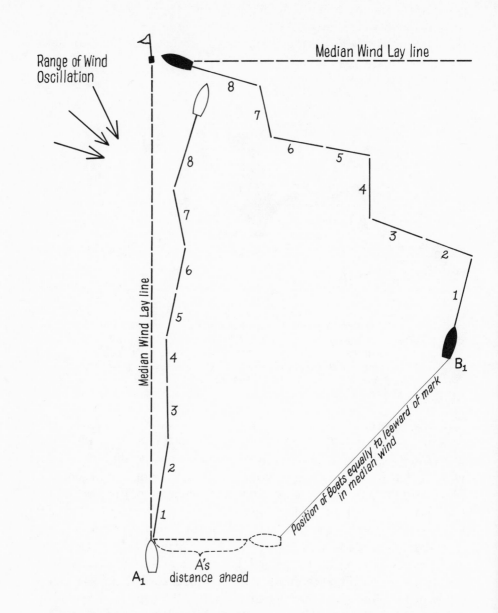

Range of Wind Oscillation

Median Wind Lay line

Median Wind Lay line

8
7
6
5
4
3
2
1

8
7
6
5
4
3
2
1

B₁

Position of Boats equally to leeward of mark in median wind

A₁

A's distance ahead

In an oscillating wind the first boat (**A**) to the lay line loses. Thereafter as boats to leeward (**B**) gain on each header, she is unable to gain on any. Her remaining distance can only be lengthened by further shifts—deviating her course from the straight line!

gain for a time, my moment should have followed. Perhaps I'd just been stupid—tacked in some lifts or after some minor headers that were followed by far greater major headers? I couldn't remember doing so. In fact I'd sailed through a number of minor headers waiting for a good one, recognizing that it was less harmful to miss a header than to tack in a lift away from the direction of the next header. Perhaps the geography of the situation resulted in an altered wind direction along the shore? No, this wasn't evident, and the windward shore was so far away that it couldn't have affected the local conditions. Perhaps inadequate boat speed? She hadn't felt as well balanced with the light-weight crew I'd had aboard. Perhaps I should have made some further sail and centerboard adjustments? But when we were near other boats we seemed to be going as rapidly as they and pointing considerably higher.

Pointing considerably higher! Perhaps pointing high was a defect in oscillating winds in which the ideal was always to be ahead and to leeward of the competition so as to receive the new heading shift (which you hoped you were always sailing toward!) first. However, when I worked this possibility out on paper, with two boats each receiving simultaneous and identical oscillating shifts, the high-pointing boat retained its expected advantage. Perhaps the boat to leeward did receive the new wind seconds sooner as a puff spread across the water, but those few seconds didn't create the lead that I was beaten by and would have been at least offset by my pointing advantage.

So not the wind (forget luck!), not the geography, not the boat, not the relation of the boat to her competitors. Perhaps the relationship of the boat to the mark! Ah, light dawns! Who was always first to the lay line—to the near lay line on the minor tack—while the others continued up the major tack well below this lay line, often ignoring headers that I had tacked upon? Me! And after I'd reached that lay line what was in store—the last mile of that long beat. What did I gain from further shifts? Nothing! A lift and I was overstanding; a header and I lost a little from the direct course. The lay line was already the shortest straight-line distance to the mark, and with any and every shift my course could only grow longer! While below me my rivals went on tacking in their headers—and gained with every shift—*for until they reached the lay line every shift produced a gain so long as they kept to the lifted tack!* And I could only lose—and the last boat to the lay line (everything else being equal) could only win!

The lesson learned then is to avoid the lay line at all costs in oscillating winds, to be on the lookout for it, and to be aware that when the wind is oscillating 30° (or more) that the lay line after the next shift may be 10°, 20°, or 30° below the 90° bearing that one usually expects. Essentially this precept indicates that it is dangerous to wander much beyond the 60° (30° either side of the rhumb line) arc to leeward of the weather mark. It is wise to tack against even a major lift well before the 90° lay line as the subsequent header will otherwise cause overstanding and allow boats behind to tack in beneath and ahead. (Of course, the opposite pertains in covering a single opponent who, if he carries on to the lay line, should be accompanied, as once on the lay line no shift can help him, and the covering may be considered complete.)

The principle of avoiding the lay lines as long as possible must be correlated with the precepts of tacking on all major headers in oscillating winds so as to be always on the lifted tack sailing toward the next header. The reasonable compromise is to initiate each leg on the lifted tack and to adhere entirely to this precept until approaching the 60° line to the weather mark. As this position is approached, on the *minor* tack (heading relatively more away from the mark), lesser and lesser degrees of heading must be considered sufficient justification for tacking, and once beyond the 60° line even a return of the median wind must be accepted as sufficient justification. If no return of a heading shift ever appears, a tack should be made at approximately the 75° line. When returning on the major tack, tacking should only be considered in association with major headers until the rhumb line is past. Thereafter, when once again on the minor tack, tacking on progressively less significant headers should be contemplated until beyond the opposite 75° line when tacking again becomes obligatory, regardless of the wind direction.

In oscillating winds the lay line must be avoided; the boat on the lay line loses with any subsequent wind shift.

G. The Dangerous Lay Line

"It is better to stick to your guns. If you are religious you may pray for your wind to come back."
—JACK KNIGHT

After starting at the far end of the "gate" at the 1962 Canadian Dinghy Association Regatta, we tacked up the middle of the weather leg. A general shift to port provided a major advantage to the boats that had started early and held on starboard out towards the port-tack lay line. We attempted to salvage what little position remained by tacking towards the new wind and then, tacking near the lay line, we sailed up under the mass of the fleet now approaching the mark on the starboard lay line. We were about to be overrun, trampled under the dense dacron and foaming bow waves. Surrounded by shouts of "starboard" and with no room to bear away astern, we tacked to starboard. Now barely on the lay line but within the mass we were backwinded, blanketed, slammed back by the stern waves, and smothered by the wakes. It was soon evident that we would be unable to make the mark. We slowed so as to drop back behind the boat just to weather, tacked, bore away behind the sterns of two others, and finally tacked in the clear above the mass. We had lost at least ten places in about two minutes.

For the leading boat on the lay line to the weather mark, any shift in the wind is dangerous. She can only lose in a lift or in a header; she can't cover her competitors; and, if she makes her tack from afar, she may misjudge the sailing angle so as to require

153

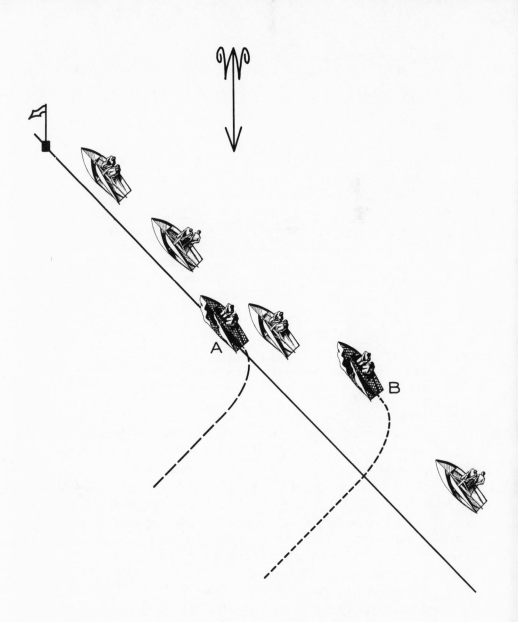

A tacks ahead and to leeward, risking a pinching situation at the mark in the backwind of the boats ahead from which there may be no escape. B assumes a far safer course, crossing astern and tacking far enough to windward to allow for the damaging effect of backwind ahead.

excessive bearing away or two extra tacks. Hence the classic rules: never stray more than three points beyond the median wind line; stay on the "major" tack, *i.e.* don't reach the lay line until close aboard the mark.

When in doubt these are good maxims, but, as with every rule, there are exceptions. If the wind is steady (is it ever?), if one side of the course is distinctly favored by a geographic wind shift relative to a shore, by a less adverse or more favorable tide, or by less sea, the first boat to the favored lay line should be the first boat to the weather mark. When these conditions exist, it will pay to tack immediately from the starting line, in one long hitch, to reach the lay line first. If this maneuver will not result in being the first or second boat there, however, some think it wiser to adhere to the maxims above, tack earlier, hope for a significant lift on the final approach, and avoid the long line of backwind from half the fleet along the lay line.

That long inescapable line of boats that accumulate along the starboard-tack lay line when large fleets of closely competitive boats race over short courses creates the problem. Breaking through from beneath is readily accomplished when the rounding is to starboard, and the starboard-tack boats must keep clear of the port tackers while tacking. But when the rounding is to port there is no easy solution. If attempting to join the starboard fleet late, it will pay to hold back and to look for a clear area, free of excessive wind interference, before sailing into the mass on port—but there may be no such clearing. Often the safer solution, despite the drawbacks of massive interference and strategic hazard, is to join early and to establish a rightful place in that unhappy train. A late port tacker may have to bear away behind a whole fleet, unless the starboard tackers have overstood, and she can tack into a safe leeward. The latter maneuver is dangerous, however, as the starboard tacker may romp over, blanket, and leave the original port tacker floundering and unable to make the mark. As soon as the tack is completed, the yacht tacking to leeward acquires right-of-way advantages and must also be granted room at the mark. If, while pinching up to clear the mark, she hits the windward boat, or the windward boat *and* the mark, it is the windward boat that will be disqualified.

If the mark is to be rounded to starboard, there are significant advantages to the port-tack approach (in addition to avoiding the mass on the starboard-tack lay line). In this case overstand the lay line a bit before tacking, so as to have sufficient freedom to bear away behind a starboard tacker (who must tack to round and who cannot tack close ahead). If the starboard-tack approach is favored for strategic reasons, be certain to go well out to the lay line so that no boats will be likely to tack on your windward quarter. Any such boats can pin you down to tacking after they tack, or even force you about twice, if you foolishly attempt to come about on port beyond the mark.

If you can induce your nearby competitors to come to the lay line with you, then do so every time. Once behind you on the lay line, they are well covered and lose no more and no less than you do in a windshift. As they cross your stern, eyeing your lay line course in order to decide when to tack, bear away a bit to convince them that you are unable to lay the mark and so make them overstand! Your extra speed will compensate for the slight loss to windward, and you'll add several boat lengths to your lead. However, if racing in a small fleet, don't be misled into sailing out to the lay line sooner than your competitors (unless you are certain that they are gullible enough to follow). Tack early, preferably before you are more than three points beyond the median wind line, and hope for that wind shift. If it lifts, you may be able to lay the mark; if it heads, you're to leeward and will gain.

Arrange an appropriate approach to the weather mark sufficiently far in advance so as to insure a controlling relationship to the massed competitors on the lay line.

H. *Classification of Wind Shifts*

*"With any fair gift of wind prophecy, a yachtsman can
win races. Even without the gift of prophecy, he can place
his craft advantageously so as to gain to some degree on any
wind shift of any magnitude. With a sound strategy based
upon an accurate guess, he will win against faster yachts that
are better sailed."*

—H. A. CALAHAN

RELEVANT CONSIDERATIONS

I. PERSISTENT SHIFTS
  A. Primary Consideration: determine direction of new wind
    1. *Sail toward direction from which new wind is emanating*
    2. *Avoid initially evident lifted tack as indicated by compass*
    3. *Sail well into area in which new wind is active—into
       header—before tacking to lifted tack*
    4. *Keep inside and to windward of competitors*
  B. Classification of Persistent Shifts
    1. *Thermal shifts*
      a) Creation of wind by thermal effect
        (i) sea breeze—general and local
        (ii) land breeze—local

b) Modification of wind strength and direction by thermal effect
    (i) Diminution of vertically stable wind strength by cold water surface
    (ii) Enhancement of vertically unstable wind strength by warm land surface
2. *Geographic shifts*: modification of wind strength and direction by terrain features
    a) Refraction: change in direction of offshore wind by "refraction"
    b) Friction (blanketing and elevating effects at windward and lee shores)
        (i) vertically stable air—enhanced blanketing and elevating
        (ii) vertically unstable air—diminished blanketing and elevating
    c) Channeling effects
        (i) vertically stable air—moderate channeling
        (ii) vertically unstable air—marked channeling
3. *Weather-system shifts*
    a) Movement of existing weather system
        (i) direction alteration relative to clockwise rotation of wind about high
        (ii) direction alteration relative to counterclockwise rotation of wind about low
    b) Modification of weather-system winds by geographic factors
        (i) enhancement or suppression of winds created by thermal or terrain effects
        (ii) diurnal variation in thermal effects—weather-system winds more evident morning and evening
    c) Appearance of new weather systems
        (i) sudden shift with the appearance of a high following a low "front"
        (ii) gradual shift with the appearance of a low following a high
        (iii) arrival of storm system
    d) Modification of strength and direction of weather-system winds by prevailing wind. In temperate zone westerlies enhanced, easterlies diminished

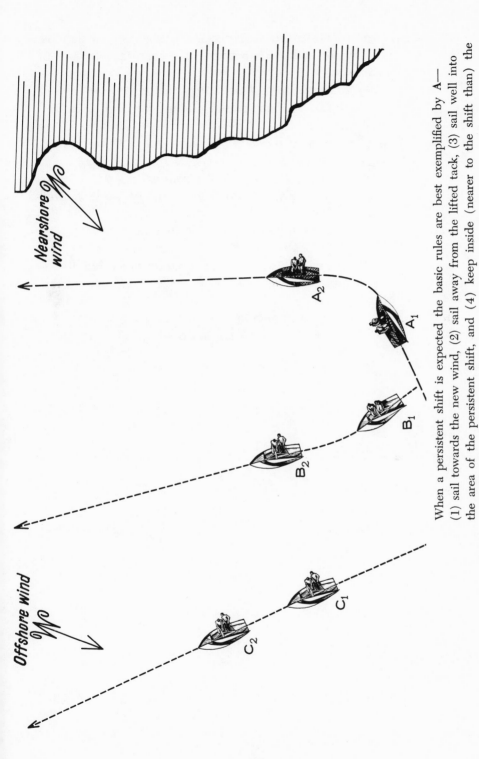

When a persistent shift is expected the basic rules are best exemplified by A— (1) sail towards the new wind, (2) sail away from the lifted tack, (3) sail well into the area of the persistent shift, and (4) keep inside (nearer to the shift than) the competition.

159

II. OSCILLATING SHIFTS—VERTICALLY UNSTABLE AIR
   A. Primary Considerations: determine range of oscillations, median wind, and median course for each tack by use of the compass
      1. *Keep to the lifted tack as indicated by compass* (expect gradual lift, sudden header, sailing through localized puffs)
      2. *Sail (farthest to the side of course) toward the next expected header*
      3. *Keep ahead and to leeward of competitors*
   B. Exceptions to the Primary Considerations: be wary of lifted tack if there is:
      1. A long time interval between oscillations with
         a) A short beat
         b) Duration of beat less than equal to interval multiples
      2. An inequality of shift experience, *i.e.*, a widespread distribution of competitors
         a) Starting location and tack varied
         b) Time of initiation of second beat varied

I. When the Wind Shifts the Wrong Way

"You can never afford to just look for temporal variations, and if there aren't any, just assume that you can sail along watching the scenery. If you do, the scenery is likely to suddenly consist of boats now ahead of you that you had written off long ago."

—TED WELLS

"Now that I'm in this mess what can I do about it?" The question erupts when far to starboard of the fleet and halfway up the beat it becomes evident that the boats to weather on port tack are in a tremendous lift. In addition to the reasonable "d--n"s and the unreasonable demands that the crew "start" hiking, the first attempt at solution is a kaliedoscopic review of how the "h--l" it happened.

The wind should certainly be stronger to starboard and the current more favorable and your position seems quite justifiable until you remember that you told the crew before the race that there would be a significant shift coming perpendicularly off that port shore and that you had better stay over there! Most of the fleet went that way and you now kick yourself for not believing that they just might have known what they were doing. You don't want to admit *that*, of course, but still when you were leading shortly after the start, you could have tacked to cover.

And so the skipper muses, "Well, you can't always be right." No, but you don't have to be this wrong either! You could have tacked at about the 60° angle to the mark—as the book says—and not have gone quite this far down the drain!

But there's no use kicking yourself forever; what are you going to do? No, wishful thinking won't help; the shift has occurred and if the wind remains just as it is, the positions of all boats will be fixed in their present relationships. The situation is as if we were starting the race now and those boats were starting that much farther up towards the windward end of the line. Nothing can be done to compensate for this loss . . . except. . . . They're pointing higher, therefore you're in a relative header. You should tack and take advantage of this as soon as possible! Don't you remember—"whenever boats to windward on the same tack are pointing higher than you, tack to cover"? And the boats up there on the opposite tack have been pointing at greater than 90° to your course for some time —that should have been a good enough reason to tack in the first place! Ready about!

Now let's think this through calmly. You've tacked; you're in a relative lift on starboard tack now; but you'll soon be in their wind. After that nothing will improve, you've had it . . . unless . . . unless the wind shifts again! But which way will it shift? This is not a vertically unstable wind; there's no hope of its shifting back. If it were, you should have continued on port to the expected lay line and short tacked along it awaiting the header. If it shifts again due to the shore effect, it will only shift further; the closer you approach the shore the more perpendicular to the shore the wind will become. If it is a general shift due to a movement of the weather system, it will again be a further shift in the same direction; it certainly won't shift back. So it's probably going to shift further—if at all.

The farther you are to the side of the course when the shift arrives, the more benefit you will receive. Therefore, you'll have to get over to the other side as soon as possible—continue your present tack to the opposite lay line. You've nothing to lose by getting over there, and if it does shift further you may at least gain something back— or go no farther down the drain than you are already!

Such are the considerations of every skipper who awakens sometime after the start to recognize that he's on the wrong side of the course. In an oscillating wind disaster is only temporary; hanging on may yet redeem the loss—if the beat is long enough. But if this is a permanent shift, geographic or weather system, there is no redemption. There is only exacerbation or attenuation. Subsequent tactics may increase the loss or curtail it; no restitution is possible. Recognition of this fact is extremely difficult for most skippers. Many continue their predetermined course on the wrong side of the beat in an attempt to deny the loss and their responsibility for

162

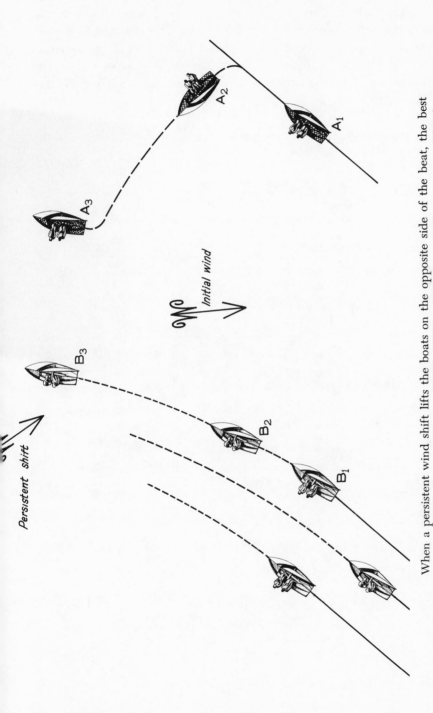

When a persistent wind shift lifts the boats on the opposite side of the beat, the best defensive maneuver is to tack immediately to take advantage of the relative lift of the opposite tack and to reach the area of the persistent shift as soon as possible.

163

it—in direct opposition to the rational solution.

Losses must be accepted in racing; no skipper can always be right. Multiple considerations integral to all tactical actions necessitate risks that result in statistically certain errors. The reasonable skipper learns to accept such consequences and learns to act immediately to limit the resultant losses. The unreasonable skipper denies the error and continues the action which initiated the loss, thus enhancing it.

The inevitability of loss must be accepted; confine its degree, once recognized, by immediate compensating action.

J. Planning for Shifts

"When the wind backs round against the sun,
Trust it not, for back it will run."
—TRADITIONAL

The observed wind (a result of the strongest general influence creating pressure alteration) is usually consequent to the weather-system
wind modified in strength and direction by the prevailing wind and
by the sea breeze (if any) and locally modified by thermal and
contour effects.

In planning a race consider the vertical stability of the wind first.
Oscillating wind shifts are only significant in vertically unstable
wind typically produced by the cold air of a weather system flowing
over warm land when the rising warm surface air brings down puffs
of rapidly moving cold upper air. When vertical instability is reduced or absent and the surface air becomes (in overcast or at
night), or is, as cold or colder than the upper air, the upper air
remains aloft, and the surface air becomes stagnant. If a sufficiently
large body of thermally stable water exists and if the temperature
of the thermally unstable land changes sufficiently during the day
(or night), vertical instability may also be created and produce a
sea (or land) breeze.

Secondly, consider the relation of the strength and direction of the
weather-system wind to the prevailing wind and any diurnally produced thermal winds. Except with marked barometric variations as
in storms (which may produce strong easterlies), the strongest

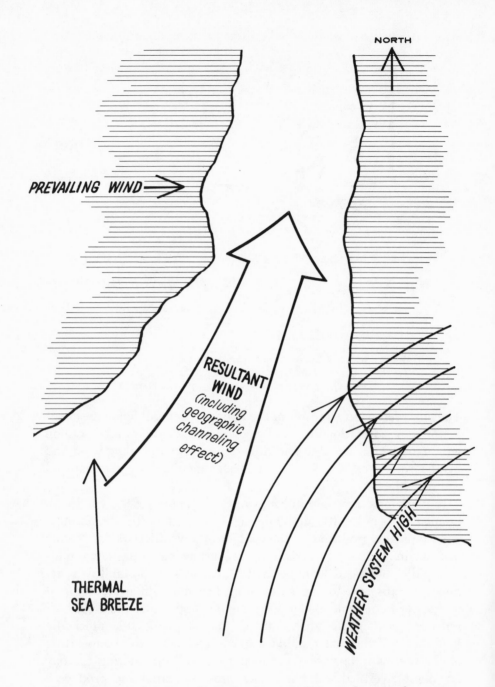

The resultant wind is a combination of a prevailing wind, a weather system wind, and a thermal wind modified by the regional topography.

winds are usually produced when the weather system creates westerly winds that supplement rather than oppose the prevailing westerlies. In areas where a sea breeze supplements the prevailing westerly and when the weather system is also producing a westerly—a summer high to the east of Buzzard's Bay for instance—maximum wind strength is produced, and the wind direction is a composite of the influence of all three factors. The greater the thermal difference, the hotter the air ashore, the colder the water (as with a flood tide) the more effective the sea breeze in Buzzard's Bay, the more the southwester will shift south (offshore), while the stronger the weather system and the less the thermal effect, in the morning or late in the day, the more the wind will shift westerly.

Thirdly, an evaluation of the weather system itself and of the rapidity of its movement must be considered. If the weather system is moving rapidly, a gradual change in the wind direction must be expected during the course of the race; this alteration in direction is dependent upon the geographic relationship of the racing area to the center of the system and upon whether the system is a high or a low. If a new weather system, a storm, thundersquall or hurricane, or the passage of a front appears during a race, an abrupt and major wind shift must be expected. An examination of the most recent weather map and an evaluation of a reliable local forecast are essential preparations.

Fourthly, regardless of whether the wind is derived from the weather system or from thermal influences and regardless of whether it is vertically stable or unstable, if it is onshore, its strength and direction will be modified by friction, and if offshore, by both the refraction and friction of the shore contours. Seek the windward shore in vertically unstable offshore winds as the warm surface air over the land brings stronger wind to the surface, and avoid the windward shore in vertically stable winds as the cool water holds a stagnant pool along the bank beneath the wind aloft. Expect the strongest vertically stable winds to appear offshore where the friction is least or at the mouth of creeks and valleys where it will be channeled along the axis of the depression. Expect vertically unstable winds to be strongest close to shore and particularly near high points and projections of the shore where the warm air rises most effectively to be replaced by puffs of variably directed upper cold air.

Plan for wind shifts; the wind at any time is a combination of a prevailing wind, a weather-system wind, and a local thermal wind modified by the vertical stability of the air and the local geography.

K. Wind-Shift Considerations— Order of Precedence

"One false decision and the race goes, if not down the drain, at least perilously near it."
—C. STANLEY OGILVY

A complete evaluation of wind conditions should be attempted before a race in addition to a consideration of terrain, wave, and current factors that may influence strategic plans. Although such considerations may require modification during the race, modifications should be consequent to developments for which one is adequately prepared. If the factors creating the present wind are recognized, then all possible variations and deviations can be reasonably evaluated. All influences that pertain to wind production and deviation should be analyzed and their relative significance during the period of the race assessed. An essential determination is the detection of the presence or expected presence of an oscillating wind as the tactics of sailing to windward in an oscillating wind are diametrically opposed to those required in sailing in all other winds, which shift only in a persistent manner. Whether or not the primary wind due to the weather system is vertically unstable and thus oscillating, the factors that may cause persistent shifts—thermal, geographic, or weather system—must also be considered. If these latter factors result in significant wind deviation during the course of the race, they will affect its outcome to a far greater degree than the super-imposed oscillating shifts and thus must be given primary consideration in the planning.

Recognition of all the possible factors that might result in wind deviation does not necessarily provide sufficient information to determine which of the influences will be dominant at a specific time or location on the race course. Although all possible effort including early arrival and reconnaisance in the racing area should be made to acquire the needed information, the subsequent combinations of thermal, terrain, weather-system, and oscillating influences cannot be accurately predicted. It is thus reasonable to establish a general plan that accords each influence an order of precedence and to utilize this plan in a conservative manner, which will obviate major losses if the combinations are incorrectly predicted but which will still provide the major advantages to be expected if they are correctly predicted.

I. *Thermal, Geographic Shifts or Weather-System Shifts*
1. Select and assume the side of the course near the predicted shift(s)
2. Sail towards such shift(s) and keep nearer to such shift(s) than any other competitor
3. If oscillating shifts occur simultaneously, keep to the lifted tack, but sail farther towards the expected geographic or weather-system shift(s) than your significant competitors whenever they tack towards such shifts or whenever a lift that carries you away diminishes.
4. Unless certain of the character of geographic or weather-system shift(s), do not sail beyond the 60° angles to the weather mark (except in drifting conditions to achieve clear air).

II. *Oscillating Shifts*
Keep to the lifted tack, and always sail towards the next expected header *except*:
1. On short beats or when the lay line will be reached before the expected time of the next header, do not sail beyond the 60° angle to the weather mark and stay between your most significant competitors and the mark.
2. When your competitors are sailing in a wind of different direction tack to cover:

169

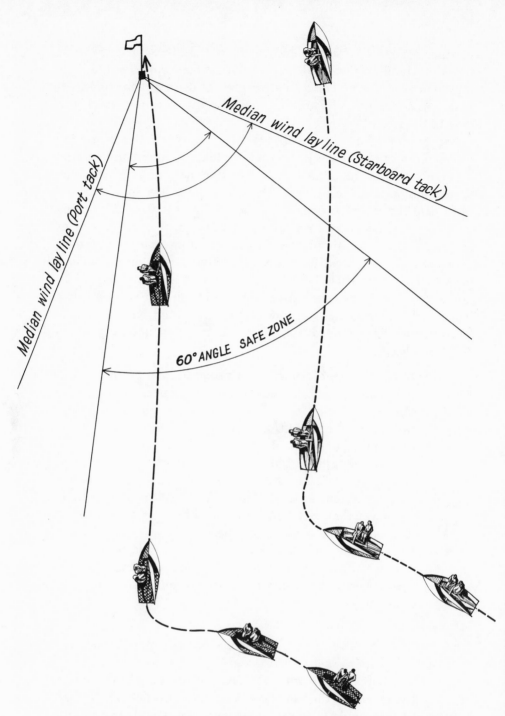

Median wind lay line (Port tack)

Median wind lay line (Starboard tack)

60° ANGLE SAFE ZONE

Tacking to the lifted tack and holding a lift beyond the 60° angle "safe zone" to the weather mark is dangerous on a short beat in an oscillating wind as the lifted boat may sail a great circle course around the mark before the next header arrives—and will overstand when it does!

a) if boats to windward on the same tack are sailing higher than you;

b) if boats to windward on the opposite tack are sailing at greater than 90° to your course.

3. In light air avoid the middle, the frequent tacking, the close covering; keep her moving and sail away from the fleet until you can tack with a clear lead to cover.

Plans will not always be consistent with actual developments. Errors must be expected and arrangements must be provided to protect against excessive resultant losses. The first way to reduce loss is to avoid excessive risk; proceed no farther into an area or phase of wind deviation than necessary to obtain a slightly greater advantage than any of the competitors. Don't be greedy. Second, be capable of recognizing errors when they occur and be willing to admit them by an immediate compensating alteration in plan and action.

III. *Positional Error Recognized*
1. If a thermal, geographic, or weather-system shift to the opposite side of the course becomes evident, tack immediately to reduce the loss in expectation of a further shift

2. If sailing in an oscillating wind but in doubt as to the presence of an oscillating header or a header only recognized after prolonged exposure, continue without tacking, expecting to compensate in the next expected header when far to the preferred side of the course.

3. If approaching the lay line in a lift of an oscillating wind, tack just beyond the future lay line predicted for the desired header, and tack along such lay line hoping for a salvaging header

Plan to obtain greater advantage than any of the competitors from wind shifts by a full evaluation of their possible occurrence and an assignment of precedence to their significance, but take no excessive risks, and be willing to recognize and compensate immediately for any errors which may result.

L. Racing
with a Compass

"The yacht that gains on the first shift of a double wind shift consolidates her gains only if she can achieve split tacks and sail towards the direction of the second shift."
—H. A. CALAHAN

Wind strength, a major racing variable, is not difficult to determine and to utilize by sailing in zones of optimal wind force. But the other major variable that determines the strategy of the race, wind *direction*, is not so easy to ascertain. Oh, the direction of the apparent wind is obvious enough, as it effects the sails and the wind pennants, but relative to the geography of the area, relative to the rhumb line to the weather mark, the true wind direction is an elusive matter. And this elusive matter determines the outcome of all races when the wind is shifting significantly and of many races when the wind seems steady! The course and its turning marks are established geographically, and it is the relationship of the true wind direction to the geography of the area that determines the favored tack and the shortest sailing distance between two marks.

Before the start the true wind direction should be determined in terms of the close-hauled courses. Both starboard and port tacks should be assumed repeatedly and compass readings noted to determine the consistency of the wind direction. Even an apparently steady wind will shift from 5° to 10°, and a vertically unstable wind, typically the "northwester" that follows a front, may shift through a range of 60° to 90° in a few minutes. The directions of the close-hauled courses indicated by the compass will determine the range through which the wind may be expected to shift during the race.

The median wind direction, midway between the extremes of the range, or the median close-hauled course for each tack should be determined in advance so that each subsequent heading may be evaluated in relation thereto. If any subsequent course is outside the median it is a headed course; if inside the median, it is a lifted course. Future reference to the compass may then indicate whether the close-hauled course relative to the true wind direction at any moment is lifted or headed relative to the expected wind variations.

Lifting or heading of the starboard-tack course at the start may thus be determined instantly and a decision made as to whether an immediate tack or continuance is indicated. In the melee of a crowded start and deflected wind, only the compass will accurately indicate the true wind direction and permit a change in tactical plan to start on port or to seek an opening elsewhere on the line. Continuing for even a short distance after the start in a starboard-tack header may result in a disastrous loss, whereas an immediate tack may produce an insurmountable lead.

In oscillating winds repeated referral to the compass during the windward leg is essential to the success of the leg. As was true of the starting tack, persistent sailing in a header, at an angle outside the median close-hauled course previously established, results in a major loss, while tacking immediately in a header produces a major gain. Only the compass can make an accurate distinction between the significant header and the minor header that will be followed by a subsequent further header in the same direction and thus permit the immediate, appropriate decision to tack or continue.

The boat that refrains from tacking in a minor header, awaiting a more obvious and extreme header, may sail a headed course for several minutes and lose steadily during this period on all boats sailing the lifted tack. The boat that tacks in a minor header, inside the median course established for the tack, will be even more harmfully affected, as she will be sailing away from the significant header that will follow and thus be farther away from this shift when it appears.

It must be remembered that with each heading shift of an oscillating wind the boat closest to the side of the course from which the shift appears will gain the most, and any boat sailing away from the shift when it appears will be sailing a circular course of greatly increased length. *It is thus far more disastrous to tack in a minor header than to ignore a major one.* The boat that refrains from tacking gains nothing but will recoup much of her relative loss by sailing farther to the side of the course so as to be even better positioned than the tacking boats for a subsequent major shift in the same direction.

The compass should be checked at the initiation of each tack and the course evaluated relative to the previously established median close-hauled course. In an oscillating wind if the tack is lifted above the established median, it should be continued. The crew should read the compass repeatedly and call out the changes in heading as a 5° lift, a 2° lift, at the median (or expected), a 2° header, a 5° header, and so on. The compass probably cannot be read accurately within 5° so that the course should be continued until the presence of a significant header is established by a 20 to 30 second persistence of a reading 5° or more beyond the median. This accuracy is far greater than the unaided eye can achieve and will prevent tacking in minor headers and permit tacking appropriately in major headers far sooner than the unaided skipper. The same sequence of compass observations is repeated for each tack, and in oscillating wind its application will insure the shortest possible distance sailed to the windward mark.

The compass permits sailing the windward leg without regard to other boats, concentrating on sailing the shortest possible course. In an oscillating wind a studied disregard of the competition is often commendable. In the presence of persistent shifts and when the compass shows a doubtful oscillating shift, however, it is safer to utilize competitor's positions as determinants of tactics. In general, if boats on the opposite tack are sailing at an angle of greater than 90° to your course, you are sailing in a header and should tack. If boats on the same tack are sailing significantly higher than you, you are sailing in a header and should tack. These are effective axioms, particularly in short races, but are only indicative of relative position and therefore may cause tacking in minor headers that may result in major losses. Only the compass tells the story relative to the total pattern of the leg *in an oscillating wind* and permits sailing the shortest course to the mark.

Perhaps the start of the second weather leg in a twice-around or Gold Cup course provides the most impressive indication of the value of the compass. After rounding on to the wind at the leeward mark, the crew notes the compass course and determines whether the tack is headed or lifted compared to the previous median wind. Continuance on or tacking to the lifted tack is thus possible immediately with no time or distance lost sailing in a header. In the 1961 Viscount Alexander or Tunis Trophy Race (five times around a three-mile triangle), I was able to detect the lifted tack with the aid of the compass and sailed from fifth to first, with a 100 yard lead, on the third beat. As this race was held in an onshore wind on Lake Ontario, the true wind direction could not have been detected without the compass.

The compass is essential in determining the favored tack in an oscillating wind by indicating the degree and direction of variation of any shift from the median wind direction.

A tacks away from the further header in a minor shift. **B** carries on in the minor header and tacks in the major header farther to the side of the course from which the new wind appears, thereby achieving a major gain.

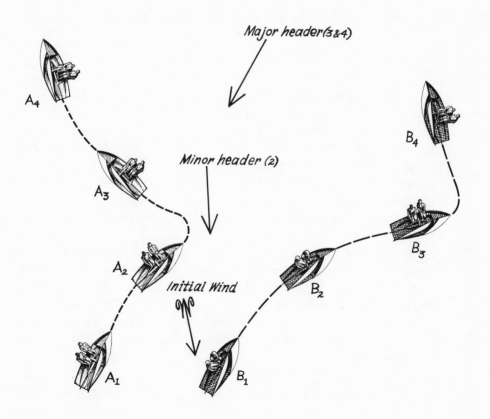

175

M. When Not to Use the Compass

"The most dangerous thing about using a compass while racing is that it is easy to become so engrossed in doing what the compass says to do that you may forget to watch the other boats carefully enough."

—TED WELLS

Added to the skepticism of the many who have never used a compass in small-boat racing is the confusion of the many who have! Concentration on any single element of yacht racing to the exclusion of other considerations is always dangerous; boat speed, current tactical considerations, free air, and a host of other factors require attention. The compass cannot be blamed for all errors to windward (though it does provide a great excuse). However, it may be directly misleading at times in indicating an apparently favored tack that in fact provides a longer rather than a shorter course to the weather mark.

The major danger in sailing to windward in shifting winds is the failure to distinguish a persistent shift consequent to an alteration in a weather system or thermal wind pattern or to the presence of a terrain feature from an oscillating wind shift. In oscillating winds the lifted tack provides the short course to the weather mark and to the next beneficial header. In a persistent shifting wind the lifted tack provides the long course in a great circle around the weather mark. Unfortunately the compass cannot make the distinction; this is up to the skipper. Even in an oscillating wind, however, discretion in clinging to the lifted tack as indicated by the compass is warranted.

The primary use of the compass is in determining the median wind direction and/or the range of the possible sailing angles when close-hauled on each tack in an oscillating wind. This determination permits tacking or retention of a tack in winds of varying direction so as always to be on the lifted tack—that tack that permits sailing closest to the median wind direction, *i.e.* that permits movement farthest upwind in the overall wind pattern of the period during which the weather leg was undertaken. The use of the compass is thus predicated on knowledge previously gained as to what the range of shifts has been and the supposition that shifts in both directions over this same range will continue. The oscillating variation of a typical north-westerly always provides a subsequent shift back in the reverse direction so that a boat sailing on a significantly lifted tack is always sailing *toward the next heading shift* and will be closest to the direction of the new shift when it arrives. This sequence ideally provides a major reduction in distance sailed to the weather mark as the boat is always sailing at less than the usual 45° angle from the direct course to windward.

It is obvious that the boat sailed on a lifted tack depends upon a subsequent header to provide the desired lifted approach to the mark on the opposite tack—and that, if this header fails to appear, she may have to sail well beyond the normal lay line and make her final approach on a headed tack sailing at greater than 45° to the median wind direction. Thus, if the lift continues and requires sailing to a lay line farther upwind (referrable to the median wind) than would have been required in the initial or previous wind direction, more may be lost in the final stages of the leg than was gained initially. All boats to windward of a lifted boat gain by sailing a shorter, more direct final tack, while the lifted boat sails a great circle around the mark, actually sailing farther and farther to reach the mark as the lift increases. Thus, if a lift fails to be succeeded by a header, the boat following the dictates of the compass to sail the lifted tack may lose to all her competitors who (by ignorance or design!) have sailed in a prior header so as to be farther to windward in the final lift.

A long beat will usually permit an equalization of the effects of successive oscillating shifts. However, if the total number of shifts is odd or the number experienced by individual boats is different, the final shift and the position of the competing boats when this shift occurs may determine the outcome of the entire leg. Two principles logically follow from this recognition: (1) one should avoid blindly following the compass indications to sail a lifted tack far to the side

177

of the course if the beat is short, and (2) one should try to cover one's competitors so that if no subsequent header appears no boats will be so far to windward that a major loss will result. To accomplish these ends one should first avoid sailing beyond the 60° angle to the weather mark (30° to each side of the median wind line) particularly on a short beat. The conservative boat in this position will never give too great an advantage to the daring souls who risk all by continuing to the extreme lay lines and there find a header awaiting them at the ideal moment. Such conservatism may not win the race, but it will more often win the series! Secondly, one should tack in relation to the competitors, rather than in relation to the compass indications, (particularly on short beats) before sailing beyond the 60° lines. If boats to windward on the same tack are sailing significantly higher than you, tack, as you are in a header relative to their wind, and they are in a threatening position if the lift continues. If boats to windward on the opposite tack are point-

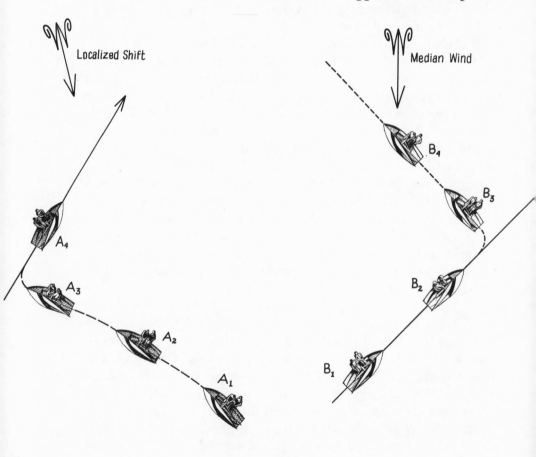

Localized Shift

Median Wind

ing lower than you, either you are in a header or they are(!) and if the latter, you had better tack to reach their header as soon as possible. If boats to leeward on the same tack are pointing higher or boats to leeward on the opposite tack pointing lower, it may be preferable to continue in your relative header until they tack or cross your stern, thereby maintaining the cover.

It is thus evident that the compass may be extremely misleading even in an oscillating wind, when it is most valuable and when other considerations rarely take precedence. It is even more evident that, if a shift of a fixed type occurs, due to geographic or thermal factors or a major movement of the weather system, the compass, which suggests sailing the "lifted" tack, will lead straight away from the new wind into a great circle disaster!

When using the compass distinguish persistent shifts from transient oscillations; assume the opposite tack from any persistent lift as soon as it is detected!

B, noting that A on the opposite tack is sailing into a header, tacks to cover in her relative port-tack lift. If, relying on her compass alone, B had continued to sail away from A's heading shift she would have lost drastically.

N. Against the Tide

> "The general principle of sailing in adverse current is thus to 'keep her moving.' Increased duration of exposure consequent to excessive tacking, wind interference, and pinching is far more harmful in adverse current and results in major differences in boat speed and major losses in distance gained over the ground."
>
> —THOMAS MARSTON

Everyone always (well almost always) remembers to ask about the tide—and always (well almost always) forgets all about it when on the course. The general principles that are recognized are that when the tidal current is adverse one should sail out of the strength of it as rapidly as possible and stay out of it as much of the leg as possible and that if the current is favorable one should sail into the strength of it as soon as possible and stay in it for as much of the leg as possible. Even though all boats may be equally affected by the current and other factors such as variation in wind strength may be of far greater significance, the effects of the current must not be underestimated.

Current is of the greatest importance on the beat for three reasons: (1) more time is spent on the beat than on any other equivalent length of course (2) there is a greater possibility of major variation in current strength between boats at the extremities of each tack than on any other leg, and (3) boat speed over the bottom and through the air will vary on each tack and thus create greater boat-speed differentials than on any other leg. Adverse current multiplies this significance as it increases the time spent in these conditions and thereby multiplies the differential effects upon boats in various positions on the leg. The dramatic effects of current in determining the outcome of a race are most obvious in light air (because of the increased duration of exposure), but they are significant at all times regardless of the wind strength.

It is usually possible even in open water to find variations in the current strength, particularly over shoals where friction reduces the flow. In the long 1964 Connecticut Cup Race, after falling over a mile behind the leaders, we were able to catch up and go on to win by short tacking up Long Sand Shoal, a narrow sand bar well off-shore in Long Island Sound. The leaders had thoughtlessly struck off for shore after rounding the mark, hoping for less current along the beach but forgetting the one-mile crosstide leg in and back out to reach the mark at the shoal's eastern end. There may have been even less tide close in on the beach but not sufficiently less to compensate for miles of extra distance and the double crossing of a strong tidal flow. However, if the beginning or ending mark of the beat is close to the shore, the decreased current along shore may more than make up for the short exposed crossings. The entire leg must be viewed in terms of exposure and every effort made to keep to the "protected" waters overlying shoals, off beaches, and behind obstructions such as breakwaters.

When it is impossible to find "protected" water, the advantages and disadvantages of the uptide or crosstide tacks must be considered. The fundamental advantages of the lee-bow current and of making progress towards the mark must be recognized. Whenever it is possible to have the current on your lee bow assume that tack until the mark can be laid. It is, of course, essential to tack early, well below the wind lay line, if approaching the mark with a lee-bow tide to avoid overstanding. Bearing away against the tide after such overstanding can be fatal; it is far better to take an extra tack or two so as to remain downtide on the approach. The advantages of the lee-bow-to-the-tide position usually take precedence over all other considerations, unless it is possible to get into an area of less current on the opposite tack. The lee-bow tack if available should usually be assumed immediately after the start of the leg so as to achieve the maximum gain (and a certain gain) early. The vicissitudes of wind variation may mean that the lee-bow effect will not be available later and/or that the wind variation itself must be given preferential consideration.

The lee-bow-to-the-tide tack is advantageous because the current is deviating the boat to windward of its headed course while the boat on the opposite tack is being deviated to leeward of its course. The degree of deviation varies with the angle to the tide being sailed, the current causing the greatest slowing at slight sailing angles to its flow and the greatest deviation at right angles to its flow. The dramatic advantage of the lee-bow effect is evident to a boat sailing almost dead into the current; she seems almost to be shot to windward as she points just a degree or two higher and acquires a lee-bow current. The dramatic benefit is not the consequence of any mysterious squeezing but is consequent to the *doubled* difference between a leeward deviation at any angle less than head on to the current and a windward deviation at any angle above. A little judicious pinching and/or tacking after slight headers to achieve this effect may pay big dividends. In that Connecticut Cup Race we were frequently able to pinch up in a wind shift sufficiently to lee-bow the current and were rewarded by dramatically working up beneath the major portion of the fleet far to weather.

If avoiding the current and lee-bowing it are both impossible which tack is favored? If conditions remain the same and both boats have to sail uptide and crosstide equal distances there are no advantages to either tack. Whichever tack takes the boat more directly to the mark should be assumed first. Although the deviation of the adverse current is fixed, the deviation of the adverse wind is unpredictable and at any time may change to permit the boat nearer the mark or all boats to lay the mark thereby allowing the nearer boat to take the lead. Thus the more uptide tack has significant advantages in the presence of wind variations (which may be reasonably expected). If the wind heads the uptide tack, then the boat longest on this tack, being ahead and to leeward of his competitors, gains the most. And if the wind lifts, the boat on the uptide tack may reach the lee-bow-to-the-tide position while the cross-tide boats, tacking to windward, overstand. The percentages in a shifting wind are thus distinctly with the boat on the uptide tack.

On the other hand the boat on the uptide tack is making significantly less progress over the bottom and because of her decreased apparent wind is also making less progress through the water. If speed is desired to permit the rapid acquisition of a desired position, *i.e.* to reach a position out of the adverse current over a shoal or along the shore or to approach the mark when the major tack is crosstide, then the crosstide tack should be selected—immediately. After rounding a mark out in the current at the end of a reach, tack as soon as it is possible to clear the mark safely and come racing back, crosstide to the protection of the shore. On the other hand,

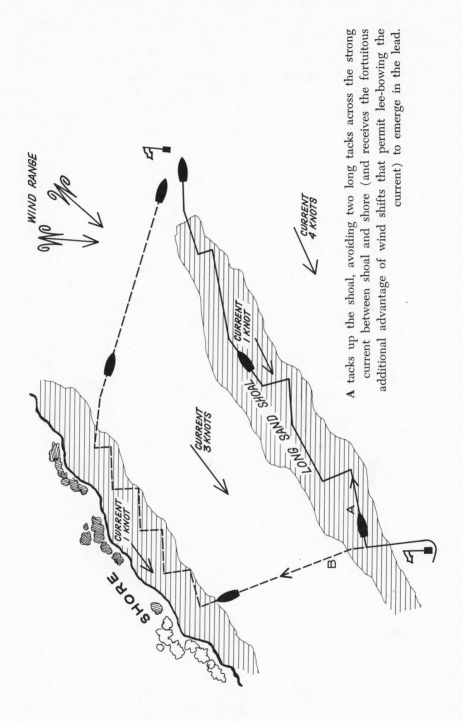

A tacks up the shoal, avoiding two long tacks across the strong current between shoal and shore (and receives the fortuitous additional advantage of wind shifts that permit lee-bowing the current) to emerge in the lead.

WIND RANGE

CURRENT 4 KNOTS

CURRENT 1 KNOT

LONG SAND SHOAL

CURRENT 3 KNOTS

CURRENT 1 KNOT

SHORE

B

A

183

if there's no avoiding the current and the uptide tack is heading nearest to the mark, assume it and keep plugging along—any windshift will be beneficial.

When beating against the tide one should sail directly to the area of the beat with the least unfavorable current and short tack in this area until a sufficient distance beyond the lay line is reached to permit recrossing the current and rounding the mark.

O. Along the Shore in Unfavorable Current

*"When beating down the shore off Egypt Point against
a foul tide and a vile sea, I stood in too close. We were
hung up for a long time and chucked the race. I aggrievedly
complained that since my last visit they must have moved
the Isle of Wight two feet further to the eastward."*
—SHERMAN HOYT

When racing in a stream, tidal or otherwise, the major determinant
of victory will be the current. Duration of exposure to the current is
the key, and as duration is markedly increased when sailing against
the current, current becomes most significant on the upstream beat.
It is evident that sailing in shallow water along the shore provides
protection and that the shallower the water (or the closer to shore)
the less the current and that the deeper the water (or farther from
shore) the greater the current. On this course marked variations in
current strength effect boats at slight distances from each other,
and each boat sails through a constantly changing rate of flow.
Thus, at a rate dependent upon the angle of shoaling, the boat on
the tack approaching shore is sailing in progressively less adverse
current, and the boat sailing on the tack away from the shore is
sailing in progressively more adverse current.

It seems reasonable to conclude that the boat should remain as
close to the shore as possible and sail out as little as possible on the
away-from-shore tack before tacking in again. This thesis must be
modified by at least two major factors—the rate of shoaling of the
bank, and thus the rate of current increase as the boat leaves the
shore, and the loss of boat speed in each tack. A good tack results
in the loss of at least one boat length. (Did you ever try tacking
exactly one boat length dead ahead of a boat approaching on the

185

opposite tack?) All boats in the same current strength are being set back equally regardless of whether they are sailing uptide, crosstide, or are tacking, but boats tacking in strong current are spending more time in the stronger current (with boat speed reduced during tacking) and are therefore losing more than boats in the same current not tacking or than boats in lesser current which are tacking.

If boat speed is 4 knots, a 30 second tack away from the shore will carry a boat 200 feet through the water. If during this run, the boat leaves an adverse current near shore of ¼ knot, sails into an adverse current of 1¼ knots, tacks, and sails back she will lose 100 feet to windward on the two legs consequent to the excess current (presuming wind and current to be in the same direction). A competitor who makes two additional tacks to avoid leaving the ¼ knot adverse current zone gains the 100 feet but loses two boat lengths, 30 to 40 feet while tacking. The boat in the stronger current has an additional excess loss due to her lengthened exposure while making her tack, the amount of which will depend upon her boat speed.

LOSSES TO WINDWARD	BOAT IN 1¼ KNOT ADVERSE CURRENT	BOAT IN ¼ KNOT ADVERSE CURRENT
Current losses		
While sailing 400 ft. at		
4 knots in 60 seconds	125 ft.	25 ft.
While tacking in 3 seconds	6 ft. (1 tack)	1½ ft. (3 tacks)
Boat speed losses		
While tacking	20 ft. (1 tack)	60 ft. (3 tacks)
Totals	151 ft.	86½ ft.
Current losses		
While sailing 133 ft. at		
4 knots in 20 seconds	42 ft.	8 ft.
While tacking in 3 seconds	6 ft. (1 tack)	1½ ft. (3 tacks)
Boat speed losses		
While tacking	20 ft. (1 tack)	60 ft. (3 tacks)
Totals	68 ft.	69½ ft.

It is thus evident that sailing at 4 knots for more than 20 seconds into a current one knot greater than that experienced by a competitor who tacks will cause progressive loss, increasing steadily thereafter, but that if 3, instead of one, tacks will be required to sail the same distance up to 20 seconds of exposure to the increased current may be warranted. It must be emphasized that the critical factor is time, the duration of exposure, not the boat speed or the distance sailed. With lesser boat speed shorter legs and more tacks will be required,

186

although the danger of more prolonged exposure is somewhat offset by the increased loss in boat speed when tacking at slower speeds (in light air or heavy seas). With lesser current differences more prolonged exposure can be tolerated (and vice versa); the more gradual the shoaling, the fewer the tacks indicated, the steeper the bank the more tacks required.

General rules:

1. It will pay to continue out into the current for as long as 20 seconds if no more than a one-knot current difference results in order to save 2 extra tacks when rounding points, piers, and so on (with the additional assurance that at such points the current differential will be slight, *i.e.* it will be increased near shore, and thus the tolerable duration of exposure is increased).

2. Unless it is evident that competitors will have to make 2 or more extra tacks, any distance sailed farther offshore than they will result in a loss. So long as no extra tack is entailed, stay closer to shore than your nearest competitors and tack back in before they do.

3. If the shoreline is irregular, tack in whenever an indentation can be laid that permits the longest possible inshore tack. Try to arrange to reach the lay line at the farthest feasible inshore position of an inshore tack, thus making the fewest possible total tacks and remaining in the least adverse current for the maximum possible time.

It may pay to overstand the weather mark significantly, particularly if the offshore tack is at only a slight angle to the shore. The inshore overstanding boat in less tide may be able to move at a speed over the bottom sufficiently greater than the offshore boat on the lay line that the distance wasted to weather is more than compensated. An inshore boat 100 feet to windward traveling at 4 knots in one knot less current gains the 100 feet in one minute or 400 feet of sailing and from then on is going away.

The approach to the mark must be made in the most favorable conditions. If no shoaling limitations exist, it is best to sail out of the current to or beyond the lay line on a single hitch from the starting line, remembering that because of the adverse current the lay line will be considerably above the 90° line to the initial tack course. Tacking, if possible, should only be done once and then as far out of the tide as possible. No compromise that requires additional tacks further into the current than the competitors should be undertaken regardless of disturbed air, need to cover, or other tactical considerations. Let the competition be the first to tack out, the

Boat **A** loses 151 feet in sailing 400 feet at 4 knots due to the 1¼ knot average current and the slowing consequent to making one tack while boat **B** loses 86½ feet while sailing the same distance in the ¼ knot average current and making three tacks, a gain for boat **B** of 64½ feet.

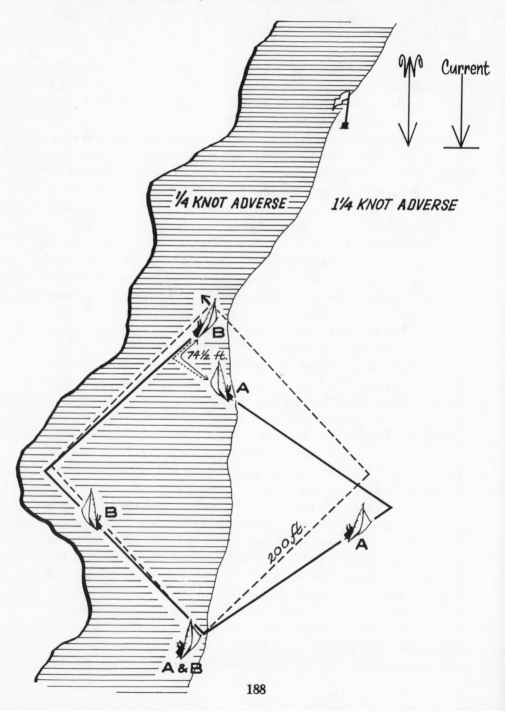

first to test the current out in the mainstream; it often pays to be a little behind so as to observe the leaders peel off and be swept away and thus to judge the optimal lay-line approach.

Once out in the major current approaching the mark, boats on the crosstide tack may be moving at two, three, or more times the speed of boats on the uptide tack. Indeed, boats having approached across tide may be unable to achieve any forward progress at all after tacking to the uptide tack near the mark. They may then have to watch their competitors, who continued but a few feet beyond them on the initial tack out of the current, sweep above them and round the mark well in the lead. The difference in boat speed on the two tacks is the major determinant of the racing results in these conditions. Every precaution should be taken to insure that the up-tide tack is taken entirely out of the main current and that nothing remains but the rounding once the mark is reached. Sailing 100 yards too far before tacking for the cross-tide approach is a negligible loss compared to tacking 10 yards too early and being almost unable to make any forward progress at all uptide in the vicinity of the mark. If a tack must be made to round, there must, of course, be at least enough wind to permit some progress uptide. Often in light air, although the mark can be reached on the offshore approach, the distance that must be sailed beyond the mark in order to clear it carries the boat out into such an increased current that no upcurrent progress is possible and the mark cannot be cleared! It may pay if the wind is extremely light to hang back (another "Slow up and win!"), proceeding on the cross-tack approach very slowly, waiting for the necessary puff to swoop down and around.

The final consideration on the beat against the current is tacking to round the mark. How far must one sail past the mark before it is safe to tack and clear it? As indicated in the table while tacking in 3 seconds in a 1¼ knot current a boat loses 6 feet downcurrent and while sailing one boat length at 4 knots which requires an additional 3 seconds, she will lose another 6 feet downcurrent. Thus tacking 12 feet beyond the mark when close aboard on the approach is probably the minimum reasonable allowance to permit completion of the tack and forward movement sufficient to clear the stern in a 1¼ knot current. If the current is stronger and/or the boat's tacking ability or speed less, proportionately greater distance must be allowed.

Once out in the current it may be too late to get back; the decision to initiate the cross-tide-approach tack is the crucial one. Not only does the uptide boat have markedly reduced boat speed over the bottom but markedly reduced boat speed through the air, reducing her apparent wind. She is thus helpless against the properly executed approach of a cross-tide boat coming down on a puff!

When beating along the shore against the tide, one should tack as infrequently as possible consistent with keeping farther into the slack water than the competition.

P. To Windward with the Current

"Good luck should not be unduly rewarded nor bad luck unduly penalized, the purpose of a scoring system being to reflect skill rather than luck."

—GREGG BEMIS

After a few experiences in battling to windward against the current —tacking in and out of the rocks along the beach, searching for the shoal in a confused sea, or working up behind a point ¼ mile beyond the lay line—an opportunity to rush up to the weather mark in a favorable current seems a welcome relief. But the danger of differential benefits in varying parts of the course and the risk of being set beyond the windward mark are disguised in the apparent ease of this prospect, perhaps even more important to the result, the shortened duration of the weather leg greatly increases the significance of any error.

Consider the following situations, which will demonstrate the problems of controlling the rushing sea beneath:

1. A beat across the mouth of Chichester Harbor as the water rushed out of the western channel revealed the necessity of remaining in mid-channel. Crossing the narrow outlet of the harbor on port provided the full advantage of maximum current sweeping the boat ahead and to windward, while the starboard tack *almost* directly down channel provided the full advantage of forward movement at the expense of slight

deviation to leeward. It seemed essential to remain in the deep water along the outside of the bend, but as this position could only be maintained on starboard tack, it resulted in a net loss due to the leeward deviation. We tried the port tack repeatedly but continually found ourselves running out of the current over the deceptive shoal along the inner border of the harbor bend.

2. We once beat up the Chesapeake Bay's main channel off Annapolis in a 25 knot northeasterly which was producing extremely large waves. We tacked out from the leeward mark towards the center of the Bay to take full advantage of the flood tide. In the steep sea created by wind against current we were alternately stopped and periodically immersed. It was soon evident that the boats in shore *out of the favorable current* were making better progress.

3. In a P.O.W. Practice Race we tacked out to sea on starboard in the weather going tide to obtain the maximum current advantage and did not come about till just short of the lay line. We thought we had allowed for the cross set of the current while approaching the mark but soon recognized that we had overstood and that the mass of the fleet on the starboard lay line would come up under us as we bore away up tide at the last. It had been impossible to accurately estimate the extent of the windward deviation from ¾ mile away.

4. At Essex we tacked to the port downcurrent (downriver) lay line from close aboard. Although we were approaching almost on the direct line of the current, we suddenly recognized at the mark that a significant lee-bow vector was present and that we were being swept into the mark. Only by jerking up the board so as to bear away abruptly were we able to clear it.

5. In the race for the Hunstanton Town Trophy off Lowestoft we took the starboard tack across the weather-going tide and made but a few short hitches to port in adjusting to moderate wind shifts. We tacked ahead and beneath the fleet approaching the mark on the port-tack lay line to prevent overstanding and soon found ourselves coming up close to the lay line. A final tack on starboard from about 100 feet to leeward permitted an accurate final approach without wasting more than a few inches of favorable set.

6. In the final race of the P.O.W. Week we started from the leeward end of the line in an easterly wind with the south-flowing current under our lee bow. Expecting the southerly

Salute took off on starboard tack, lee bow to the adverse current, on the first round, to overstand the mark for the port-tack, cross-current approach. Beyond the shoals however, the current had not yet turned south so *Salute* had to work upcurrent and downwind to the mark while the fleet roared up the starboard-tack lay line in favorable current below her.

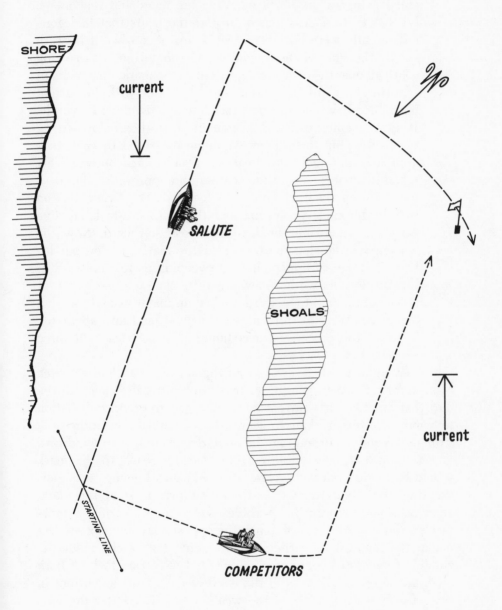

flow to be present throughout the first round we overstood the mark to allow for the adverse set on the cross-tide approach. We congratulated ourselves on the excellent uptide position we had achieved and presumed that we were well in the lead. But much to our chagrin we discovered that the current was still flowing to the north out near the mark and that as we bore away to a dead reach on port the boats that had gone out initially were now being swept up on starboard beneath us! By the time of the second round the current was flowing south all over the course except right at the mark, which meant that the starboard tack was almost across tide with the current on the lee bow and the port tack was almost dead downtide. It again seemed essential to remain on starboard for as long as possible, but in so doing we again overstood the port-tack approach and again lost boats that had more conservatively taken some of their port tack earlier and approached the mark more accurately from farther to seaward. To obviate this on the third round we approached the starboard-tack lay line early and made our final approach on starboard. Now the current was flowing south even at the mark and, on our lee bow on the final approach, was sweeping us to windward of the lay line. As we bore away a third time another group of boats behind and to leeward worked up under us and rounded alongside. We had thrown away a good lead and about ten boats in the process of overstanding on each tack in three successive approaches.

It is essential to break away from the starting line into the area of maximum weather-going tide. It is also essential to keep to the tack that provides that current on the lee bow to produce deviation to windward rather than to leeward as leeward deviation in a strongly favorable current may be more detrimental than windward deviation in a less favorable current. The approach to the mark should be made from well below the lay line with complete understanding of the variations of current that may exist at the mark, allowing a large margin for possible error. The final lee-bow cross tack should be made so as to reach the opposite lay line close to but not at the mark. This permits the rounding tack to be made accurately from close aboard on a lee-bow-to-the-current tack (if both tacks are so oriented) or with the windward bow to the current in case of a current flow across the weather leg. The latter provides complete control at the mark utilizing the boats full windward ability to the end and prevents the disaster of overstanding and working downwind and upcurrent at the last. If both tacks are lee-bow to the current great care must be exercised to make the final approach below the lay line. If the rounding itself is to be made uptide overstanding is all that need be feared; if the rounding is downtide then additional care is necessary to avoid being swept into the mark while rounding.

Take full advantage of the area of maximum favorable current by remaining in it and retaining its lee-bow deviating effect as long as possible, but avoid overstanding at all costs, and make the final approach tack from close aboard on the tack with the least lee-bow deviation.

Q. Racing along the Shore

"I have been sailing on many race courses around the world with a good deal of success because I have trained myself to take the trouble to learn the local wind and current conditions."

—PAUL ELVSTROM

Variations in wind direction and wind strength caused by the shore are often the major determinants of the outcome of races held in rivers, lakes, and small harbors. Such races are often held in offshore breezes, which, along the East Coast at least, are usually vertically unstable and subject to periodic shifting. The oscillating shifts of a vertically unstable wind must be distinguished from the fixed shifts created by the proximity of a shore.

The accepted dicta of "tacking on headers," "keeping on the tack directed toward the next header," and "keeping farthest to the side of the course from which the next header is expected" do not apply in the usual manner to adjustments to geographic wind shifts. Tacking as soon as a header caused by the configuration of the shore is detected may result in sailing right out of an advantageous shift. In general one should plan in advance to sail well into the area where a geographic shift is operative to insure that its beneficial effects are acquired as completely by you as by any other competitor. Short tacks to accommodate for the directional changes caused by oscillating winds may have to be superimposed upon the general plan to go farther in to the area of a geographic wind shift but should not interfere with the primary utilization of the geographic deviation.

When sailing upwind on a river (or any narrow body of water) remember that the wind direction will twist to follow the long axis

The median wind is deviated to the east in midchannel and to the south along the shore. To take advantage of these persistent geographic shifts, the boat must be sailed on the headed tack well into the area of the shift (towards the deviated wind direction), finally approaching the mark on the lifted tack.

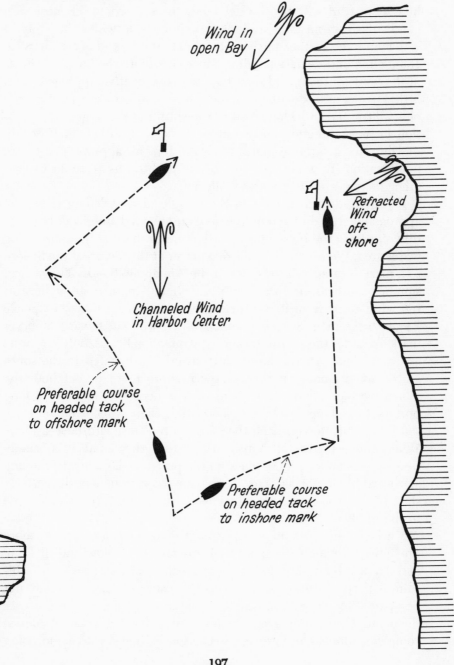

Wind in open Bay

Refracted Wind off-shore

Channeled Wind in Harbor Center

Preferable course on headed tack to offshore mark

Preferable course on headed tack to inshore mark

of the water, particularly if the shoreline is elevated. It is important therefore to be on the inside at any major bends, so that you will be nearest to the expected shift around the bend. The wind will tend to blow down the long axis of entering creeks, coves, or even dry valleys so that being near their openings may provide beneficial lifts. The wind will also be deviated, so as to come off more perpendicularly, from long straight shorelines. The wider the body of water and the farther offshore the boat, the less effect such wind channeling and deviation will produce. Evaluate the possible effects of the land contours, and then take the conservative approach: go a little farther into the advantageous shift than your competitors but only a little farther! The extent of the shift and the degree of alteration in wind direction and strength associated with it may be impossible to determine until too late for an appropriate course modification. It is always best to risk as little as possible in case other factors are of greater significance.

If the windward mark is in the middle of a widening river, the approach tactics dictated by the geographic wind shifts will be quite different from those used for a mark close to shore or in a narrowing water area. We frequently race downriver at the mouth of the Severn to a mark located well offshore in the Annapolis Roads. The typical summer southeasterly seabreeze is deviated more easterly here as the wind turns from its southeasterly direction up the Chesapeake Bay into the main Severn channel. When we beat towards another mark up under the southern shore of Annapolis Roads, only a ½ mile away, we find that the same southeasterly is deviated to the south as the wind comes off that southern shore more perpendicularly. When we race for the inshore mark it is necessary to make a long port tack well up under the shore and, then when well into the southerly shift, to approach the mark on the starboard-tack lay line. When racing for the offshore mark on the other hand, it is usually necessary to approach the mark on the port-tack lay line after a long starboard hitch that picks up the maximum advantage of the easterly shift in the river's center when well to north of the rhumb line to the mark.

Marked variations in wind strength are associated with shore proximity. A windward shore will obstruct wind flow and, if high, may have a zone of almost complete calm in close proximity. This calm is particularly evident in vertically stable winds, but may not be evident in vertically unstable conditions. A leeward shore causes the wind to lift and again, if high, may have a zone of almost complete calm in close proximity. Obviously, one should avoid going too close to either shore. This is particularly a problem when the course deviates around a point or an island to windward. In vertically stable wind it is best to hold a course well offshore on the approach, only gingerly closing the shore, and never going in more than a little distance closer than your nearest competitors. When warm air flows over cool air pocketed against a windward shore many places can often be picked up (or lost) in relation to a boat that attempts a short cut around a promontory to windward.

A boat in close proximity to shore risks the dangers of disturbed wind flow from blanketing, lifting, or eddy formation and the dangers of running aground. Running aground seems of minimum consequence until experienced. I recently lost several boats and 100 feet by cutting across a point too close aboard. Not only does the boat stop, but she suffers the consequences of attempting to reinitiate forward motion with the board up at a time when maximum lateral resistance is needed. This results in marked leeway while the crew is floundering in the bilge with both his hands on the board tackle and the jib sheet flogging about in his teeth. It is also usually necessary to tack to get clear when grounding occurs on the windward leg, which means that the boat is suddenly flung about on to the "wrong" tack and often in the backwind, blanket zone, or direct path of a right-of-way yacht. At the best it ruins a strategic plan, at the worst it produces a disqualification. The best principle that can be derived is to avoid running aground. The next best is to be prepared for the possibility, to have the board started up as you go in, and to be prepared to tack without confusion at the first touch. This is particularly important over soft muddy bottoms when the boat may be completely stopped if the centerboard digs in without a warning sign. Remember that you needn't run aground before demanding room to tack from a boat behind and to weather (unless he can clear the obstructing shore); take no chances, demand the room and take it—well in advance.

The wind deviations produced by proximity to the shore overwhelm the effects of all other wind shifts, determine the distance sailed to the weather mark, and usually determine the outcome of races conducted along the shore even when unassociated with the catastrophic consequences of running aground.

Geographic wind deviations deserve primary consideration whenever they are present; plan to approach the shore so as to obtain maximum advantage from the deviation expected.

R. Racing in the River

"Suffering is an intensely interesting subject and close to the heart if not to the experience of most and there is something about it which rings true of every sufferer alike. If one facet of the agony is suddenly relieved, then the morale rises with a crescendo astonishingly disproportionate with the actual respite given."

—KEITH SHACKLETON

We frequently race in the rivers at Essex, at Annapolis, and in Washington. Once each year on New Year's Day we race up the Severn River around St. Helena Island in Round Bay, and return, a distance of about 12 miles. The high shores of the Severn are indented by coves and creeks and by irregular promotories that deviate the winds along the main axis of the channel. In 1965 we raced in a light varying northwesterly that funneled down the river to provide a 4 mile initial beat.

We started at the headed, upwind, port end of the line but were unable to break away to the port tack. Those who were able to do so were well to starboard of the fleet and gained significantly when the subsequent shift to starboard appeared. As we tacked up the straight main channel of the lower river in the oscillating wind, we gradually improved our position by judicious use of the compass. As the river gradually bent to the north we worked towards the northerly (starboard) bank and were rewarded by a permanent shift from this direction, which gave us the lead. We tacked to cover the fleet and continued on starboard tack in the progressive lift.

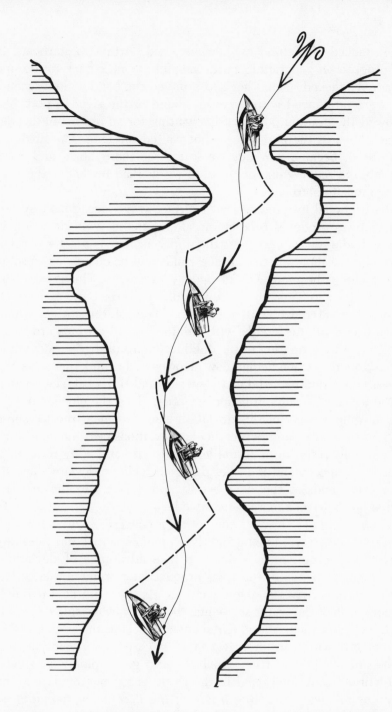

By working to the side of the course toward which the river is deviating and by tacking close under each promontory (on the inside of each bend), it is possible to obtain full advantage of each wind deviation produced by the bending of the river channel.

Goose tacked off behind us, however, and, farther to starboard in the progressive geographic shift, was able to tack back inside and ahead. We tacked behind her and rounded the bend a close second. We were now faced with a gradual bend of the river to port. We followed the gradual port-tack lift waiting for an oscillating header to tack towards the port shore—but waited too long. The lift held, progressed, became marked; we lost three more boats and were only able to recover one of these as we worked up under the next promontory to starboard.

The frictional interference with surface winds occasioned by terrain features produces predictable alterations in wind direction in narrow bodies of water. Unless the upper air flow is exactly perpendicular to the shoreline the surface winds will be channeled to some degree along the main axis of open water areas. The greater the height of the shore and the more irregular its surface the greater the frictional interference with the normal flow of the surface wind. Initial frictional interference with oblique flow off a windward shore results in eddy formation to the oblique side resulting in a deviation towards more perpendicular flow. However, beyond this zone the decreased friction over the water surface and the resistance created by the lee shore results in major deviation along the elongated axis. The maximum effect of this deviation is evident near the lee shore whereas blanketing and perpendicular deviations near the windward shore usually result in undesirable interference and eddy formation. Thus, in each segment of a river the wind tends to deviate along its main axis, bends as the river bends, and deviates to the greatest degree on the river's more leeward side.

When racing in a river the competitor is concerned with variations from the median wind along the river's main channel and therefore must place himself in a position to take advantage of deviations consequent to bends in the river produced by promontories, creek entries, or major river course deviations. As the wind flow parallels the long axis of the water segments, the wind always shifts towards the direction of the next segmental deviation. Thus the strategic plan for racing to windward in a river must be based upon being nearest to the side of the river from which the next geographic wind deviation will occur at each bend in the river. The general rule may be stated as follows: *Be on the inside of the fleet when rounding all major bends in a river* (or similar body of water). The position on the inside, of course, must be sought consistent with the recognized wind disturbance close to the windward shore; if the bend produces any significant blanketing effect it should not be approached too closely. All promontories of the shoreline should be approached from beneath (downwind) on the most direct tack. This approach will permit tacking out from under the point, close aboard, on the tack that will be progressively lifted as the boat emerges into the new channel (or altered main axis). The boat making this approach will always be on the inside, to windward of her competitors, short-cutting across the great circle being sailed by boats on the outside at the bend.

Geographical shifts of this nature will effect all boats in the fleet and are not remedied by oscillation back in the opposite direction (unless the river bends back) and thus take precedence over all other wind-shift considerations. The presence of an oscillating wind superimposed upon the terrain shifts will require modification of tacking to conform to such temporal deviations but should never prevent adherence to the fundamental rule given above. If I had paid less attention to the superimposed oscillations indicated by the compass and more to being in the right location to take advantage of the shifts created by the deviations of the river, less carrying on in a lift on the outside of the bends and more tacking, in an oscillating header if necessary, to be inside at the bends, I might have won the Ice Bowl again.

As shifts created by the river channel are persistent in a given area, relationships with other boats become meaningful indicators of progress, and such indications should be utilized to determine the need for covering tacks. Boats on the same tack that are being lifted as compared to your course (particularly those behind and to windward) indicate that you are sailing in a relative header—tack and cover them, *i.e.* get inside for their lift. Boats on the opposite tack that are sailing at an angle greater than 90° to your course indicate that you are again sailing in a relative header—tack and cover them, *i.e.* get inside for your own lift! Disregard nearby boats whose courses will be determined by the same wind and oscillations that effect you. Look for boats at a distance and utilize their experiences to indicate what is to be expected. Don't allow yourself to become preoccupied with neighboring competitors and immediate tactical problems.

Keep to the side of the river from which channeled wind will next emerge, and be on the inside of the fleet when rounding all major bends.

S. Upwind and Upwave

"It will be the races in the big winds that will live in your memory, not the days spent in the lee scuppers with one eye on the jib, the other on the tell tale, and zinc oxide on your nose!"

— JACK KNIGHTS

Modern small-boat racers, usually performing on sheltered waters, have become preoccupied with wind and current and have given little thought to the effect of surface waves. The traditional concept of "men against the sea" has been replaced by one of men manipulating the vagaries of mass air and water movements to their own purposes. In open water in a big breeze, however, the power of the sea becomes apparent, and the struggle against its superficial contortions may well decide the race. Here the intellectual subtleties of outguessing the shifts and shoals are swept aside by the immediacy of contention with the waves. It is the waves whose recurrent blows thrust us back on the beat and whose foaming surfaces sweep our hull out from under us on the reaches. It is the waves that bring us to a jarring halt as we tack and trip us into the brine as we jibe. Although waves remain unpredictable, much is now known about them that can lead to their successful conquest. This mastery permits defensive maneuvering to escape their damaging effects to windward.

At the start of the fourth race of the 1961 Princess Elizabeth Series in Bermuda's Great Sound the series leader was eliminated when a competitor, reaching the line too soon, attempted to tack, was stopped by a big sea, fell back in irons, and crashed into him. The collision tore away his jibstay, and his mast came thundering down into the starting melee. We barely escaped by bearing away beneath his stern and were forced to fight our way slowly back into clear air. We finally cleared our weather quarter and were able to

204

tack to port towards the center of the Sound. The wind had been blowing at about 25 knots all the day, and by this time big seas were rolling in from the Somerset shore 3 miles away. We could see that most of the fleet, scudding away to leeward on starboard tack, was heading for the lee of the islands that would shelter them on the port-tack lay line. A wind shift to starboard seemed possible, however, so we elected to continue on port. The boats nearby were being periodically set back by breaking seas; by comparison to them we seemed to be going well. Half way up the 1½ mile leg, we passed the last boat that remained ahead of us, a top Canadian helmsman, and tacked inshore to cover the remainder of the fleet. As we approached the port-tack lay line just beyond the shelter of the islands, we could see that one American boat would be ahead of us and that some of the weaker sailors who had taken off on starboard initially would come out ahead of the tough competitors we had passed en route through the big seas on port tack. The leader who crossed us about 100 feet ahead had taken off from the leeward end of the line, headed straight for the islands on starboard tack and had short-tacked up the shore in their lee. We took over the lead on the second reach and headed directly for the islands after rounding the leeward mark. The Canadian who had been beaten in the big seas was now moving faster in the smoother water and was barely ahead of us at the second weather mark. The three leaders having sailed the protected route on the second buck were now far ahead of the remainder of the fleet, particularly of the few who had elected to go out into the big seas for the second time. (We had difficulty with the spinnaker on the way home, elected to be safe rather than sorry, finished second, and thus were safe and sorry.)

This race illustrates the fundamental tactical principles of sailing to windward in big waves. Avoid late maneuvers (fraught with the dangers of stopping and losing control) on the starting line, keep clear of other boats at the start and during the leg, and seek the sheltered side of the course as rapidly as possible. Regardless of ability or of wind-and-current conditions the boat bucking against big seas is being slowed and is occasionally stopped by them. It may be possible to parry the blows, and such a technique must be developed, but their successive appearance, hammering the boat back again and again, results in a net slowing far better avoided than fought. To leeward the boat encounters but a few waves and utilizes them to sweep her onward; to windward she is met by blow after blow, the second of which may slam her back before she can recover from the first.

As breaking waves produce the worst possible obstruction to forward progress, shoal water directly exposed to the wind force (a lee shore or an underwater bar or reef) should be avoided at all costs. When starting from a lee shore the tack that takes the boat most rapidly offshore is usually to be preferred, and when an underwater shoal exists in some portion of the weather leg it should be circumvented. When the wind parallels or strikes a shore obliquely the refraction of the waves may be utilized to advantage. The inshore tack may then be preferred, as long as it is not continued into breaking waves, as the refraction produced by the shoaling turns the wave front more parallel to the shore. This means that the boat on the inshore tack is crossing the waves more obliquely while the boat on the offshore tack is bucking more directly into them. The irregularities of the shoreline may often be effectively utilized to permit keeping to the inshore tack, which confronts the waves more obliquely until a variation in the underwater contours permits coming offshore in an area where the waves are less deviated or deviated in the opposite direction, *i.e.* at a headland. The more paramount concern should, of course, be to avoid breakers regardless of the deviation of the wave fronts.

Whenever possible big waves should be avoided even when they are not breaking, and this may be achieved best by seeking the lee of a windward shore. Even a small promontory extending across the wind may be helpful as the diffracted waves beneath it are smaller. The largest seas, with their increased "slope drag" (the horizontal vector of buoyancy and gravity), wind exposure, and filling capacity are found wherever the greatest fetch exists. Thus the areas nearest the shores of an ovoid or otherwise irregular body of water may present considerably smaller waves than the center. The windward leg should be sailed whenever possible across areas having the least fetch from the windward shore.

If there is no way of avoiding the big waves, they should be sailed through so as to reduce as completely as possible the period of exposure to the undesirable "slope drag," backward orbiting crest particles, and enhanced windage in the crest. This requires bearing away slightly in the troughs to increase speed and maintain the advantage of the forward (for the boat) moving water in the trough for as long as possible and then heading up to slice through the crest and its backward moving water as rapidly as possible. By this means the wave crest, which is usually moving at a far greater speed than the boat, is rapidly passed. At the same time the boat is less exposed on the crest top to the slowing effect of the wind as

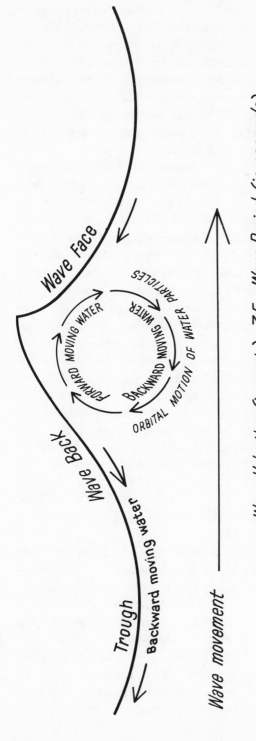

Wave Face

ORBITAL MOTION OF WATER PARTICLES

FORWARD MOVING WATER

BACKWARD MOVING WATER

Wave Back

Trough

Backward moving water

Wave movement

Wave Velocity (in knots) = 3.5 x Wave Period (in seconds)

Wave Period = Time required for passage of one Wave Length

Wave Length = Distance between successive Crests

The essential element of wave movement is the orbital motion of water particles.

she meets it more perpendicularly. A good hike as the boat rises to the crest is invaluable as it further reduces the windage of the exposed hull and permits a more effective drive through the backward moving water. Even more important, if the wave happens to break—and even in open water the superimposition of turbulent wave systems from multiple sources (previously deviant wind direction, reflection, and so on) may produce an occasional breaker—the boat heading more directly into the smashing mass will be less adversely affected than the boat hit broadside.

Inasmuch as wave systems may be refracted even in fairly open water so that they are no longer perpendicular to the wind's axis, an advantage in meeting the waves obliquely may be evident on one tack. On this tack, although windage in the crest is not reduced (indeed it may be enhanced), and the technique of heading up in the crests and bearing away in the troughs should still be utilized, the harmful effects of "slope drag" are reduced. As the boat rises obliquely on the wave face, "slope drag" increases its leeway relative to the bottom but does not slow its forward progress as in a perpendicular attack on the wave. Thus aerodynamic force continues to be successfully used in forward thrust, and less side force and forward resistance result. In addition, the longer the interval between meeting successive wave crests, as in a long sea, the better the boat may be prepared for meeting each successive crest. The *sine qua non* of beating in a breeze is to keep her moving; this is accomplished more readily in oblique than in perpendicular seas. Whenever possible the oblique tack should be selected for critical times, immediately after the start, when approaching the weather mark, and when near other boats that might interfere. The perpendicular tack should be taken where, if possible, the seas are least severe, and freedom to maneuver is not obstructed.

When racing to windward in large waves, avoid contact with other boats, tacking, and slowing, which increase side force and ultimately forward resistance and which interfere with freedom to maneuver. Avoid breaking waves completely, if possible, and the areas of the weather leg in which the seas are the largest. Utilize wave refraction to retain the tack that meets the waves obliquely at critical times and for as great a portion of the leg as possible. Keep the boat moving by bearing away in the troughs and slicing perpendicularly through the crests when orbiting water, windage, and even breaking may cause excessive slowing.

T. Tactics to Weather When Behind

> "It has often been said that the best way to win a race is to get out in front at the start and steadily improve your position. . . . The ones who win the most regattas are the ones who can't be counted on to stay bottled up when their situation looks hopeless."
>
> —TED WELLS

There are many possibilities for controlling the boat ahead on a windward leg. Tacking and port-tack restrictions may often be successfully utilized by a following boat to permit passing the leader.

When close astern or to windward the following boat may prevent the leading boat from tacking. This may be particularly valuable at the end of the weather leg, permitting the second boat to force the leader to sail well past the mark, unable to tack to round until she does so herself. It may also be applied at the initiation of a windward leg or at any time during it, if the following boat can maintain her position or if she can pinch out to weather. The leader unable to tack may then be forced beyond the lay line and the follower tacking first, when ideally positioned, will be in the safe leeward spot and certain of victory. I neglected this technique at the initiation of a final weather leg at the Corsica River Yacht Club Regatta, when following closely, I tacked for the line (which could be laid) immediately upon rounding. Unfortunately the other end was farther downwind, and I had freed my opponent to tack for that favored end! I should have continued the initial tack, forced him beyond the lay line to the favored end, and then tacked—to certain victory.

If following, but not close enough to prevent tacking, it may be possible to pinch out to weather or otherwise place oneself in a position to approach the mark on starboard while the opponent ahead and to leeward must cross again on port. If the port-tack boat elects to come in on the lay line when the mark is to be rounded to starboard, the meeting should be so timed that if he bears away to pass astern, he will be unable to lay the mark thereafter. If he attempts to hover ahead waiting for the starboard-tack boat to tack first, he may be forced completely about. This may require judicious slowing but not an alteration of course, which would constitute a balk. By such slowing he may be caught so as to have no option, other than to bear off below the lay line or to be forced about. The wiser solution for the leader, of course, is to tack earlier below the lay line, pass astern, tack again to weather, and catch the opponent on port, right at the mark. Which establishes a fundamental principle of rounding a mark to starboard: *approach on starboard as close aboard the mark as possible so that no one to weather can prevent your tacking.*

When rounding a mark to port, the port-tack follower may be able to prevent a leader close ahead from tacking to round. The defensive technique for the leader is to bear away below the course of the follower, then to tack, and *after completing the tack* to catch the follower port-starboard at the mark.

When well behind but in a situation where the leading boat is preoccupied by covering ahead and to windward, it may be possible to sail the leader beyond the lay line. If the leader can be induced to continue, not tacking until the follower does, and particularly if the follower can pinch up across her stern, the conditions achieved by the close-astern follower can be acquired. When both boats, even if in line astern, tack at or beyond the lay line, they are even, and the leeward boat has the advantage of the lee-bow position in the final stage of the approach.

Misleading the leading boat or inducing him to maneuver inappropriately is more readily accomplished in a shifting wind. Multiple short tacks may result in a sufficient loss to the leader that he eventually gives up the exercise. If he can be induced to give up while on the headed tack much can be gained. It must be recognized that any wind shift helps a following boat that is directly to leeward, and any boat that attempts close covering in a shifting wind will lose with each shift. If there is a preferred side of the course, a series of tacks may be initiated and continued until the leader ceases to cover while proceeding in the opposite direction. A false tack may

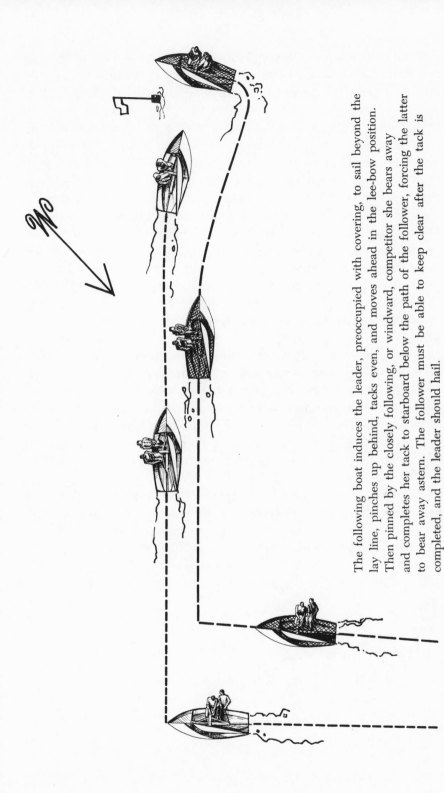

The following boat induces the leader, preoccupied with covering, to sail beyond the lay line, pinches up behind, tacks even, and moves ahead in the lee-bow position. Then pinned by the closely following, or windward, competitor she bears away and completes her tack to starboard below the path of the follower, forcing the latter to bear away astern. The follower must be able to keep clear after the tack is completed, and the leader should hail.

sometimes accomplish this end. Few small-boat sailors are willing to admit they've been fooled, consequently they complete a "covering" tack as if they'd intended it anyway and sail off attempting to appear unconcerned.

Following tactics should be modified to conform to the performance characteristics of one's boat. A boat that foots well but points poorly must avoid, in close quarters particularly, the presence of other boats on her lee bow. She must immediately bear away astern, pick up clear air to leeward, and go; any dawdling in a leeward boat's backwind merely expends valuable time needed to pick up distance. Such a boat should always tack on the lee bow of her opponent and never allow herself to be caught to windward. A high pointer on the other hand should pinch out across the leeward boat's transom, pin her to an unfavorable tack, or break clear to tack at will when advantages appear. In the 1964 Douglas Trophy Match Race my opponent was in the lead at the start of the second buck so that I needed my high pointing ability to break through. I initiated a series of short tacks that brought *Salute* close up under the Canadian. Each time he would bear away across my bow to take my wind until finally I was so close that I barely missed his transom as I swung away on the new tack. When he tacked close to cover we were bow to bow, he was unable to hold course above me, and soon was forced to luff to keep clear of fouling. (Unfortunately he later passed me on the close reach—but we took all the beats!)

The race is not won until the finish line is crossed; much can be done from behind on the beats. Avoid preoccupation with the mistakes that left you behind; concentrate on manipulating the situation to control the opponent ahead. He can be beaten.

U. Luffing on the Windward Leg

*"Let me say that the rules were invented to keep people
out of trouble with their competitors; tactics were invented
to make as much trouble for them as possible."*
—GORDON C. AYMAR

(I have the feeling that this will be a chapter I'll wish I'd never
written. My only hope is that my competitors don't read, as I'm
going to feel awfully silly swimming about my capsized boat knowing that I gave them the idea!)

Luffing as a defensive technique is difficult to apply on a reach or
run and had better be avoided on these legs if the overtaking
boat is actually faster. To windward, however, it may be extremely
effective, even against a much faster boat. On the beat even a minor
deviation to windward from the critical sailing angle required will
result in a major variation in boat speed. A boat luffed on the weather
leg may come to an abrupt halt while a boat luffed on a reach may
actually increase its speed (at least initially). Bud Whittaker, the
RCYC 14 star, says that the greatest source of untapped revenue in
small-boat racing is the luff on the windward leg.

In the crowded conditions after the start, as boats ahead and/or
to leeward kill their weather competitors with backwind, boats
farther to weather may romp over and by. The boats on the lee bow
are lost anyway, but losing those to windward as well may be
disastrous. A sharp luff after the start will usually so halt a boat
overtaking to weather that she will fall back into a hopeless backwind position. The general dictum after a congested start is to bear
off and "foot." This obviously results in bearing down on boats to
leeward, attempting to waltz over them with increased speed. The

only defense for the leeward yacht, if pinned by boats farther to leeward, is a sharp luff.

An even more dramatic utilization of the sharp luff to windward is in the breakaway from an undesirable lee-bow position. A boat ahead and to leeward may wish to tack to lay the mark, to change to the favored tack after a header, or to reach a more favored side of the course but be unable to clear the controlling boat in the weather-quarter position while tacking or after tacking to port. An abrupt luff even from a half-boat length to leeward may catch the windward boat unawares and force her head to wind, so that, with jib aback, she flounders in stays or even falls off on the other tack. The luffing boat with jib freed initially, sheets in her headsail, bears away smoothly and then tacks in the clear before her opponent recovers. The luff must be done abruptly and head to wind to be successful, but it seems only sporting to hail "coming up" as the luff begins. If caught completely unawares without a hail the windward boat may be fouled out or even, with jib aback, capsized. As the intent of racing is to compete, preferably against close competition, such an elimination of the closest competitor of all makes little sense!

The effectiveness of the windward-quarter or close-astern control position to windward is dependent upon the resultant restriction on tacking that requires the leeward or leading boat to continue the tack against her will. If the controlling boat is more than a boat length to windward it may be possible for the leeward boat to tack and pass astern (or if no boat is close to leeward to bear away and then to tack and pass astern). Otherwise the leeward boat may be forced to continue her tack until she works far enough ahead to tack in the clear, a consequent delay that may be intolerable, permitting, as it may, not only the opportunity for the controlling boat to gain and pass but the opportunity for many boats on the opposite side of the course to reap the full advantage of favorable geographic conditions. All this unless—unless the leeward boat is willing to sacrifice immediate position relative to her attacker for ultimate gain. As soon as the advantages of tacking are recognized, the distance to be lost by continuing must be weighed against the distance to be lost by dropping back to luff or pass astern. The escape maneuver that will lose the least is the sharp luff. It may often be justified to drop back considerably by slowing and/or pinching to acquire a position from which the luff will be successful. Depending upon the nature of the opposing helmsman and the abilities of his boat, it may be more reasonable to slow so as to permit a tack astern of him or to

214

pinch up to force him to fall astern and to leeward. If tacking to pass astern results in the continuing advantage of the weather boat, the luff should be selected as the preferable maneuver.

The most desirable breakaway technique from the lee-bow position on the windward leg is often the sharp luff.

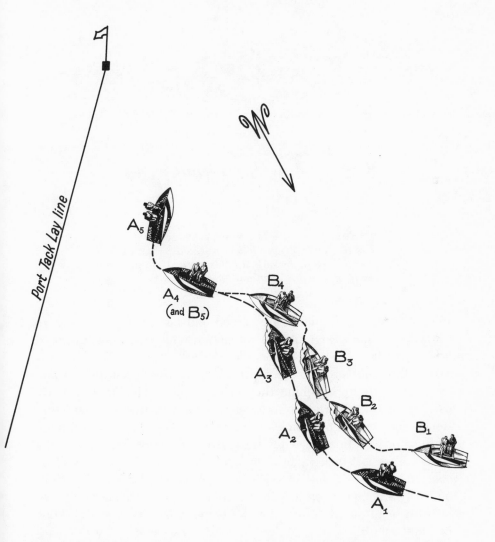

A, pinned in the lee-bow position, may be forced beyond the port-tack lay line, permitting **B** to tack for the mark in the lead. **A** may escape, however, by a sharp luff that leaves **B** in stays and permits **A** to bear away and then tack clear ahead.

V. Rounding the Weather Mark

"I believe that if we had to name the moment in a race nearest to the heart of satisfaction, it would be the rounding of the weather mark, because it holds more of the potential ingredients of pleasure than any other phase."
—KEITH SHACKLETON

In large fleets many places are gained and lost on the approach to the weather mark. The mass of the fleet usually seeks the starboard lay line early and creates a parade of starboard-tack boats on the final 100 to 200 yards of the approach. It is usually sensible to join this parade by approaching the lay line and tacking for the mark early so as to have right of way at the mark. Under some circumstances, however, a port-tack approach may be necessary or desirable because of variations in wind and current on opposite sides of the course. The port-tack yacht approaching the weather mark will be confronted with the line of starboard tackers. Her choice, if a yacht on starboard tack is on a collision course, is to tack ahead and to leeward or to pass astern and tack behind and to windward. When in doubt as to the ability of the starboard-tack yacht to lay the mark or one's own ability to attain the safe leeward position, it is better to pass astern and tack to weather. A second tack, necessitated by failure to lay the mark (tacking too soon or being overrun by the boat to weather), is disastrous in a large fleet.

The pass-astern-and-tack maneuver loses many boat lengths as it necessitates bearing away, crossing, tacking in disturbed water, and then sailing in backwind for the final yards of the approach. Recognition of this frequently encourages the port-tack skipper to risk the tack ahead and to leeward. If many boats on starboard are crowding closely and/or it is essential to remain ahead of a particular competitor, it may be reasonable to take the chance. The initial dangers include tacking too close (the tack must be completed prior to interference with the overtaking yacht) and establishing an overlap to leeward without giving the windward yacht "ample room and opportunity to keep clear." The sudden establishment of a leeward overlap by tacking to leeward may be completed with the windward yacht so close aboard that she is unable to keep clear. If the yachts are gunwale to gunwale as a result of the tack, the windward yacht may be unable to luff or tack to keep clear and, in the interference zone of the leeward yacht, may fall off and collide. If she can prove that she was not given "ample room" to keep clear, the windward yacht may disqualify the leeward.

After the overlap is established, further dangers appear. If the windward yacht drives over the blanketed leeward yacht, the latter may be unable to lay the mark. This danger is increased by the leeway consequent to an adverse tide or heavy sea. Under these circumstances, the leeward yacht may take the windward to a disqualification with her. If she persists in maintaining her right to the inside overlap at the mark but is unable to clear it she may cause the windward yacht, caught in her backwind, to collide with her in the rounding attempt. Although the windward yacht may feel that the leeward yacht is not justified in forcing her buoy-room rights when she is unable to clear the mark, she is obligated to keep clear and give the room. Her only proper recourse, if she sees that she will be unable to clear the mark and the interposed leeward yacht, is to tack away.

In smaller fleets control techniques other than the application of starboard-tack or lee-bow positions may be useful to insure rounding the weather mark in the lead. Complete control of a boat on the same tack may be achieved from close abeam to windward or from the weather-quarter or close-astern position. The leeward yacht may then be forced to continue on the same tack and, if unable to lay the mark, be forced beyond the lay line. The weather-quarter position or the close-astern position may be difficult to maintain due to the injurious backwind effects of the leading yacht but should be clung to at all costs if near the lay line. If the leader can be prevented from tacking, the windward yacht may tack first on the lay line and then arrive at the mark in the inside lee-bow or clear-ahead position. If the competitor is ahead when crossing on the approach, passing astern and tacking on her windward quarter may provide this same control. The windward-quarter or close-astern position only provides adequate control on the approach tack heading towards the lay line, which permits rounding without tacking. If forcing a competitor to the starboard-tack lay line for rounding to starboard or the port-tack lay line for rounding to port, however, the control may be lost after the tack as the competitor exchanges her lee-bow position for a controlling windward-quarter position thus preventing the final rounding tack until she tacks first and ahead. In these circumstances the weather-quarter control must be continued far enough beyond the lay line so that the windward boat tacks well ahead or forces the leeward boat to jibe away or slow up and tack away astern. If the rounding is to port and the leading boat is pinned on the port-tack lay line, she may bear away below the lay line and tack to starboard to catch the follower port-starboard at the mark. This, of course, requires a sufficient lead to permit completing the tack before interfering with the oncoming port tacker.

When farther ahead on the approach the close-abeam-to-windward position may be acquired by crossing ahead of a competitor and tacking immediately after clearing. It may be necessary to delay the crossing or slow the tack to insure that the tack is completed close aboard, but it must be completed sufficiently rapidly to prevent falling back into a backwinded position. Once this position has been achieved the leeward yacht is unable to tack and, unless she has luffing rights and can luff sharply or drops back to tack astern, can be pinned until the windward yacht can tack for the mark in the lead. This maneuver should be applied against a competitor who, although behind, will have subsequent right-of-way advantages at the time of rounding, *i.e.* should be applied to a boat approaching the port-tack lay line when the rounding is to starboard or a boat approaching the starboard-tack lay line when the rounding is to port. In either instance failure to control the competitor crossing behind may result in being forced to give way at the weather mark and to lose the lead. When a competitor is approaching the starboard-tack lay line, her cross-and-tack close-abeam-to-windward control maneuver may be thwarted by initiating a tack to starboard before she completes hers to port. As the boat to starboard has right of way when two boats are tacking simultaneously, this maneuver should force the attacker back to her original starboard tack and

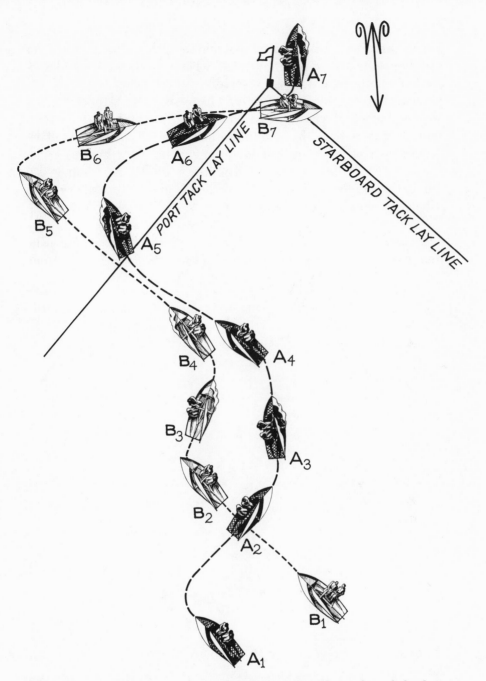

A breaks away from her lee-bow controlled position by tacking behind B. As B tacks to maintain control, A tacks simultaneously (with right of way as she is to starboard) forcing B to fall back to her initial tack. (Hail!) A then forces B beyond the lay line, tacking ahead for the mark. As A cannot tack at the mark directly ahead of B she luffs till B is forced astern and then completes her tack.

permit carrying *her* beyond the lay line from the windward-quarter control position. It is essential to hail when attempting a simultaneous tack; no tactical purpose is served by a collision.

Control techniques are effective chiefly because skippers resent any semblance of control, and thus, in an attempt to deny their controlled condition, they continue their directed course. No effort to escape is usually initiated as dropping astern or bearing away would admit the fact of control. The necessary defense is obviously the ability to recognize the controlled state and to breakaway from it before permanent damage results.

When approaching the weather mark, acquire a controlling position to insure rounding ahead of nearby competitors.

W. Tactical Control

"Marks should always be approached on starboard tack unless the way is so clear that there is no possibility of entanglements."

—GEORGE (BUD) WHITTAKER

Under a number of circumstances it is possible for one competitor to control another. Such control may be *complete*, so that the only escape is the assumption of a maneuver that either produces slowing or course lengthening, or *partial*, so that, although no course alteration is produced, the competitor's preferred course is either directed or obstructed. Partial-control techniques are always useful to induce the competitor to a more disadvantageous course and to permit retention of a more favorable one. Complete-control techniques cannot be successful for long periods and thus should only be applied at critical times such as prior to reaching the lay line, to rounding a mark, or to crossing the finish line. To windward the following control techniques are possible:

1. COMPLETE CONTROL: the competitor is unable to tack and is forced to continue his present course

    Weather-quarter, or close-astern, position—when competitor is ahead

        BREAKAWAY—sharp luff

                bear away and tack to starboard

                jibe away

    Close-abeam-to-windward position—when competitor is behind

        BREAKAWAY—pinch to safe leeward and luff

                drop back and tack astern

                jibe away

                exchange lee-bow or abeam to leeward-controlled position for dead-astern controlling position

221

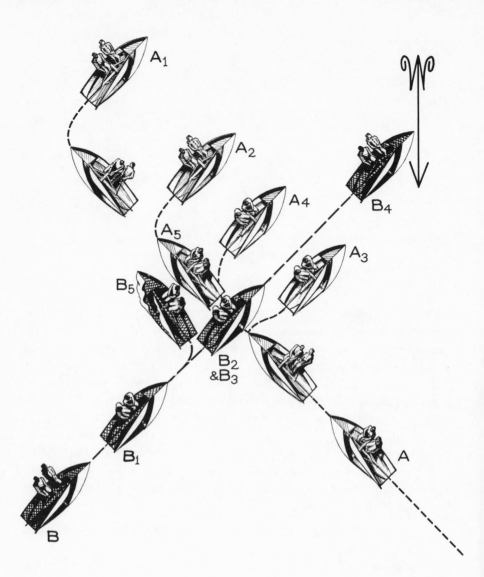

The starboard-tack boat **A** has five options when meeting a port-tack boat **B** which may provide tactical control if properly executed. She may (1) tack ahead and to windward for partial control, (2) close abeam for complete control, (3) to the lee bow for backwind effect, (4) to the weather quarter for partial control, or (5) force the port-tack boat to tack to starboard.

2. PARTIAL CONTROL: the competitor is induced to assume a less advantageous course or is covered so as to prevent subsequent acquisition of an advantageous course, when competitor is behind

Wind Interference

> *Lee-bow position*—force competitor to tack or to fall astern; utilize on the lay line or early on a long tack, *otherwise dangerous*
>> BREAKAWAY—tack away
>>> fall astern to controlling "weather-quarter position"
>
> *Dead to windward position*—force competitor to disadvantageous tack or to fall astern
>> BREAKAWAY—tack away or bear away

No Wind Interference

> *Distant abeam to windward position*—cover bulk of fleet en masse without interference (which might induce tacking and fleet splitting)
>> BREAKAWAY—not necessary
>
> *Distant ahead or ahead to leeward position*—cover bulk of fleet en masse without interference; utilize to reach an area of strategic advantage first; utilize to enter oscillating shifts to maximum advantage.
>> BREAKAWAY—not necessary
>> Danger—ware control by boat gaining to "weather-quarter position"

3. CONTROL NEAR THE WEATHER MARK: the competitor is blocked and forced to round second by the use of a control position

Weather-quarter position—force competitor beyond lay line, tack inside

Close-abeam-to-windward position—force competitor beyond lay line, tack inside

Lee-bow position on lay line—hold competitors astern
> Acquire by tacking into or bearing away behind crossing competitor
> Provides inside overlap rights while rounding

Starboard tack—controls port tack competitor when rounding to port
> Advantage limited when rounding to starboard by loss of right of way while tacking
> Always preferrable when three or more boats meet

*Tacking on the competitor's starboard hand when boats are tack-
ing simultaneously*—blocks competitor's attempt to assume
"close abeam to windward position"

4. CONTROL AT CROSSING: the competitor is completely or partially
controlled by the acquisition of a control position

Starboard tack—options:

Cross and tack or tack to partial-control position
Cross ahead, tack to close-abeam position
Tack to lee-bow position
Slow up to force competitor to tack
Cross astern, tack to weather-quarter position

Port tack—options:

Cross and tack or tack to partial-control position
Cross ahead, tack to close-abeam position
Tack to lee-bow position
Cross astern, tack to weather-quarter position

Third boat present—options:

Induce competitor to tack into interference zone of third
boat or to permit escape by tacking from partial-cover-
ing position to avoid such interference
Competitor forced to tack or completely controlled by third
boat
Acquire room to tack to weather-quarter position to clear
third boat with right of way

*Complete- or partial-control positions that permit the acquisition
or maintenance of an advantage over a competitor should be sought
at critical times such as crossings and particularly when nearing the
weather mark or weather finish.*

IV. *Reaching* —

The Acquisition of Maximum Speed

A. The Principles
of Reaching

"*But the new school advocates the doctrine: 'Rather
return to your mooring than keep on a straight course.'*"
—MANFRED CURRY

The reach provides the ideal demonstration of innate boat-perform-
ance characteristics; good hulls and good sails, properly trimmed,
reach rapidly, poor ones, slowly. With well-matched boats little
speed difference is to be expected. Thus strategic advantage and tactical control are the means of converting a parade into a conquest.
All advantages consequent to wind variations, current, and waves
must be sought to insure a more effective exposure than that obtained by any other competitor. Boat-handling techniques permit
the effective exploitation of such strategic advantages.

1. The reach should be initiated by a breakaway in clear air im-
    mediately after rounding the mark towards the preferred side
    of the course.
2. The leeward side of the course provides the advantage of clear
    air with increasing boat speed owing to the progressively better
    sailing angle at the end of the leg and better opportunity for
    adjustment to wind variations—up in the lulls, down in the
    puffs.
3. The leeward position is essential on a one-leg beat or close
    reach as any wind shift will adversely affect the boat to wind-
    ward.
4. In adverse current it is essential to sail the direct course,
    sufficiently upcurrent of the rhumb line to maintain positional
    advantage at the termination of the leg.

227

5. In light air, keep the boat moving and approach the leeward mark at the highest possible sailing angle.
6. If planing or surfing is possible, initiate planing or surfing and keep her moving regardless of deviation from the rhumb line.
7. When reaching along a shoreline, stay away from a leeward shore at all times, away from a weather shore in vertically stable winds, but close to a weather shore in vertically unstable winds.
8. Arrange to cross the two-boat-length circle about the reaching mark so as to seize or break an overlap as desired.
9. Determine the control position desired for the subsequent leg and arrange to acquire it when approaching the leeward mark —an inside overlap if the next leg is a beat with the opposite tack preferred or a broad reach, an outside lee-bow position if the next leg is a one-leg beat or a close reach.

On the reach seek maximum speed in clear air to leeward and upcurrent so as to acquire a controlling position at the termination of the leg.

C breaks away immediately in a puff to leeward of the fleet. The other boats luff each other to windward of the rhumb line, while C is free to accommodate to each lull and each puff, thus continuously maintaining maximum speed.

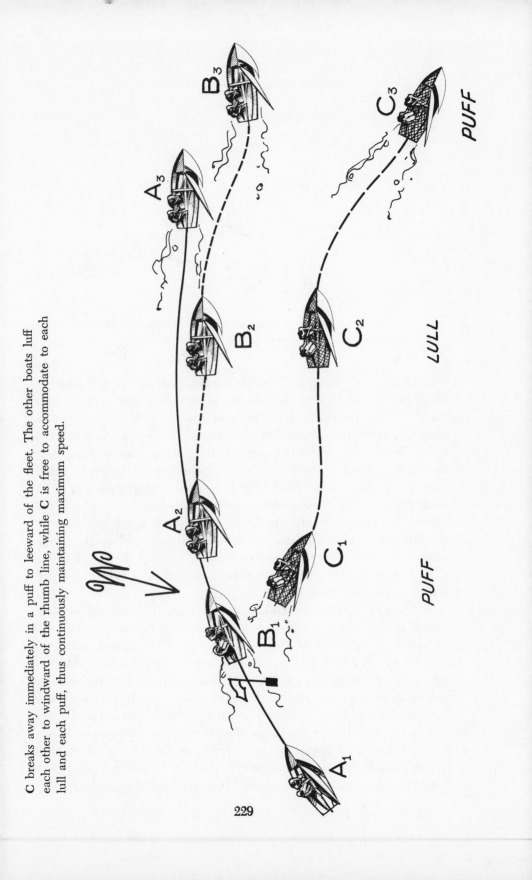

B. Initiating the Reach

"I wish to have nothing to do with any ship which does not sail fast, for I intend to go in harm's way."
—JOHN PAUL JONES

The essence of racing is thinking ahead, and the justification for these articles is to demonstrate the probability that prior understanding can be applied to thinking ahead. The reach must be planned before the weather mark is rounded. The primary decision must determine whether the shortest straight-line course is indicated or whether wind or current conditions warrant deviation to windward or leeward. Secondarily the prospective interference of other boats must be evaluated to determine whether the chosen course will be feasible. It is essential to know exactly what will be done on rounding and to avoid mere reaction to boats rounding simultaneously. The maneuver of rounding should develop directly into the tactical plan for the leg which is to obtain clear wind on the preferred side of the course.

As the rounding is undertaken, competitors close aboard must be watched carefully. If none are close, the elected course may be immediately undertaken; if one or more are close ahead, an immediate move to blanket must be weighed against the probable disadvantage of being temporarily (at least) pinned to windward; if one or more are close astern, the advantage of an immediate move to leeward must be weighed against the probable blanketing by and loss to the weather boats. If the weather side of the course is preferred because of better current, wind, or wave conditions, it is usually relatively easy to follow this preference unless a boat close ahead is a determined luffer. In light air, particularly in a temporary

230

lull, it is usually preferable to shoot to weather, maintaining speed while the boats bearing away more abruptly come to a near halt. However, when planing is possible, when the leeward side of the course is preferred for reasons of wind, wave, or current conditions, or *whenever the windward side is not distinctly advantageous*, the move must be to leeward.

It is this move to leeward that is fraught with danger. Even though it theoretically should result in far better position later in the leg and permit freedom of action during the course of the reach, the initial loss may exceed the gain unless properly executed. Particularly as the movement to leeward is through a greater arc than any other, retention of speed is difficult but essential. The board should be coming up with the rounding, the boat well hiked, and the main eased rapidly, as nothing kills speed more quickly than the sharp rudder action necessary to combat a board full down, heeling, and a tight main when bearing away. If speed can be retained from the rounding, it may be possible to slip out from the otherwise inevitable blanket of a closely following weather boat or to break sufficiently wide as to obtain clear air to leeward of a boat ahead. If the boat ahead rounds poorly and slows while making rig adjustments or setting the spinnaker, it may be wise to shoot on to weather, stop her completely, and then bear away across her bow. If the boat behind rounds poorly it is safe to go for the leeward berth, but if she rounds well it may be essential to hold the straight-line or windward course awaiting a more optimal moment. As soon as she slows with rig adjustment or on the back of a wave, the move to leeward may be undertaken. Any slowing creates vulnerability to similar moves by the opposition so that all slowing maneuvers or manipulations should be carefully timed to moments when the competitor is already slowed.

I remember so vividly times when, intent on being the first boat to have the spinnaker up and drawing, I've sailed off into a hole and slowed the boat so drastically with the crew movements associated with hoisting that a fleet has moved by to weather. How much wiser, if less dramatic, to hold the hoist until the rounding is completed with jib, main, and board well trimmed, nearby boats controlled by blanket or better boat speed, and the intended course to leeward (or to weather) properly embarked upon. Then, as the leader bears off to hoist and slows or the followers give up their threatening posture, the spinnaker goes up in clear air with minimal, if any, loss. More can be gained with the setting of the spinnaker than during the entire remainder of the leg if it is hoisted in proper relationship to the nearby competitors and if the skipper (or third crew member), with the sheets in his hands, breaks out the sail and has it pulling while the crew is still fiddling with pole and jib.

Integral to the breakaway maneuvering at the initiation of the reach is the maintenance of top speed. Speed is the consequence of power produced by careful attention to sail adjustment while changing course and the reduction of forward resistance to the bare minimum. At all times while reaching and particularly at the initiation of the leg, rudder action should be reduced to the minimum. Steering can be largely accomplished by hull manipulation and sail trim. To bear away she should be hiked to weather; to bring her up she should be allowed to heel to leeward. Shifting of weight and adjustment of main can and must be used all the way down the reach to permit maximum forward drive with minimum resistance. Such steering technique and its application in varied wind and wave conditions provides the dramatic difference between a properly sailed reach and the usual parade.

The essence of commencing the reach is the determined movement, under full way and in control of neighboring competitors, to achieve clear air on the preferred side of the course—fast, clean, and away.

B bears away immediately after rounding to set her spinnaker to leeward in the classic, recommended manner. As she slows, **A**, rounding less sharply and retaining her jib, slips up into a blanketing position. **A** sets her spinnaker in a puff and takes the lead.

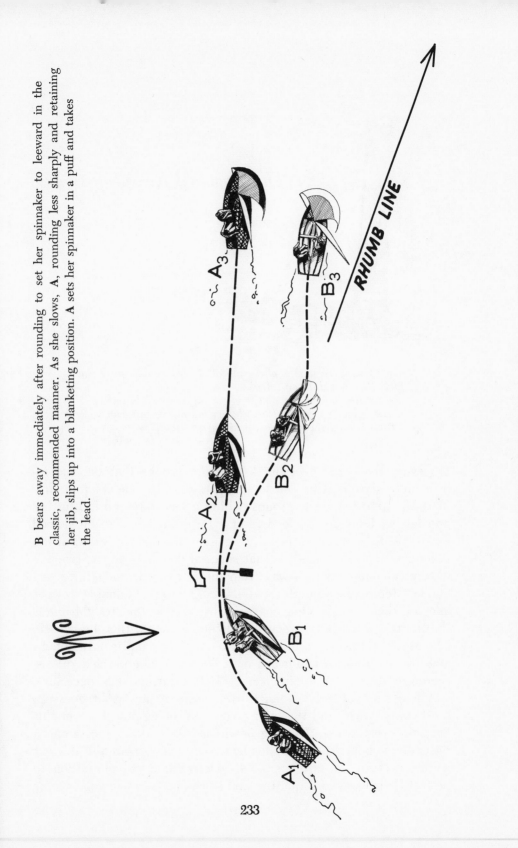

RHUMB LINE

233

C. The Leeward Reaching Course

"I suppose it is a phase we all pass through but I am glad that I learnt several years ago that if a boat is overhauling me so fast that it might be worthwhile luffing her it is much more worthwhile getting out of the way and letting her go through as quickly as possible."
—ROBIN STEAVENSON

On every reach the fleet breaks up into groups that become increasingly separated as the leg progresses. The leaders pull dramatically ahead, and the groups behind consolidate and fall farther and farther behind. The leaders of each group seem to be slowed by the boats astern, and the entire gaggle slows to the speed of the tailenders. It is thus evident that successful sailing on the reach is dependent upon getting away from the interference of other boats (and preferably being in the lead!). Clear wind is obtainable straight ahead if there are no other boats nearby, and, as the straight line is the shortest distance between two points, it should then be chosen. Whenever other boats are near, however, clear wind is only obtainable by deviation to windward or to leeward. The derived rule is, therefore, deviate to obtain clear air but no farther than necessary.

A long-time 14 sailor, John Carter, used to say "what goes up, must come down" and the luffing boat will unhappily discover this truth on every reach. "Coming down" is a long slow process and a bitter one as boat after boat slips by to leeward. Despite this evident truth most skippers are unable to overcome their compulsion to protect their windward quarter, and so the mass of the fleet always moves out to windward of the rhumb line. Meanwhile, boats to leeward have the two major advantages of less interference from nearby boats and a much faster course near the crucial termination of the leg.

The instinctive desire to push the helm down when an overtaking boat is discovered or approaches on the windward quarter should be tempered by the following additional considerations. Alterations in course and rudder action slow the boat; defensive maneuvering is always more abrupt and therefore more likely to produce slowing. While maneuvering to prevent a boat passing to windward, the skipper is concentrating on the other boat, not on sailing his own boat at top speed. There will be significant deviations from the straight line course with luffing maneuvers, often sharp deviations, and usually "up in the puffs, down in the lulls." And "what goes up, must come down," slowly, agonizingly. All this while other boats have been gaining, gaining, gaining, and slipping by to leeward.

In addition to these disadvantages of luffing, the cold fact of ineffectiveness must be recognized. It is almost impossible for a leading boat to prevent a following boat from passing to windward (if the following boat is fast enough to be a threat in the first place). When a luffing match does eventuate, interference between the two boats is prolonged and reduces the speed of each to the level of the slowest. Then, when finally "mast abeam" is called by the helmsman of a boat that has slashed up across the windward quarter to a blanketing position, the luffing boat is faced with prolonged blanketing and slowing until the victor breaks well ahead.

If the leg is a close reach, stay close beneath and luff the boats nearby only if necessary as the leg may become a beat. Don't let another boat sail between you and the arrival of a new wind or between you and a windward shore, if sailing close. If only a single competitor threatens and he is about to take your wind immediately after rounding a mark or at the finish line, give him a good *sharp* luff. But make it quick, be done with it, and get back to a reasonable course. (Of course, don't fail to luff on the windward legs, particularly just after the start; work up under anyone near to windward, force 'em about or to drop behind to leeward.) At all other times, keep to leeward!

Thus there are specific justifications for deviations to windward, but, particularly when they are to windward, deviations should be as limited as possible. In all other circumstances deviation to leeward is the ideal solution when other boats threaten. The problem is in deviating to leeward without losing initially to the boats that, moving faster, higher on the wind, rush up to blanket. An analysis of the prospective progress of the boats involved must be made: several boats close together will interfere with each other and deviate in sequential luffs well to weather of the course while a single boat will sail the straight line at maximum speed. Deviation to separate from the group will undoubtedly be effective as continued interference will slow all who remain to windward to the speed of the slowest. When but a single boat is near, to windward or astern, her speed will be improved by deviation of the leader to leeward, and therefore less net gain can be expected by deviation. The greater the number of nearby boats who will produce wind interference or require progressive deviation to windward to maintain clear air, the greater the need to bear away to leeward and the greater the safety in so doing. The fewer the threatening boats the lesser the need to deviate and the greater the risk in deviating; one boat freed of the leeward yachts' interference may readily romp down the leg to victory.

From the leeward position, without restriction by the right-of-way rules or by wind interference from other boats, it is possible to adhere to the other major precept of reaching, "bear away in the puffs, ride up in the lulls." The ability of the leeward boat to sail her own race, adjusting course to the variations in the wind and the waves so as to maintain maximum possible boat speed, provides a major enhancement of performance relative to the restricted condition of the boats massed to weather. Up there, with each boat struggling to avoid the other, there is no opportunity to capitalize upon wind and wave conditions with resultant further slowing.

On the reach, after wide separation on the beat, the fleet closes together again, slows together again, and as at the start only a few break away ahead and to leeward to clear air and an unassailable lead.

When a large number of boats round close astern, they can reasonably be expected to interfere with, slow, and luff each other well to weather of the rhumb line. Under these circumstances it becomes possible to escape to leeward, permitting the acquisition of clear air, course adjustment to wind velocity variations, and a faster sailing angle at the termination of the leg—advantages unavailable to the windward fleet.

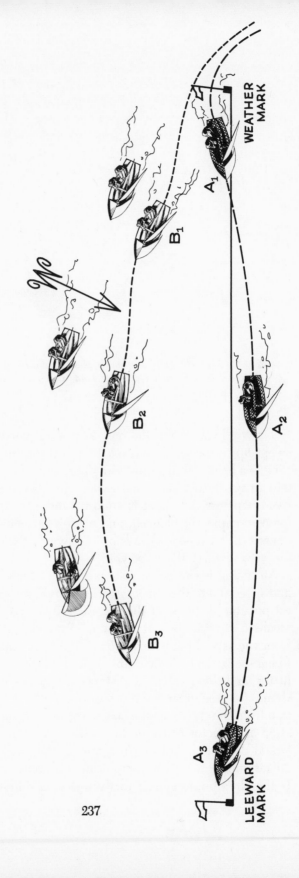

D. Up the Reach

"An old sailor's proverb, that is confirmed by experience, puts it: 'The speed of your boat increases with your own confidence.'"

—MANFRED CURRY

For a windward boat, the only sensation worse than that of being swept up to the windward mark by a favorable tide is that of stopping in a head tide after rounding it. As the entire fleet jams up astern and to windward and a hard won lead disintegrates, the prospects seem hopeless. The fleet is almost standing still, the available wind seems completely blocked, and there's no evident way to extricate oneself. But someone always breaks away, finds clear wind, and races away to victory. Why not you?

All racing is composed of two essential variables—distance sailed and speed—and their successful resolution requires sailing the shortest possible distance at the fastest possible pace. On the reach this means a straight line at maximum boat speed, and any deviation from the straight line demands a significant increase in boat speed to compensate. In unfavorable tide duration of exposure is the key factor, and the greater the distance sailed due to deviation from the rhumb line the greater the exposure and the consequent loss. Deviation from the direct uptide course exposes the boat to a further deviation as a vector of the unfavorable tide is now acting to produce lateral deviation. Thus even minimal deviation produces enhanced deviation due to current, significantly increasing the distance sailed. If the rhumb-line course to the mark is different from the direct uptide course, current deviation laterally will occur and must be compensated for. Any consequent deviation is deviation downtide, resulting in a more uptide ultimate course to the mark.

As in sailing to windward so in sailing against the current, the boat most upcurrent ("upwind") is the farthest ahead. The upcurrent reach should be sailed in a straight line that compensates for any current flowing across the leg or as directly into the current as possible consistent with that resultant straight line. Any boats working out to windward—and "downtide"—or jibing to tack downwind and "downtide" or bearing abruptly away to leeward—and "downtide"—i.e. any significant deviation from that straight line uptide course are bound to lose. Just as one cannot afford to throw away pointing ability on the windward leg (when sailing 500 yards through the water to make 300 over the bottom), one cannot afford to throw away uptide position on the reach.

But how can one keep up boat speed on that desired straight line uptide course when everyone else wants to sail the same course and is taking all the wind? Some sacrifice of the straight line must be accepted to achieve speed, as in a mass of dacron (which is ever increasing in density as each boat behind progressively blankets and slows each boat ahead) boat speed may be reduced below current speed. Look for a hole in a direction as uptide as possible, preferably to leeward, and break free as quickly as possible. Deviate as little as possible—but get clear wind—and then keep it, and keep to the straight line as closely as possible thereafter.

In the Weymouth Town Trophy Race at Lowestoft, England, I rounded the weather mark with a good lead over 84 starters and bore off against the tide. Unable to see the mark, I sailed well to windward of the rhumb-line course until my followers rounded and bore away correctly on the direct course to the mark almost directly uptide. I bore away to "cover" but discovered that now, not only downwind at a better sailing angle but uptide, the "followers" were already ahead. Even without knowing the location of the mark, I should have known that where I wanted to be was uptide and should have borne away to the most directly uptide course. From my uptide vantage point I could have then covered the fleet and sorted out the most direct and fastest course to the reaching mark at my leisure.

I deviated back to the rhumb line and found that the current now deviated my boat back towards the rhumb line but that while sailing the longer deviated course I was set back farther than the boats moving directly uptide. When I finally reached the rhumb line, two boats were well ahead with the clear air I should have had, and the mass of the fleet was just astern taking my wind. The resolution of my error was, reasonably, to return to the rhumb line, direct uptide course as rapidly as possible so as to reduce the consequent current deviation and course lengthening to the absolute minimum. But now that I was back, there was no wind! Unfortunately *some* deviation was necessary. I jibed away to the opposite slightly uptide side of the rhumb line, cleared the air astern, found 100 feet of open space, and jibed back. The first two boats rounded the leeward mark a mere 50 feet ahead, but were off in the favorable current of the second reach—never to be caught.

When reaching upcurrent, keep upcurrent and deviate as little as possible from the straight-line course (which allows for lateral current deviation) consistent with retaining clear air.

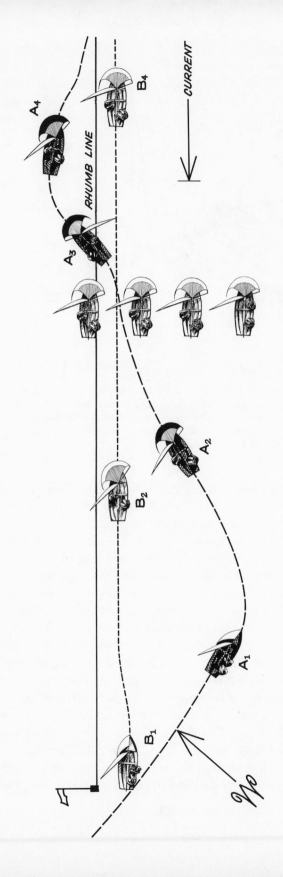

A mistakenly sails to windward and down tide from the rhumb line. In working back downwind and uptide she loses the lead to **B** and ultimately has to jibe away from the blanketing mass astern to obtain clear air. When in doubt the leader should assume a downwind, uptide course that provides continuous positional advantage. All deviations from the rhumb line are deleterious when sailing against the current.

E. The One-Leg Beat

*"Always take the tack which is closest to your mark.
Never take the short hitch first, unless you are in an awful
hole or have no choice. During the period of time required
to make the longer board, conditions (which never remain
stable for long) may change."*

—ARTHUR KNAPP

We had turned the last mark of the 1964 Severn Trophy Race, and I was in second, close behind Dave Kirby. Dave was 2½ points behind in the series so that I needed but to hold the position—or even drop another boat—to win the series and, with the series, the Governor's Trophy, emblematic of the best standing in the major East Coast regattas of the year. Bob Empey had been gaining on the last few legs of the 15 mile race and was close astern as we rounded for the 3 mile one-leg beat to the finish. Don Doyle was just behind Bob after a seesaw battle between us in the 12 to 15 knot varying westerly. No one else was close. We seemed to be holding Dave though we were but 50 feet astern in his wake and his backwind, but Don was working out on our windward quarter, and Bob Empey seemed to be moving up to leeward. The distant mark looked to be a ¼ mile to weather of the course we were making on port, and the wind was (for a change) fairly steady, near its median direction. We would not be able to pass Dave from dead astern, and Don Doyle, who we reckoned was the more dangerous of our attackers, was lifting to weather. We decided to take a short covering hitch and came about again 50 feet to weather of Don's course. We had no sooner completed the tack when a header appeared, and we fell down on Dave, who seemed much less affected, and Don. Don was moving very well and gradually came up beneath us. For a ½ mile or more we were less than a boat's length apart bow even with bow. We'd work out ahead hiking as hard as we could to keep her vertical; he'd fall off to leeward to clear his air and then come working back up. Finally another slight header provided the edge he needed, he drove up hard, and we were in his backwind—and forced to tack. We tacked far enough to completely clear our air and then came around—now in a lift. We were overstanding the mark by at least 100 yards! We cracked sheets a bit in an attempt to drive in over them in the last mile. But Don could lay the mark, and Bob Empey needed only a short hitch to tack beneath and about a boat's length ahead as we approach the mark. And that, after 15 miles, 5 races (with 3 firsts), and an entire season of racing, was that. We'd thrown away the lot on one long one-leg beat!

Stupid? Or a deliberate attempt to throw it away? Or a slower boat? But it could have been saved. Dave came out ahead with an even greater lead; I should have merely stayed with him. ("Don't be greedy." Settle for the series, the season's trophy; forget the single race even if it was for the Severn Trophy.) But next time would I take that first tack to cover Don Doyle? It has often been said that one should keep to windward on a close reach as it may turn into a beat, but there are a number of basic principles that deny this. Stay between your opponents and the mark. It is difficult to do this by working to windward when the mark is almost dead ahead! Avoid the lay line. When almost on it already what possible advantage is there in getting even closer?

The one possible circumstance on a one-leg beat in which a position to windward will be advantageous is when a lift appears (and all boats to windward gain in lifts) that permits precise laying of the mark. In any greater lift boats to leeward will also be able to lay the mark, thus counteracting the initial advantage. In any header boats to windward will lose, and all boats ahead and to leeward will gain. Only a few degrees separate the course of a one-leg beat from a course of overstanding and to hope that a shifting wind will select this narrow arc for one's private benefit is a bit unrealistic. The boat to leeward, however, is aided by any wind direction heading the existing course and any wind direction lifting beyond that sufficient to permit the windward boat to lay the mark.

One can't always be right, but one is a lot more likely to be if he stays with the odds. I obviously should have borne away to leeward for my attempt to pass Dave Kirby. From the leeward position the boat can be sailed free, adjusting to wave and wind conditions without interference. Don Doyle could never have come up on my lee bow forcing me to pinch—and eventually to tack—at a time when I no longer dared drop behind and to leeward.

Sailing in a parade is better than being passed, and it is better to accept a passive sailing technique than to attack when the odds strongly favor a loss. The only time a lay line is safe is when one is in his desired position with everyone else on the lay line as well. And this is the condition of the one-leg beat or close reach. Relax and enjoy it! If you must attack, do it to leeward!

On a close reach or a one-leg beat stay to leeward.

A tacks to cover **B** and then, in a heading shift, falls down on **B** as **C** and **D**, ahead and to leeward, gain. **A** tacks again to clear **B** on her lee bow and in a subsequent lift overstands while **B** and **D** lay the mark and **C** almost does the same. Were she sailing to windward **A** would have done well; near the lay line she loses disastrously.

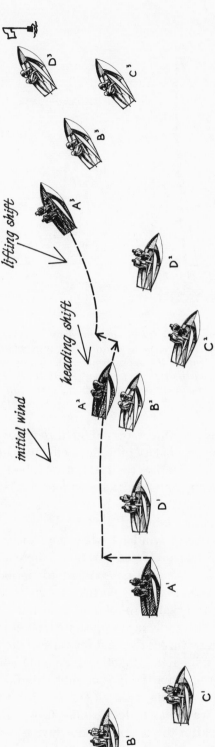

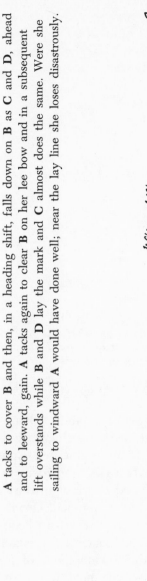

lifting shift

heading shift

initial wind

245

F. Wave Riding

*"Ahead as each untrammeled wave rises before her, she
bursts upon it, scattering it into whiteness to either side.
This is the most exhilarating living while it lasts, for it has
all the right constituents—exertion against the elements, a
challenge of concentration, insecurity of tenure."*
—KEITH SHACKLETON

The disadvantages of sailing through waves to windward are the
advantages that permit their effective utilization to leeward. Then
instead of fighting the crest, it may be ridden; an unequal exposure
to orbiting water particles is beneficial when the time spent in the
forward motion of the crest can be extended and that in the backward water motion of the trough diminished or avoided. Downwind
the increased windage when high on the crest serves to keep the
boat in this preferred position. There is no concern for increased
forward resistance consequent to periodic development of excess
side force. Breaking waves merely thrust the boat more rapidly
ahead and water smashing aboard is drained out by the suction
bailers as rapidly as it appears. Slope drag, the nemesis of windward
work, now surges the boat forward as the resultant force of buoyancy
and gravity acting together produce a horizontal vector forward and
down the wave face. But more significant than all of these advantages of racing in waves to leeward is wave velocity. The velocity
of the wave has little meaning to windward when the waves rush
by one after the other, but downwind, where only a few waves may
be met during an entire leg, velocity has significance!

In one race of the 1962 Buzzard's Bay Bowl series we rounded the weather mark in second place, gained all the way down the close reach, and were right on the *Chief*'s transom as we reached the jibing mark. The *Chief* jibed on the face of a wave, oscillated a bit in the 20-knot breeze, and shot away on the broad reach. We swung up to avoid the *Chief*'s transon (as we had missed the overlap), slowed on the back of a wave, and jibed in the trough. We tried to round up to a faster course, but our bow was well dug in the trough. By the time the jib was organized and adequate boat speed was achieved on a course well above the lay line the wave behind had slipped from under us. While we struggled to reacquire the speed necessary to hold a position on the wave face, the *Chief*, still on his private wave, shot away to a 50 yard lead. We spent the entire remainder of the leg, capturing wave after wave, to make up our loss and barely nick the *Chief* at the line.

The energy, kinetic in wave velocity and potential in water elevation, in a wave system is proportional to the square of the wave height and to the wave length. Full generation of waves from a 20 knot wind may require an exposure of 10 hours over a fetch (or exposed water distance) of 75 miles indicating that the transfer of wind energy is dependent upon duration and fetch as well as wind velocity. The wave velocity in knots is approximately $3.5 \times$ the wave period in seconds (the time for a wave crest to travel a distance equal to one wave length). The wave period for chop is from one to 6 seconds providing a wave velocity of approximately 3 to 20 knots whereas open sea waves have a wave period of from 6 to 12 seconds providing a wave velocity of approximately 20 to 40 knots. Thus, if a boat can maintain position on the forward surface of large chop or sea waves, it can reach a speed in excess of 20 knots. This position maintenance is the major determinant of success in racing downwind in a sea.

When the forward vector of gravity and buoyancy forces (the "slope drag"), exceeds the skin friction, the boat slides forward down the wave. The combination of this force, the forward motion of the orbiting water in the crest, and the aerodynamic force achieved by the sails is often sufficient to maintain position on the wave face. When the elevation of the wave and/or the aerodynamic force fall below a critical level, the boat will cease to maintain its position, and the wave crest will slip on ahead. When wave elevation and/or aerodynamic force exceed a critical level the boat will surge down the face into the trough ahead. The loss of slope drag and the backward movement of water particles in the trough slow the boat and prevent ready reestablishment of position on the wave face ahead or behind.

The water surface in a strong wind is composed of many superimposed layers of sine waves, layers of water particles orbiting under the influence of myriad impulses in varied directions and with varying energy. Just as the wind varies in intensity and direction so the resultant waves vary in height, length, and period. The superimposition of these random impulses produces markedly irregular wave patterns even in the open sea with segments of waves disintegrating, reappearing, and altering in direction. Attempting to maintain position on the upper wave face while sailing through these irregular mounds and troughs is difficult in even a steady wind. The necessity of maintaining forward speed, through the development of aerodynamic force and the utilization of slope drag, at a level sufficient to maintain wave position under these circumstances is near impossible. Constant adjustment of course to obtain maximum forward thrust from the wind, higher in the lulls, off in the puffs, and constant search for steep wave faces to obtain maximum benefit from slope drag must be combined. A planing position must be maintained on the wave crest until a deeper trough appears ahead. Then any course deviation may be justified to acquire the slope drag provided by heading down that slope. Always dive for the holes. When the wind is strong, the boat fast, or the waves steep, it may be necessary to hold back so as to avoid being swept beyond the wave face. This is usually best achieved by riding the wave diagonally. Once off the wave it may be difficult to reachieve position as the irregular mounds disintegrate and reappear, and boat speed sufficient to maintain wave position may not be reacquired until another puff or an unusually steep wave reappears.

The tactical requirements of downwind sailing in waves include initiating the leg with a fast breakaway maneuver utilizing a wave face if possible. To initiate surfing combine bearing away perpendicularly down a wave face to obtain the maximum benefit of slope drag with hiking to break frictional resistance with pumping the main, jib and/or spinnaker. To maintain surfing trim the sails constantly to adjust to the variations in boat speed. Ease the sheets as the boat slows or bears away and tighten them as she surges ahead with wave velocity or turns higher on the wind. Modify the course continually to bear away down the steepest wave face as the wind drops, and come up across the wave face as the wind and boat speed increase. Steering should be achieved by altered hull immersion whenever possible without deleterious rudder drag and

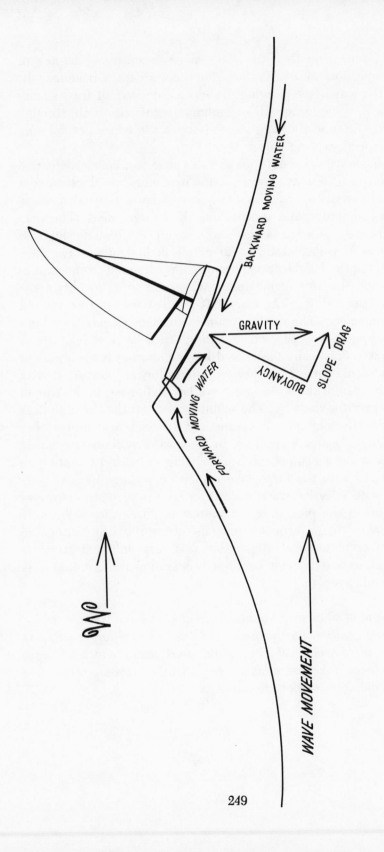

The combination of aerodynamic force, forward moving water, and slope drag on the wave face permits the boat to reach the velocity of the wave and to maintain position on the upper wave face.

the sails pumped for the little extra speed necessary to acquire or maintain position on a wave face. By these means a boat may be kept on the wave face, surging ahead continuously at the velocity of the wave, through periods of minimum wave elevation, through the troughs, around the heights, and across the wind, never losing the boat speed once acquired.

With major wind strength and wave variations, course deviation should be arranged so as to preserve the maximum speed advantages for critical moments, when breaking away from the weather mark, passing a competitor, and approaching the leeward mark. This may require taking a leeward course early, saving the planing, high on the wind, with sufficient thrust to permit holding the wave face, for the end of the leg. Or it may require deviating out from a shore-line to reach the area of maximum wave size so as to obtain the necessary "slope drag." The essentials at all times are free air and room to maneuver. The marked course variations essential to maintenance of wave-face position and the critical level of boat speed necessary are drastically obstructed by neighboring boats ahead or astern. A blanket may not merely reduce forward thrust, it may spill the boat from the wave and leave her wallowing in the trough as the competitor roars by. The inability of a weather boat to bear away under the rules when a competitor is nearby may prevent her from seizing a major wave face to leeward. Preoccupation either with preventing a competitor from passing or with attempting to pass him and with the responsive maneuvers so required can only interfere with effective wave utilization. The immediate maneuver after rounding the preceding mark must be to deviate sufficiently from the evident or expected courses of nearby competitors, to windward or to leeward, depending upon the inherent strategic advantages, so as to provide continued separation and absolute freedom for maneuver.

The essential element of racing downwind in a sea is wave riding, maintaining position on the forward upper face of large waves in order to utilize wave velocity. Continuous maintenance of wave position should take precedence over all other considerations and requires complete freedom to maneuver.

G. Shorelines

"It is essential for a leading boat closely followed by a group to avoid being drawn into a luffing match and particularly to avoid losing one! The leading boat is best advised to keep to leeward and let the next boat take over the role of 'defender of the wind.'"

—ROBERT EMPEY

In the race for the Royal Bermuda Yacht Club Trophy at Itchenor we raced up and down the narrow reaches of winding Chichester Harbor, and at the end of the day I longed for a Gold Cup course in the open sea. We had led to the weather mark, going away from the fleet with ease, but on the dozen (it seemed like more) successive reaches lost boat after boat to salvage a poor eighth at the finish. On the first reach we bounced off the shoals on the leeward shore while our close competitors planed past out of the adverse current on the windward shore. On the way back down we selected the windward side of the deep-water channel, and they planed through us to leeward. And when we rounded East Head for the reach back up the eastern channel, we bore away for the leeward shore, and they planed by to windward again!

Current considerations must take precedence when sailing along the shore as flow differences may be extreme at varying distances from the shore. But if only one shore is present or if both shores provide equal current advantages, the preferable course must be chosen dependent upon wind conditions. The course may well be devious, dog-legged, or curved along the shore that creates different

251

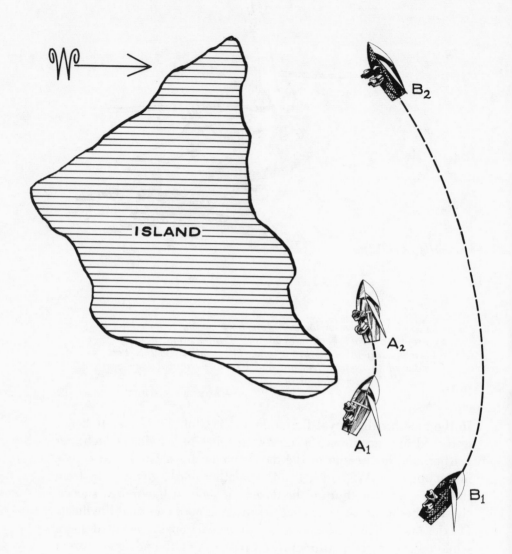

In a vertically stable wind the warm air flow remains aloft, riding over the cool surface air pocketed against the weather shore. Boat **A**, cutting the turn closely, stops in this area of flat calm while **B**, farther offshore, slips past. If the wind had been vertically unstable, a sea breeze or a northwesterly, the air flow close to the weather shore would have been enhanced by rising thermals over the land, and the inside course would have been preferred.

segments of the leg. Modification of the course due to these geographical requirements must be coördinated with tactical requirements created by the proximity of other boats. Far more significant, however, is the effect of the shore on the wind system and the necessity of adjusting course to utilize the resultant wind modifications most effectively. In vertically unstable winds (cold air aloft) consequent to an approaching cold front (a "varying northwesterly") or to a sea breeze, the strength of the cold flow aloft is brought to the surface by mixing with warm air rising over the land, and thus the maximum strength of the wind is felt close to the windward shore. In vertically stable winds the warm air aloft slides over the pool of cooler air on the surface of the water and may not reach the surface until well offshore. This pattern is, of course, typical of the effect of a lee shore where air cooled by passage over the water surface remains pocketed, forcing the warmer wind to rise above the surface. Thus a close approach to the windward shore must be avoided in vertically stable winds and to the leeward shore in all winds. Even in vertically unstable winds a close approach to the windward shore must be avoided if the bank is high and produces a blanketing effect.

At Tom's River we have often raced down the bay around a major point at the river's mouth in a northwesterly. Under these conditions each boat attempts the shortest course around the low marshy headland limited only by the depth of water. As there is no recourse from the complete blanket produced by a following boat's intervention close to shore and as the vertically unstable wind is at maximum strength nearest the beach, each boat holds as tightly as possible to the shore. Although the racing rules only permit a yacht clear astern to establish an overlap between a leading yacht and a shoreline when there is room for her to do so in safety, few competitors are inhibited unless the leader approaches the shore determinedly and hails that no room remains. And while a yacht under way must keep clear of a yacht aground, she will not be penalized for fouling one that goes aground immediately ahead of her! Thus a yacht astern will not be intimidated from following closely to intervene between the leader and the shore if the opportunity arises. At Tom's River if the opportunity is granted, the intervention is accomplished, and the boat ahead is passed and beaten.

The boat that approaches St. Helena Island too closely is often left behind when we race for the Ice Bowl. The temptation to take the short cut around a point, or an island, or along a curving shore can lead into a zone completely devoid of surface wind. The high shores of St. Helena produce a complete blanket for 100 feet or more offshore and even near its low areas in a vertically stable wind the warm air may lift above the cool surface leaving a void near the shore. George Moffat once chanced an inside course across the back of St. Helena, went from second to last, and might still be slatting there if a stray puff hadn't arrived at last. One possible advantage of a shoreline, to windward or to leeward, in a very light vertically stable wind is the development of a minimal sea breeze close along the beach. When all the sea is glass and even when the basic wind is off the shore, close in there may be an onshore whisper, which may spell victory.

There may be danger along the lee shore as well because its proximity restricts any breakaway opportunity to leeward. When other boats press close astern or to windward and the course bends around a promontory to leeward, there may be no means of maintaining the preferred leeward and shorter course without being trapped by the dacron to weather. Coming down the Severn on a broad spinnaker reach we sought to keep to leeward of the fleet one day in hopes of holding the sailing angle advantage at the finish. Unfortunately we were forced to come up beneath the fleet at each point and around each buoy. With each such return to the disturbed air of the massed fleet we lost another boat. As we had discovered at Itchenor, the utilization of the theoretically ideal route must be modified by the necessity of avoiding disturbed air and a poor sailing angle at the critical moment. It doesn't pay to bear away to a slowed course or into a wind trap after rounding a mark in hopes of some future advantage while losing half the fleet. When danger looms and the fleet congeals, get out in the wind and worry about the strategic advantage when the crisis is past.

Consider the effect of the shoreline on the wind and the course, and plan to utilize or avoid the affected zone along the shore.

H. Two Boat Lengths

*"After the race was over I could catch all of the boats
that had passed me during the race, but unfortunately they
didn't give any trophies for getting back to the Yacht Club
first."*

—TED WELLS

We were swooping across Buzzard's Bay on the second leg, a broad
reach in a 20 to 25 knot sou'wester, and riding the big gray seas.
We had set the red-white-and-blue spinnaker, which was pulling
beautifully now with the pole almost against the stay. St. John was
flat out on the weather rail with the guy wrapped around one wrist
and the sheet around the other. As we surged down the face of a
wave he'd strain the sheet in and ease the pole, and as we occasionally slowed to climb onto the next he'd work the pole back. We
rushed along leaving most of the fleet far astern, but *Stormalong*
was staying with us and perhaps gaining a little. As we approached
the jibing mark, she surged down a big one and was now close to
an overlap inside and to leeward. We weren't certain whether the
chute could be carried on the third leg but knew that if we dropped
it now *Stormalong* would be inside at the mark, would jibe to
windward of us, and be off in a cloud of spray while we wallowed
in her blanket. Now the question was whether we could prevent
her from acquiring that overlap at the two-boat-lengths line.

As we were sailing parallel courses, she could acquire the overlap
when she reached a position perpendicular to our course and even
with our rudder. If we sailed higher on the wind as she closed
with us, we could move the overlap line, perpendicular to our
transom, farther ahead. But if we tried to sail higher we might lose
the wave we were riding, and she would surge up inside. Everything depended upon the wave configuration as we reached the
two-boat-lengths line. A big wave arrived just as we closed in. We

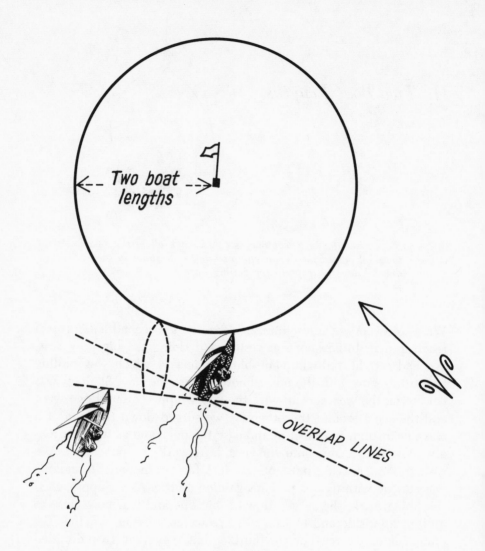

The ability of the following boat to establish an overlap at the two-boat-length circle is modified by the angle of approach of the leading boat. The latter may successfully prevent the establishment of an overlap by deviating away from the rhumb line as she approaches the circle.

bore away straight down its face before *Stormalong* picked it up, and then, almost in the trough, we headed up across its face. We were at two boat lengths from the mark and there was no overlap! I called "No room!" and bore away again on to the back of the wave ahead with the stern and rudder well down, fortunately, for the jibe. As St. John flung the boom across, and I countered her swing with a quick dip back against the turning moment, *Stormalong* shot across our stern outside. We gathered up the disordered strings and shot off ahead.

The two-boat-lengths line is a circle about the mark, and inside overlaps are gained or lost at the moment that the leading boat's bow reaches any point on that circle. Inasmuch as the overlap is determined by a line projected abeam from the aftermost point of the leading boat, the angle at which the leading boat approaches the two-boat-length line becomes extremely significant. Any boat coming in towards the mark from a position wide of the rhumb line, *i.e.* deviating at an angle towards the rhumb line, grants an overlap early. Any boat approaching the two-boat-lengths circle on a course parallel to the rhumb line grants an overlap later and unrelated to his position lateral to the rhumb line. Any boat deviating from the rhumb-line course as she approaches the two-boat-lengths line grants an overlap even later to a degree dependent upon her degree of deviation. Thus, a leading boat wishing to prevent the establishment of an overlap should deviate away from the rhumb line as she approaches the two-boat-lengths line and a following boat wishing to establish an overlap should force, by any means at her disposal (luffing, windward quarter interference, within three lengths to leeward control, and so forth), the leading boat to approach the mark from a deviated position toward the rhumb line.

The conditions established at the two-boat-lengths line are considered to continue until after the rounding, *i.e.* an overlap established, even though subsequently lost, remains in effect, and an overlap missed or lost may not be subsequently established. This provides significant advantage to a leading boat that, preoccupied with stowing the spinnaker or slowing for a jibe, no longer need worry about a follower planing in to establish a last second overlap. There is also some advantage to the following boat that might otherwise lose an established overlap while preparing for the rounding after the two-boat-lengths line. This immunity acquired after passing the two-boat-lengths line creates a new opportunity for the acquisition of tactical control. If an overlap has been established, no manipulation of the circumstance is possible; the follower has the tactical control after the rounding, and a wide swing by the leader will only salvage a safe lee-bow position. If the overlap has not been established, the leading boat may swing wide to round as she pleases except that as a right-of-way yacht she must not balk or prevent the following boat from keeping clear. Gregg Bemis has pointed out that a marked lateral deviation from an inside position might foil the following boat in her attempt to keep clear astern inside the two-boat-lengths line. The leading boat should hail, as is recommended whenever a right-of-way yacht alters course in a manner that may not be foreseen, and may not alter course so drastically that in fact the yacht required to keep clear is prevented from doing so. If freedom to tack after the rounding is desired the leading boat gains little by preventing the establishment of an inside overlap; she must free her stern as well. To this purpose once within the safety of the two-boat-lengths line she may slow up so as to force the following boat to breakaway in the only direction remaining to her—outside. If the follower can then be pinned outside during and after the rounding the leader will be free to tack at will.

When the rounding from the reach requires a tack instead of a jibe, the inside overlap becomes all the more essential. Under the 1965 rules the boat ahead when tacking is subject to the tacking and opposite tack right-of-way rules. The following boat is thus granted significant control—either with an inside overlap or even from a close astern position. It is essential for the leading boat to force the continuance or development of an outside overlap prior to reaching the two-boat-lengths line or to slow up after reaching the two-boat-lengths line to force the follower outside if she is following closely astern. When preventing or breaking the inside overlap is in doubt and an option exists it may be better to drop back to the close-astern position, control the leader, and tack inside. If, unfortunately, trapped in the close-ahead position and unable to tack freely, the solution is a luff close to the mark, head to wind, retaining right of way until the follower is forced to go behind and outside.

The two-boat-lengths overlap limitation significantly alters the tactics of rounding the downwind mark. Seek an appropriate deviation when approaching the two-boat-lengths line to control the development of an inside overlap and utilize the immunity acquired beyond this line to arrange the most effective rounding.

I. The Inside Overlap

*"Yachting is a sport for gentlemen, not as distinguished
from ladies, but as distinguished from the unsportsmanlike."*
—GORDON C. AYMAR

After concentrating on the breakaway maneuver initiating the leg
and keeping the boat moving at top speed in free air, the imminent
rounding of the leeward mark suddenly demands a new plan and
a new tactical decision. The inside overlap may be the key to the
leg—perhaps to the entire race. But does everything depend upon
it? How much should be risked to obtain it? Perhaps a wide swing
outside coming up fast to leeward would be preferable? Should one
try for clear ahead if there is a chance of crossing ahead or hang
back and slip across behind for the inside overlap?

At the jibing mark, the inside overlap is essential because of
the much wider swing required of the outside boat while the inner
one jibes. When many boats are rounding together the distance
traveled by the outer one becomes even greater; it is then worth
giving up several boat lengths to cross astern for the inside position.
After the jibe the inside boat is to windward with clear air and
the opportunity to blanket the outside boats down the subsequent
broad reach. If, of course, the subsequent leg is a close reach, the
inside overlap is useless as it leaves the inside boat in the backwind
of the outside. It is often wise when jibing to a close reach to
force the leader tight by threatening the inside overlap, then to

swing wide and come out on *her* lee bow. At a tacking mark from reach to reach the inside overlap has become even more valuable than it used to be as the new rules require the leading boat to keep clear while tacking.

Imagine yourself at the leeward mark when the next leg is a one-leg beat to the finish—on the opposite tack. To be free to tack, as you must immediately after rounding, and to prevent your chief competitor *Rowdy,* now to windward, from tacking, you *must* have the inside overlap. A close clear-astern position would be better than clear ahead, which would pin you to a continuance of the wrong tack at the mercy of *Rowdy* behind. Your leeward position should provide good boat speed on the approach, so you should have an option. Can you cross ahead, come up across her bow, and then force her outside? You are probably only a boat length ahead now and even with improved boat speed may not be able to break through *Rowdy*'s wind shadow as you converge. (One should have two boat lengths ahead and to leeward to insure a break-through when crossing a blanket zone close aboard.) If you don't make it, and she ends up with the inside overlap, you're through. And as you swing wide from below you grant her that overlap early and easily.

If you do break through and come out clear ahead, you may or may not be able to force *Rowdy* to go outside. The new rule is helpful; *Rowdy* will not be allowed to establish an inside overlap after she comes within two boat lengths of the mark. If she's close astern, as she will probably be at that time, you can slow up and force her outside. She'll have no other place to go. But suppose she slows up too and just waits for you to go round; then you're nailed again, unable to tack. You'd better forget the cross-ahead maneuver and come up across her stern now.

But suppose after you come up across *Rowdy*'s stern she luffs, breaks away, and forces *you* outside? Perhaps it would be safer for you to come up to leeward, to try to break through, and if you don't make it, to luff *Rowdy* instead of giving her the chance. A good sharp luff should stop her in her tracks head to wind, then you can break away clear ahead, and subsequently force her outside by the slow-up maneuver inside the two-boat-lengths line. There are no other boats anywhere near so that, if you can't break away with the sharp luff, and *Rowdy* retains the inside overlap, you can always take her the wrong side of the mark! You'll have to hail her as you start up or you'll be disqualified for balking (Appeal 53). If you take her high enough you should be able to bear

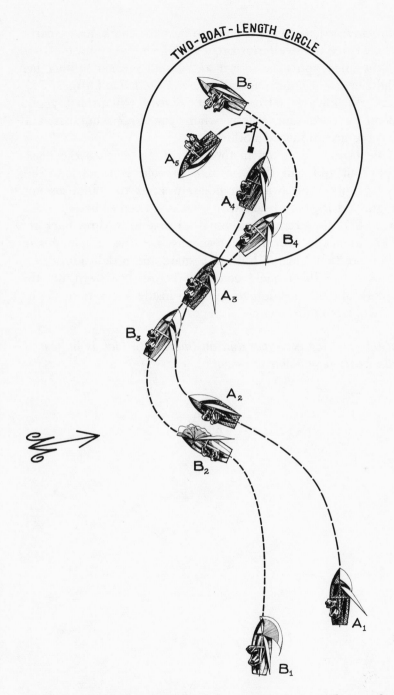

To insure the inside position and the opportunity to tack immediately after rounding, **A** luffs **B**, breaks away to a "no overlap" position at the two-boat-length circle, and then slows to force **B** outside (once safely within the two-boat-length circle).

away suddenly or jibe away, if you are past the mark, and emerge clear ahead. Once the overlap is broken (prior to reaching the two-boat-lengths line) you may return and round without giving her room whether or not you've actually passed the mark (Appeal 57). Unfortunately, however, after all that, *Rowdy* will probably end up right on your transom, exactly where you don't want her, and you will have accomplished nothing.

She may, in fact, hang on in the luff till she reaches the mast-abeam position and will then be able to hold you outside. She, of course, cannot bear away immediately so as to collide as you must be granted room to bear away *after* she reaches mast abeam. But in the short time remaining you'll be unable to drop back for another try at inside. All of which means that the advantages of the outside position and the luff are a snare and a delusion.

You had better drop back, come up across her stern for the blanket, and take that inside overlap from inside and astern. "In on the jib! Hike! Going up—now!"

When the next leg is a beat and an immediate tack is indicated, the inside overlap position is essential.

v. *Running—*

The Search for Clear Air

A. The Principles of Running

"*An increase of wind nearly always favors the yacht astern appreciably, and even the failure of the wind can do likewise. It is very important to remember that such flukes are much more likely downwind than up because the rate at which the wind is passing you is much smaller and consequently the chances of your carrying a different wind along with you are much greater downwind than up.*"
—JOHN ILLINGWORTH

With sails operating at the stall, the run is the most inefficient point of sailing. Usually the aerodynamic force is insufficient to produce maximum displacement speed or, when planing, maximum planing speed. Significant speed increases are therefore possible (and essential) through increases in aerodynamic force produced and reduction in forward resistance. Hull and fin trim and steering techniques that avoid excessive rudder use are valuable in reducing frictional resistance. Additional sail (the spinnaker) and the application of effective sailing angles are valuable in increasing aerodynamic force. Most essential is the acquisition and maintenance of clear air to insure the continued production of the greatest aerodynamic force possible. The tactics of running are designed to achieve and maintain maximum boat speed by acquiring clear air at the best sailing angle and by utilizing current, waves, and variations in wind direction and wind distribution to the best possible advantage.

Principles

1. Initiate the run by a breakaway in clear air immediately after rounding the mark toward the preferred side of the course.
2. Maintain the momentum of the preceding leg until the breakaway is complete.
3. In strong winds, guard against capsizing usually due to uncontrolled oscillation or to sudden turning forces created in jibing, by careful fin control and steering technique.
4. Avoid loss of clear air through blanketing—the major danger on the run. Avoid being trapped in a blanket zone. Watch your wind pennant and those of your nearby competitors.
5. In favorable current, tack downwind to improve the sailing angle without a major increase in distance sailed.
6. In adverse current, seek the strategically advantageous upcurrent position by selecting the straight upcurrent course.
7. In big waves and strong winds, planing and wave riding provide such major speed increases that they must be utilized regardless of increases in the distance sailed.
8. Tactical control techniques should be utilized to acquire and retain the preferred side of the course, clear air, and the desired approach to the leeward mark.
9. Wind disturbance created by the converging of many boats at the end of the run must be avoided by maintaining a lateral position until the last second and converging at a high sailing angle.

On the run acquire clear air at the best possible sailing angle and retain it.

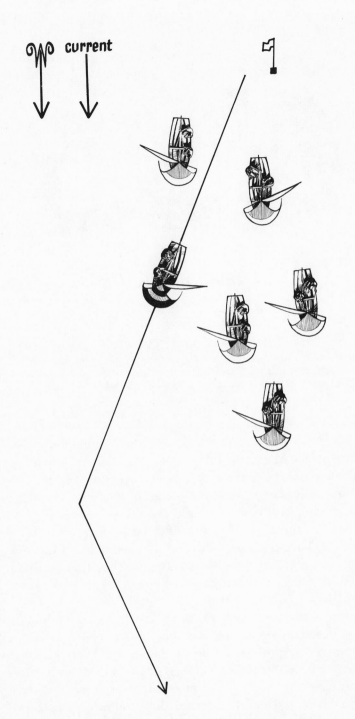

Clear air on the preferred side of the course should be sought immediately on the run and can be successfully achieved by tacking downwind in favorable current.

B. Initiating the Run

"The skill of the skipper is the decisive factor before the wind, and the boat herself, in spite of her good qualities, as the form of hull, and so forth, is quite helpless and under no circumstances to be held responsible for the final outcome."

—MANFRED CURRY

Have you been halfway down the run and suddenly wished that you were on the other side of the fleet? And have you realized how difficult it would be to get there? If you cross ahead of the nearest boats, they will blanket you en route (and you will be violating the cardinal principle of running!), and if you cross astern you will have to give away your lead. The start of a leg is always its most significant aspect, but on no leg is this more true than on the run. This leg must be planned, planned to assume the strategically proper side of the course, planned to avoid conflict with other boats, and planned to keep one's wind clear.

The culmination of such planning is a decisive and immediate move upon rounding to assume the desired course and position. If a strategically preferred side of the course exists (better wind, better current, better sea conditions, or an immediate or ultimately better sailing angle) deviate immediately to windward or to leeward in such a decisive manner that following boats will not attempt to either follow closely or to outdo you. It is patently illegal to deviate below a proper course if a boat, following within three boat lengths, desires to deviate to leeward of your course;

thus, an immediate and decisive deviation prior to the follower's rounding is essential if to leeward is what you wish to be. The degree of deviation to windward depends upon an understanding of the character of the skippers in the following boats but should always be as high as is necessary to discourage them from attempting to stay with you, *but no higher*, if to windward is what you wish to be.

Simultaneous consideration of the two other elements of the plan, avoidance of conflict with other boats and the acquisition of clear air, may influence the decision for deviation or modify its timing. Glen Foster was about to win the 1963 International 14 National Regatta when, in the final race, rounding the weather mark in the lead, he became preoccupied with setting his spinnaker and interfered with a starboard-tack boat on the approach. A careful watch must be kept particularly while setting the chute. Finally, the plan must include keeping one's wind clear. Downwind this means avoiding any position directly to leeward of following boats and this necessity reemphasizes the advantages of deviation to leeward or to windward. Remember, however, that the apparent wind may be significantly forward of dead astern and that boats on the weather quarter may be producing significant interference. Recognition of this effect reinforces the many other theoretic advantages of deviation to leeward. If the run is close to the jibing point, assuming the jibe other than that assumed by the majority may be the best way to obtain clear air, and, if so, an immediate jibe or retention of the initial jibe with deviation to weather will be desirable. Deviation from the straight-line course is predicated upon the avoidance of the proximity of interfering boats or the acquisition of an advantageous strategic position; it should be remembered that the straight line is still the shortest distance between two points, and that unless there is a need to do so no deviation should be attempted.

As important as the plan is the execution and, as the sharp rounding of the mark and the confusion of setting the spinnaker or rigging the whisker pole causes marked slowing, maintenance of way while adjusting to the new course is essential. In some classes (the 5.5's) the spinnaker is so much more effective than the jib that it is set while rounding. In most circumstances, however, it is best to maintain maximum hull speed by proper trimming of the main and jib until the deviation maneuver is completed. This also permits the spinnaker to be set under less disturbed conditions, better maintained hull and mainsail trim and after the boat is on the dead downwind course when weight forward is least harmful. The honor of being the first to get the spinnaker up after rounding may be an empty reward for the loss of two boats to windward, who retained their jibs awhile, and one to leeward, who jibed into clear air immediately. Watch the other boats; set your chute while they are preoccupied with setting theirs. Otherwise you may look up to find that you are completely blanketed by a following skipper who has been thinking and steering while you've been hoisting! Do not bear away to leeward (if bearing away is your desire) so far that the jib ceases to draw until the chute is up and pulling. Then bear away sharply if necessary—keep her moving. If you intend to jibe, do so quickly (there is no loss of speed in a quick jibe), and hoist the spinnaker immediately unless you expect the followers to jibe with you. In the latter instance it would either be better to refrain from jibing, again setting the spinnaker immediately, or to jibe retaining the jib and to work immediately to weather for clear air before setting the spinnaker.

One is likely to finish the run the way one started, well or poorly. Major gains or losses are possible. It is essential to choose correctly the first time, to acquire clear air, to retain it continuously, and to accomplish the initial deviation in such a manner that maximum way is maintained and the surrounding boats are controlled.

Instead of jibing to the rhumb-line course immediately, A avoids the disturbed air of the direct course, bears away on starboard jibe, sets the spinnaker, and works well to leeward of the fleet. After acquiring clear air to leeward of the fleet and an improved sailing angle, she jibes.

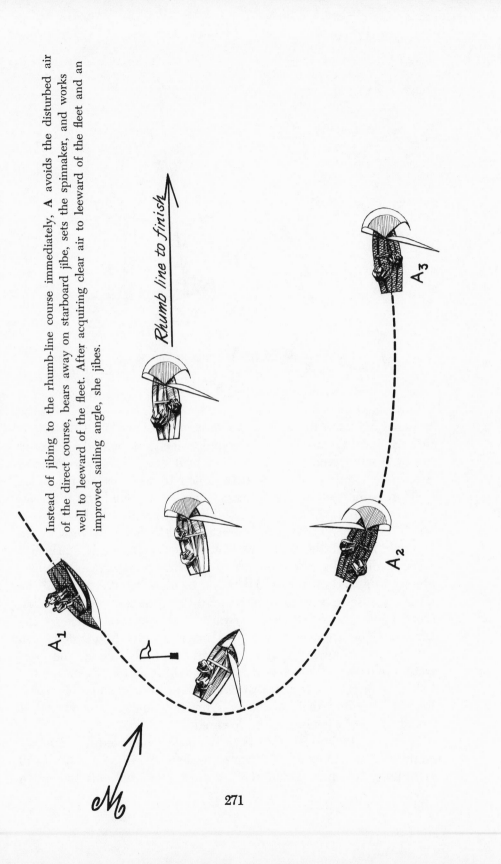

Rhumb line to finish

A₁

A₂

A₃

271

C. Capsize!

"Therefore always think how you can get the boat planing. This is the best way of getting to the head of the fleet."

—PAUL ELVSTROM

We once rounded the second weather mark of a Gold Cup course in Bermuda's Great Sound in second place, just behind the series leader. A win would give us the series lead and possibly the Princess Elizabeth Trophy. We were determined to use the spinnaker for the run home despite the 25 to 30 knot breeze and the big seas. Up it went, but, twisted from its difficult lowering on the previous reach, it wrapped about the forestay. With the crew forward to extricate the sail, the boat slowed and veered sharply to starboard. I frantically called the crew aft to give her a chance to stabilize. She straightened on course but began to oscillate. We dropped the board, she settled more quietly, and I breathed a sigh of relief. Once again the crew went forward, and I moved back to the transom. The spinnaker was now more drastically tangled than before and, billowing out in uncontrolled folds, jerked the boat from side to side. Whenever the crew would reach out to stretch the luff and free it, a vicious gust would hit, and I would shout his recall. Finally, deciding that second was better than a capsized last, I called for the spinnaker to be lowered.

In the 1959 National Regatta at Rochester we raced in a 25 knot westerly that had built up huge seas along its 75 mile fetch from Hamilton. We jibed about the reaching mark without too much difficulty and set off down the broad reach to the finish in second place. We seemed perched on a cliff as we bore away down and across a huge wave face. Rushing straight down the wave seemed dangerous due to the sudden slowing in the backward moving water of the lower face, but we had to work to leeward when we could. In the puffs we came up across the wave face to avoid being swept off the forward-moving water in the wave crest and then raced along on a full plane with the sensation of riding on spray rather than water. Suddenly the hull shot out from under us, and, before we could clamber inboard, the windward gunwale was under water and the mast crashing down on top of us. One moment everything had seemed under control while we passed the leader; the next we were trying desperately to right her. We salvaged eighth and eventually lost the series by seven points!

Adequate boat-handling technique must be acquired so that strategy is not excessively limited by fear of capsize, but there are conditions when capsize is so imminent that a conservative plan, designed to reduce the risk of capsize, is more likely to bring victory. Recognition of these circumstances is essential to their tactical modification. Capsize downwind is consequent to the seas controlling the hull rather than the rudder and hull controlling the seas. Forward motion is the prime requirement of steering and control, and thus the faster the boat is moving the less the chance of capsize. The most dangerous time is while jilling about before the start with sails luffing; a sudden gust, with no possibility of dissipation in forward movement, then blows the boat over before she can get started. Sudden slowing is even more dangerous as a planing or jibing boat suddenly smashes into the back of a wave or attempts a rapid turn. As the bow digs in from the cessation of planing or consequent to the turning force of the rudder, a pressure wave builds up along the outer face of the bow. The rig aloft tends to keep moving and/or swing centrifugally away from the direction of turning which tends to dig in the bow and heel the boat all the more. If the board is down the boat trips over its enhanced heeling moment; if it is up, she skids and begins to oscillate. Avoidance of sudden slowing or turning, particularly combinations of both as in the jibe while turning, is essential in heavy air and big seas. Inasmuch as the capsize is consequent to the pressure building up against the heeled bow sections, bow immersion must be avoided when slowing or turning. Keeping the boat parallel to the horizon when reaching and running in big waves reduces hull drag when climbing up waves and brings weight aft to free the bow when racing down their faces to a sudden slowing in the trough below.

When sailing in a sea the boat describes orbital circles just as if she were a particle on the water surface. When on the upper back or upper face (in the crest) she is moving in the direction of the wave movement and when on the lower face or lower back (in the trough) is moving against the direction of the wave movement. At the same time her buoyancy tends to keep her perpendicular to the water surface, bow down on the wave face, bow up on the wave back (when she is moving parallel to the wave movement). On a beam reach, orbital water movement causes the boat to move to leeward in the crest, decreasing lateral resistance and heeling moment, and to move to windward in the trough, increasing lateral resistance and heeling moment. Buoyancy forces on the reach, therefore, cause the boat to heel to leeward on the wave face and to windward on the wave back. Although the crew hikes strenuously to keep the boat on her feet in the trough, a sudden decrease in lateral resistance as she rises up the wave face markedly reduces hiking requirements. As the crest passes, buoyancy heels the boat to windward, which superimposed upon the marked decrease in lateral resistance due to the leeward moving water, drops the hiking crew into the sea, and sends the mast crashing down on top of them. (We once broke two diamonds capsizing to windward in the St. Lawrence!) A moderate amount of lowered centerboard increases stability and dampens oscillation but increases heeling moment and so should be utilized warily. Shift of weight on and off the rail must be synchronized with wave action while reaching; a strong hike while in the trough should be gradually reduced on the wave face and replaced by a quick move inboard as the crest passes beneath.

With moderate board down and rapid adjustment of sail trim and crew position to accommodate for fluctuations (often irregular) in wave movement, most wave conditions can be negotiated. Add a gusting wind with variable heeling, lee-bow pressure wave deviations, and oscillation associated with inappropriately coördinated hiking, and capsize may be unavoidable. Under these circumstances the spinnaker may provide additional stability (if it can be hoisted without too much difficulty and need not be lowered till after the finish). If the leg is a dead run, two long broad reaches with an intervening jibe (or tack) in a lull may provide more stability than the dead downwind course. Never allow the sails to come by the lee or the boat to heel to windward, as without any air pressure to confine its course the boat may sharply veer to leeward as the

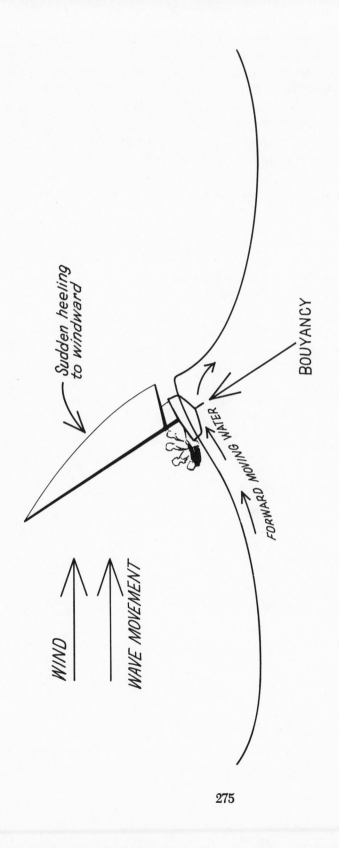

WIND

WAVE MOVEMENT

Sudden heeling
to windward

FORWARD MOVING WATER

BOUYANCY

The sudden loss of lateral resistance in the leeward-moving water of the wave crest and the windward vector of buoyancy on the wave back result in sudden heeling to windward. If the crew does not rapidly adjust to this change, the boat on a beam reach will capsize to windward.

windward bow digs in, bringing the mast over and down to wind-ward. The broad reach provides a compromise between the danger of veering to leeward and the danger of lateral-resistance loss on the beam reach. As a last resort take down the main after rounding the last weather mark; it is the lateral vector of the aerodynamic force created when it swings across the sky with the boom broad off that sets up the most uncontrollable oscillations.

In big seas capsize awaits the unwary. Accept the risk and be alert to its imminence.

D. Jibing

"The lesson to be learnt from this capsize is always jibe in a seaway as the stern squats, and not when the stern is up and the boat rushing down the face of the sea."
—UFFA FOX

At the leeward mark the jibe drastically reduces the distance sailed by utilizing the shortest course. On the run, jibing may be invaluable to permit tacking downwind. In heavy air, as the jib or spinnaker improve their effectiveness higher on the wind, tacking downwind may provide continuous planing when the dead downwind course will not. Free air may only be obtained by sailing off to the side of the fleet on the run. More favorable current or sea conditions to the side may also recommend a deviation from the dead downwind course and necessitate a jibe to return. A dead downwind course may be hazardous in big seas with resultant oscillation, particularly in boats that do not utilize the steadying effect of the spinnaker. To avoid capsize it may be necessary to sail higher than the direct course and to jibe back later. Sailing by the lee is rarely justified; even a few feet sailed in this manner will slow the boat and, of course, increase the risk of capsize in an unexpected jibe. The ability to jibe in all conditions is essential.

Involvement with neighboring boats frequently necessitates jibing to secure tactical advantage. Defensively, it is never wise to sail close across the bow and into the wind shadow of another boat on a run. In a large fleet avoidance of disturbed air may thus necessitate frequent jibing. The better solution is often to sail high of the

277

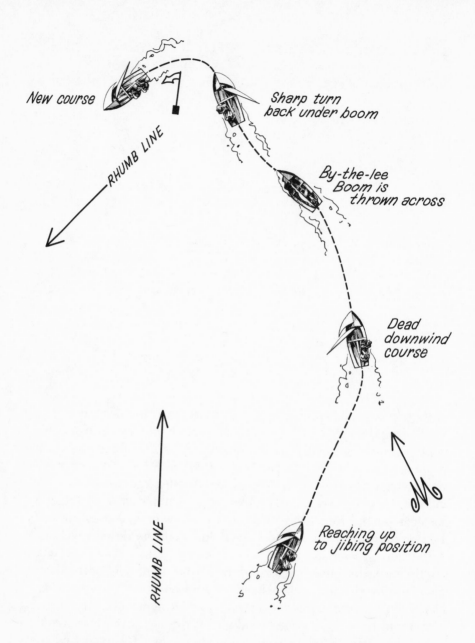

New course

RHUMB LINE

Sharp turn
back under boom

By-the-lee
Boom is
thrown across

Dead
downwind
course

RHUMB LINE

Reaching up
to jibing position

In strong winds the jibe should be made on a direct downwind line, awaiting a moment when the boat is free of oscillation and the bow is out of the water. The boom should be thrown across as the boat swings slightly by the lee. The boat is then brought sharply back under the boom before proceeding on the new course.

course on whichever jibe creates the least deviation from the rhumb line, clear of the entire fleet, and to jibe back only when the mark can be laid at a fast, safe angle on the opposite jibe. Offensively, jibing may permit approaching another boat with right of way, on starboard tack, or after the acquisition of luffing rights, an advantage that may be decisive in preventing blanketing or in finishing ahead. Remember that luffing rights may be acquired by a boat overtaking to leeward if she jibes (once or twice) so that she is forward of the windward skipper's "mast abeam" position at the completion of the jibe. Jibing technique is thus essential to tactics and should be practiced as frequently in a gale as in a drifter.

Concern over the possibility of capsize often limits the use of the jibe in strong winds. As almost no slowing or deviation from the ideal course is produced by the maneuver, it is always preferable to tacking. The danger of capsize is consequent to two factors: the centrifugal force of the rig aloft that causes heeling while turning and thus buries the lee bow and trips the boat, and the oscillation produced by the sudden movement of the boom, sail, and crew when the center of lateral resistance is high, *i.e.* the board up. *Control of these two factors is best achieved by avoiding a turn while jibing.*

Even if a jibe is required while rounding the mark, a simultaneous turn is not essential. In this instance the mark should be approached from upwind so that the jibe may be completed on a straight line final approach, or the jibe should be delayed until after the rounding when the boat is again settled on a straight-line course (if the subsequent leg is the run). In both instances this technique has the added advantage of avoiding other boats. At all other times the jibe can readily be accomplished without turning.

In preparation for a jibe in heavy air the board should be carried about one-third down (wherever oscillation is best controlled without producing weather helm). The bow should be out of the water, *i.e.* the jibe should be delayed until the boat is on top of or on the back of a wave and the crew weight moved well aft. Bear off, if necessary, to a position slightly by the lee, and have the crew seize the boom or all parts of the mainsheet while straddling the centerboard trunk (ideally performed with a mid-boom mainsheet rig). When all is stable bear off a little further before signaling him to fling the boom across. Stability is dependent upon absence of oscillation, which is dependent upon the freed bow. If there is any resistance to the bearing away maneuver, the jibe should be delayed till the bow again frees. When the helm is easy and the boat stable the helm is brought up and crew signaled "Now!" He pulls the boom

279

across with all his strength as rapidly as possible but keeps his weight low and in the centerline throughout the procedure. The sheet, of course, must be freed to permit the boom to fetch up just short of the shroud, and the sheet and the boat must be rigged so that nothing will catch en route. At the moment the boom crosses the mid-line the helm should be brought up (towards the new windward side) enough to briefly deviate the boat back in the original direction in order to counteract the centrifugal force of the boom and rig that tend to turn the boat. The crew should not jump about (which only increases the expected oscillation) but should remain in the mid-line and aft until the boat is stabilized on the new course.

This technique should be practiced whenever possible in 30 knot winds so that it is smooth and certain. Then, with confidence, the jibe may be utilized to tremendous tactical advantage, whenever required, in any condition.

My friend, Bob Empey, claims that he uses the Episcopal service in jibing. I contend that it doesn't require divine guidance, just practice.

E. Spinnaker Tactics

*"If you try to get through to leeward, you must do so
well clear of your opponent, otherwise you will get so far
and no farther, when you will find that he will be blanketing
you and you will drop back again. It is no good trying to
luff across the bow of another boat which is also running
unless you are several lengths clear."*
—HUGH SOMERVILLE

When running or broad reaching with or without spinnaker, sails
are functioning at the stall, are producing a large zone of disturbed
air to leeward, and are particularly susceptible to the effects of
blanketing. Thus, one of the most important considerations on these
points of sailing is keeping one's wind clear. The overtaking boat
has most of the advantages and can be expected to emerge victorious from any close encounter.

If unable to round the weather mark with a long lead, the major
concern downwind is to stay out from under the boats astern.
Not only the nearby blanketing boat may be lost, but, while
stopped, the leader may lose several others who take over the
blanket and slip by. As on all offwind legs working to leeward
initially is the ideal tactical solution, and this should be attempted
whenever feasible. If a dense cloud of dacron is following close
astern as you round, however, it may be necessary to luff immediately well to weather of the rhumb line so as to discourage anyone's
attempting or being capable of blanketing thereafter. The unfor-
tunate problem in luffing at all is that there always seems to be
someone who wants to go even higher, so that, once started, there
seems to be no limit. If the course is a run, it may be wise to assume
the jibe opposite to that assumed by the majority and/or to tack

281

downwind. This is a valuable technique if used under the following limitations: (1) without deviation farther from the rhumb line than necessary to keep clear wind or sails drawing well, (2) not in moderate winds when boats are at displacement hull speed dead downwind, and (3) not against a significant current.

Defensive tactics under spinnaker are primarily the avoidance of the wind shadows of following boats. Watch the masthead fly carefully to insure against sailing into a position or allowing a competitor to sail into a position that may produce wind interference. *Never cross in front of another boat* while tacking downwind, after a wind shift, to reach a favored side of the course. If a change in course or a jibe is necessary to prevent sailing by the lee, check to be certain that the change will not sail you into a blanket before acting. Sail no higher than necessary to keep your wind clear; always let the follower work a little farther upwind so that his resultant course will be slower than your own. What goes up must come down!

Offensive tactics under spinnaker, conversely, are based upon blanketing the boats ahead. Watch the masthead fly of the boat being attacked. Stay directly between her and her apparent wind. Blanket cones of sails at the stall extend for at least five boat lengths but narrow to a point at the extremity so that continuous, accurate boat manipulation, in terms of the observed masthead fly, is essential. The leeward boat should never try to pass close to leeward except at the finish or the completion of a leg when the few feet ahead, before the blanket becomes effective, may be extremely valuable.

Never try to pass close to windward either as you are likely to be luffed out of the race. Attempt the final stage of a windward pass from close aboard, high on the wind, moving rapidly and away from the overtaken boat so that as she rounds up for the luff she will almost immediately be "mast abeam." Rather than attempting the complete pass to windward, if your position is already more upwind than desirable, it may be better to feint and bear away. If you come at the boat ahead with a sudden round up to produce a roaring bow wave, her skipper will luff violently in defense. As soon as he is well up you may bear away with at least a boat length's gain and possibly enough space to leeward to break through. A major danger exists, however, in being caught to weather so close that you are unable to bear away. To avoid being caught or being carried far off the course if luffed sharply, head up sharply and let the mainsheet run. This will permit slowing and bearing off across

A hovers astern and slightly to leeway of **B**, awaiting a puff. When it arrives she slices up across **B**'s stern, forcing **B** to luff sharply. At the last moment **A** bears away sharply, jibes, blankets **B**, and forges ahead.

the leader's transom (with the added dividend of being trimmed for the new course in advance!).

On a broad reach passing to leeward is blocked by the blanket zone which a fast boat may move up into, be stopped by, and then be forced to fall back from recurrently. As the leeward boat runs into the blanket and her sails collapse, her skipper instinctively heads up, falling more deeply into the trap closer to the source of the blanket. Each effort to pass thus results in more complete obstruction unless the boat is deliberately held off despite her slowing. Three solutions exist. The simplest is to bear away at least five lengths to leeward and miss the blanket altogether. Associated slowing and other competitors may prevent this. If a third boat is in position to weather, the immediate blanketer may be feinted up under her so as to become blanketed herself. The resultant decrease in her emanating blanket zone may permit a break-through. If neither of these solutions is available, a third is possible. If arrival in the blanket zone three to four lengths to leeward can be timed with the windward boat's falling into a soft spot or with the wind shifting forward, the momentum of prior speed may be utilized to carry through. A gradual turn to weather, rounding up as speed is falling, may maintain speed sufficiently to achieve a break-through across the windward boat's bow. This must be timed to perfection as disaster is certain if all the above mentioned prerequisites are not met.

It soon becomes evident that downwind legs are treacherous, that blanket zones are everywhere—and that the only safe place for the innocent is back on the beat!

F. Traps on the Run

"Look ahead and plan ahead—ahead there's a known slow boat who has a weakness for luffing. Don't overtake him dead astern and then try to pass him. Can you see far enough ahead to know where you'll be with regard to boats around you when you get to the mark? Will you be able to get an inside berth?"

—ARTHUR KNAPP

I sailed into at least three traps on the run of the second race of a recent Spring Invitational Regatta at Annapolis and dropped from second to fifth in the process. The leeward course seemed to provide a better sailing angle and a straighter course in the light air and windward setting current. I bore away immediately after rounding the weather mark only to have the third boat move out on my quarter, take my wind, and, little by little, work past to windward. Once she was past I had clear air again and bore off farther to leeward in each successive puff. By the time I was two-thirds the way down the leg a mass of followers had worked out on my weather quarter. As we had all been set to weather by the current and had to bear away farther for the mark even the boats dead astern were now taking my wind. By the time I realized that my only way out was a jibe, I was surrounded, had lost two additional boats and as much as 100 yards on some boats that had maintained clear air throughout.

Maintaining clear air with a fleet close behind, determined to interfere with your wind and in an ideal position to do so, can be as difficult as getting away from the bar with a full glass after the Fourth of July Regatta. It is easy enough to recognize the beer slopping down your arm or the sinking sensation when your wind is gone, but protecting yourself against the catastrophe may not be nearly so simple. You may be trapped by your competitors, either deliberately or by accident, by a shift of the wind that suddenly places a competitor between you and the new wind, or, perhaps most commonly, by your own stupid maneuvering! Constant vigilance with one eye on the wind pennant and one in the back of your head is essential.

Watch out for boats working out on your weather quarter. They'll be moving more rapidly on their way out at a good sailing angle and may easily slip across your apparent wind. If they are close enough, they may trap you and slow you to such an extent that even their poor sailing angle for the latter part of the leg will bring them to the mark ahead. Unless you are convinced that the windward course is better, bear away quickly with every puff so as to get so far to leeward that the blanket effect of these boats cannot reach you. Watch out for a new wind or a stronger wind closer to the windward shore that will permit the fleet behind to move into blanketing range. If the overtaking group is not too close, a little adroit side-stepping may be all that is necessary. Watch your wind pennant and those of your competitors; place yourself in an open channel between the attackers until you can get far enough to leeward (or jibe) to break away completely. Be alert for the bright boy who may be deviating sharply to cross astern and then camp on you. One effective solution for this character is to lead him under the blanket of a third boat farther astern, which will not only stop him but markedly reduce the strength and length of his blanket zone.

Awareness of the masthead pennant is commendable, if it is associated with alertness to the competition. I've more than once been pleased at my perspicacity in detecting that I was by the lee only to be disgusted by the subsequent recognition that I had just jibed into someone's wind shadow. Variations in wind direction can suddenly place you in a blanket zone you had no thought was close. Be alert to such changes, but be not too hasty in departing from them as you may sail yourself into worse trouble as the wind shifts back or a competitor attempts his own solution!

More treacherous than the wind and the competition may be

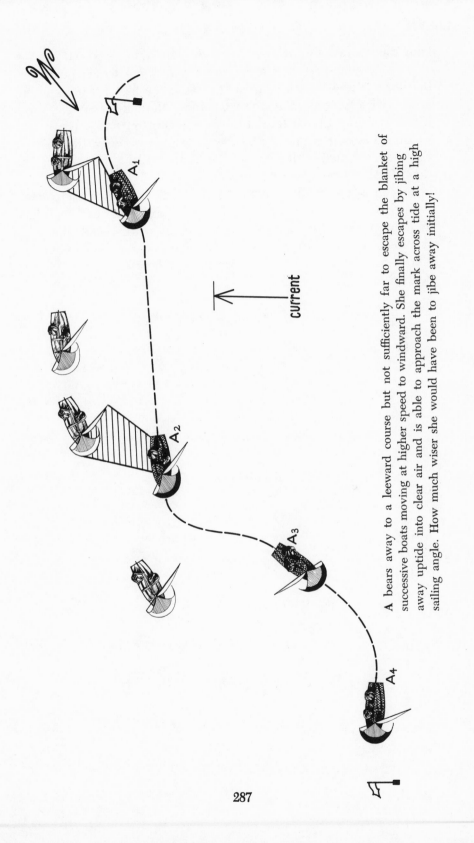

A bears away to a leeward course but not sufficiently far to escape the blanket of successive boats moving at higher speed to windward. She finally escapes by jibing away uptide into clear air and is able to approach the mark across tide at a high sailing angle. How much wiser she would have been to jibe away initially!

your own voraciousness. An awareness that the other end of the finish line is favored, that a new wind is arriving to windward, or that inside is where you must be to round the leeward mark often arrives with the greedy hope that you are the only member of the fleet to have made the fateful discovery. Desperate to salvage this treasure before the others discover it, you rush across the course. Excited, crammed with your own conceit, you have no thought for the trivial concerns of common sailors—until suddenly you are seized, impaled on the outstretched blanket zone of a mere boat from that world you had left not long before! And that boat and its uninspired skipper are going to round the mark ahead, and you, you fool, may remember to remember that one doesn't cross under other boats' noses on the run regardless of how enticingly the sea beyond may gleam.

Watch your masthead fly—and those of the boats behind.

G. *Tacking to Leeward*

*"The golden rule of all sailing is to free all your sheets
and get your sails off the centre-line as much as possible, but
this rule is more true of spinnakers than of any other sail."*
—UFFA FOX

When we race on the river at Essex, current determines the outcome. We are swept down the river willy-nilly around, past, and
sometimes into the marks. And if, after a short beat upriver, we
arrive at the weather mark with a slight lead, there remains the run
downstream with a mass of dacron astern obstructing the residual
wind. In that 3 plus knot current at peak ebb little effective wind
remains to facilitate escape, and the leader is usually passed, often
becalmed, in an apparent flat spot or in light air in the confusion
of multiple wind shifts.

One version of a yachting puzzle often discussed at the Essex
Yacht Club questions the advantage of sailing downriver with a 5
knot ebb in a breeze or in a dead calm. Would a boat reach the
leeward mark sooner in such a current if she had a 5 knot breeze
dead aft or with no wind at all? Inasmuch as the boat would have
no effective wind at all when hurtling downstream at 5 knots in a
5 knot breeze with her sails flapping, she would undoubtedly reach
the "leeward" mark sooner by beating to "windward" in a dead calm
against a 5 knot effective wind. The corollary of this thesis is that
the effective wind is always significantly diminished when sailing
with the current and that at current flows approaching wind
strength little effective driving force may remain. It is not surprising
then that on the run, as the wind varies and is obstructed by interfering boats, one seems to sail into flat spots and sometimes even

finds the wind coming from dead ahead when the remainder of the fleet still has it aft. It becomes essential in these conditions to increase the effective wind by all possible means, particularly when the possible wind variations between neighboring boats often varies upwards from zero!

Tacking to leeward is often the solution to the light-air run in no current but is the *sine qua non* of sailing downwind in favorable current. The net wind is a combination of negative wind force produced by current movement and apparent wind due to boat speed and positive wind force produced by the residual effective wind. The more the boat is deviated from the direct downcurrent course the less the effect of the current acts to reduce the residual wind force and the more the apparent wind due to boat speed is brought to act in conjunction with, rather than in opposition to, the residual wind force. The increased distance sailed when deviating from the rhumb line is infinitesimal at 5° and is of but slight significance at even 10° to 15° (in contrast to the marked increases in distance sailed when deviating a few degrees from the 45° average angle to windward). Thus, with little to lose and much to be gained, deviation from the direct course to the leeward mark makes good sense in a favorable current. And if this evidence were not enough we may add the obvious benefit of the current vector, which tends to deviate the boat back towards the direct downcurrent course and thus reduces the actual deviation or distance sailed. We can almost have our cake and eat it too; deviation produces better apparent wind consistent with the sailing angle pointed, but the current provides this advantage at a much reduced distance deviated!

The increase in speed, of course, must compensate for the extra distance sailed, and, although this results from a wide variety of deviations, there is an optimum angle of deviation and a critical angle beyond which loss must occur. The minimum is evidenced by the failure to fill the sails and see them drawing well. The maximum is evidenced by reference to the other boats; are they gaining or losing? The optimum is difficult to determine, and the reasonable rule is to deviate just a little more than one's competitors so long as this continues to produce net gains. In most light-air situations where the actual wind is barely greater than the current speed (and in any situation where the actual wind is less), the spinnaker should not be set. The jib will draw much more effectively in winds varying near zero and will, of course, be essential if the negative forces exceed the positive so that the "wind" shifts ahead.

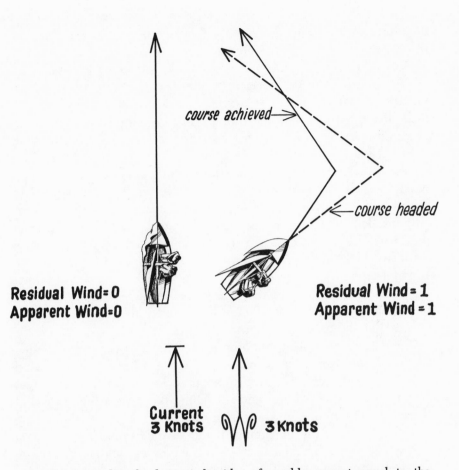

course achieved→

←course headed

Residual Wind= 0
Apparent Wind=0

Residual Wind = 1
Apparent Wind = 1

Current
3 Knots   **3 Knots**

A boat moving directly downwind with a favorable current equal to the wind strength moves at a speed equal to the current alone. A boat sailing at a higher angle moves at a speed equal to the current, and, in addition, retains some residual wind force, moves through the water producing an apparent wind, and deviates little as the current provides restorative deviation towards the rhumb line.

A number of additional advantages are inherent in course deviation with the current. Clear air, the desideratum of downwind sailing, is obviously much more readily obtainable when the fleet can split laterally across the course and in these circumstances is readily obtainable at little expense. Deviation should be exercised towards the area of maximum current flow. It is thus possible when the leeward mark is not directly downcurrent or when the current is greater offshore or off-shoal to deviate towards the preferred side of the course immediately and then to jibe over at the halfway point

291

to return, maintaining the same sailing angle, at all times within the area of most beneficial current.

Determination of the optimum angle of deviation becomes acutely pertinent in the decision to jibe back to the mark from the initially deviated course. It may be tactically more effective (as little, if any, speed is lost in jibing) to jibe many times en route. If conditions are dissimilar on either side of the course, however, a single jibe may provide the maximum advantage. The jibing point should be selected to insure an equal sailing angle to the effective wind on each jibe and thus if the effective wind is not parallel to the rhumb line, may require legs of unequal length. Other considerations that effect the decision to jibe are the need to approach the leeward mark in clear air at optimum speed and/or to obtain starboard tack, luffing rights, or an inside overlap on the approach. It may frequently be wiser to delay the jibe-back to a point at which the mark approach can be made from farther to leeward at an even higher sailing angle than previously, in order to insure speed and clear air at the crucial moment.

The danger of waiting too long cannot be overemphasized, however, and this seems the common mistake. Particularly if the wind is light and the current strong one may be swept farther downcurrent than expected and end up sailing back upcurrent to round the mark. The minimum danger in delaying the jibe is the sailing of extra distance, the maximum, being swept beyond the mark on the wrong side! The effective wind increases achieved through deviation are consequent to reductions in the effective current. Therefore, at some critical angle, usually less than 45° of deviation, the effective wind increases are negated by effective current decreases, and boats nearer to the rhumb line will arrive at the mark sooner. Remember that in the latter stages of tacking to leeward when aiming at the mark one is sailing an arc ever higher on the wind with progressive increase in leeway deviation by the current.

Deviate from the rhumb-line course and tack to leeward when running in favorable current to achieve an adequate increase in effective wind, but don't deviate too far!

H. The Long Last Inch

*"It is clear that on a run, when the boat is almost
keeping pace with the wind, it may be possible to stay inside
a dead spot for a considerable length of time. Don't wait
for it to go by, for certain other things that you are most
anxious to stay ahead of may go by first."*
—C. STANLEY OGILVY

When barely making headway against a one- or 2 knot current in
light air, we contemplate the relief of reaching that leeward mark,
shimmering in the distance. Unfortunately the mirage is often
unrealizable even at the end, as when we finally arrive we may be
unable to round. And as every moment passes, an additional boat
and an additional obstruction to the little wind astern appears. Each
robs the boat ahead of driving force until all are engulfed in an
adhesive mass that slowly floods towards the mark with a passing
puff and then ebbs away in the dying air. The only progress is
astern as the followers, and even the long tailenders, finally reach
the throng and add their "Keep up!" or "Watch out!" to the stagnant
clatter.

I had never given much thought to the solution nor to the etiology
of the problem until, while sitting out the Prince of Wales Cup
Practice Race, I saw it all develop before my eyes. The fleet of 83
boats was moving rapidly through the water and slowly over the
bottom—but steadily, and all at more or less similar speed down

293

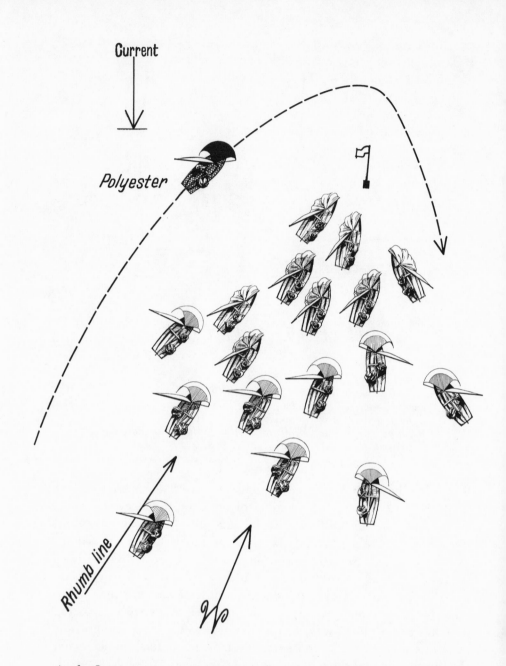

As the fleet converges and congeals in the 2 knot head tide at the end of the run, *Polyester* keeps moving in clear air, far to leeward. She sails 100 yards past the mark under spinnaker before turning to slip around to a ¼ mile lead.

the third, broad-reaching leg. They were well spread out, each seeking her preferred course and clear air. But abruptly the strangest, and yet the most familiar, phenomenon appeared. As the leaders approached the mark, they began to slow up and, finally, to stop altogether and this but a few feet from the mark! The remainder of the fleet was continuing its almost unaffected pace, but as each successive boat arrived in the vicinity of the mark it slowed and eventually halted—as if the entire fleet were theater-goers, early to the theater, awaiting the opening of the doors! Fantastic at first, it soon became evident that the slowing followed convergence towards the mark and that the boats downtide or to windward, altering course for the mark, were slowing abruptly to fall in behind those uptide and on the straight-line course. And as each additional boat fell into the double or triple line and the spread-out fleet became condensed into a smaller and smaller area, the available wind for each became less and less. Soon the line was 5 or 6 boats wide and completely halted, as the close followers slid past to leeward or to windward and then stopped as in turn their competitors astern took their wind.

Almost 80 boats were packed into a mere acre of ocean and all drifted astern as their boat speed fell below that of the 2 knot head tide; but a few were moving outside and these few rounded the mark and were off up the beat before the first of the mass broke away. They had come from far off to leeward, sailing almost straight uptide as the course angled off to windward at about 20° to the tidal flow. For awhile they had seemed far behind. (One boat I counted as fortieth a few hundred yards from the mark rounded seventh.) Then as the mass of the fleet congealed and lost their wind and/or bore away from their upwind, downtide position, the outside boats began to gain. *Polyester*, the 1963 P.O.W. winner, sailed straight uptide about 100 yards to leeward of the fleet and the mark, carried her spinnaker until she was at least 100 yards past it, then abruptly headed up and reached around in a great arc that kept her 25 to 50 yards from the fleet and the mark (except for the moment of passing). She shot away into a ¼ mile lead, and the only other boats to round in the next 15 minutes were those that had initially been well to leeward, uptide, and with clear air.

If the uptide course is to windward of the rhumb line then it is, of course, necessary to keep to windward of the fleet and sufficiently far to windward to permit an approach and a rounding that never require "pointing" uptide until the last instant. In a race we often called "The Great Veith Robbery," Joe Veith led by a ½ mile at the leeward mark in a near dead calm off Annapolis. From far astern we detected his difficulty in holding to the rhumb line towards the end of the leg and resolved to work well out to windward in advance. This course over the shoals avoided the strong current in the main channel and placed us in a nearly directly uptide position about 200 yards from the mark. While Joe vainly tried again and again to round whenever a whisper of wind appeared (only to be set downtide again at the last moment), we prepared for the final shot. We luffed along on the shoal until what we hoped was a sufficient puff appeared, bore away, shot down with the 2 knot tide, barely carried enough way to slip across Joe's bow to tack, and headed back inshore—around and ahead. Joe made it around in the same puff but only to a second-place finish, having thrown away his commanding lead by allowing himself to be caught downtide in the full strength of the current when there was insufficient wind to stem it.

Once again this vignette demonstrates the commanding advantage of the uptide (or upcurrent) position. It may not be necessary in all instances of reaching or running against the tide to bear away or head up to a directly uptide position, but whatever distance one is farther to the uptide side of the course and farther uptide than the competition, one is ahead. Bearing away with the tide is then always possible and always available as a conquering maneuver when the critical need arises. Combining the directly or more directly uptide course, which is usually at variance with the apparently direct straight-line course, with a course in clear air, free of the fleet, is the obvious solution to the problem of running against the tide and of a converging fleet at a leeward mark.

Keep uptide with clear air, to leeward best of all—and don't converge! Stay wide of the fleet even at the mark. Sail on past with everything pulling and then, from strength, play her up and across to win!

I. End of the Run

"But as interference must be accepted at the start, at the turning marks, and at the finish, a technique must be developed to make it possible to take maximum advantage of these crucial moments, to capitalize upon the slowing of the competitors, and to emerge each time with clear wind and water in the strategically desirable position."
—HOWARD GAPP

At no time save the start does there exist a greater variation in boat speed than at the time when the boats approach the leeward mark. The beat opens up the fleet, consequent to distance sailed and pointing ability, and a planing reach can separate the hawks from the geese, but the end of the run calls a complete halt to the uninitiated while the clever ones sweep on. After wide separation on both sides of the rhumb line, the boats meet in an abrupt congestion that may negate all previous gains and divulge an entirely new

297

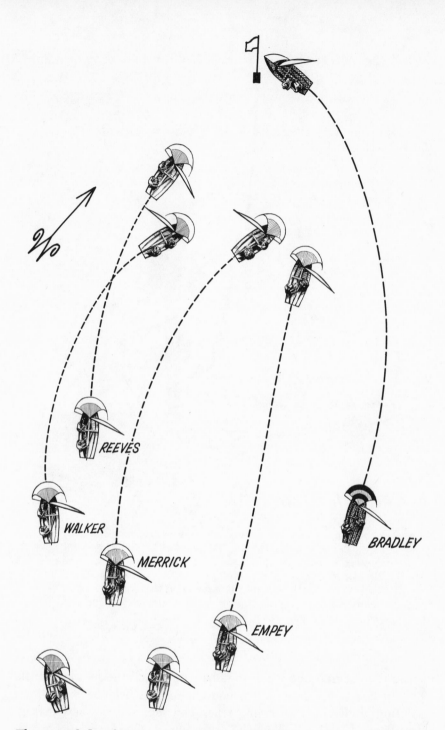

The massed fleet becomes increasingly congested as the leeward mark is neared. Bradley, who worked well to leeward initially, breaks through to the lead while the others, in increasingly disturbed air, are forced to attempt escape through a final jibe away or be overtaken.

leader. I nearly lost our 1964 Regional Regatta when, with my series rivals well behind, I stopped on the approach to the leeward mark in the last race—and eventually saw them slip by on both sides.

I had made my first mistake when I paid more attention to setting the spinnaker than to watching my competitors after rounding the weather mark in the lead. While Wendell Bradley slipped wide to leeward, Bob Reeves and Sam Merrick had cut close above and trapped me in their wind shadow. I managed to pass Sam by luffing across his stern, but this had taken both Bob Reeves and me well to weather. When we bore away for the mark, we slowed and within 100 yards nearly stopped. The wind was lifting over the sea wall not far ahead, the boats behind were interfering with what little air remained, and we were dead before it—the slowest point of sailing. The entire fleet closed up as we waited. Sam jibed away to leeward, and I followed suit, but both he and Bob Empey slipped past. I salvaged series victory by a mere ¼ point.

The start of the leg determines its completion, and when one is reduced to responsive behavior to obtain clear air, strategic plans disintegrate. However, when unavoidably high on the run, it is essential to remedy the danger early by bearing away in the puffs or jibing off in the shifts—*before entering the windless congestion on the leeward-mark approach.* If there is but a single boat ahead and no one threatens astern, this precept can be disregarded. Then coaxing the leader high permits blanketing her and acquiring the inside overlap at the mark. (His defense should, of course, be a sharp luff just before reaching the mark, then a bearing off to jibe, if necessary, to break the overlap.) If many are close astern, however, forget the boats ahead; there is little to be gained and much to be lost. If to windward, break to leeward or farther to windward immediately or jibe if necessary; acquire a better sailing angle and better boat speed even if a brief movement perpendicular to the course is required. Seek a position from which the final approach can be progressively faster and faster, higher and higher on the wind. Don't just sit there, do something!

Far better than waiting to move at the last moment, of course, is to plan the approach well in advance, to be to leeward, on one jibe or the other (preferably starboard!), and to come in low and fast from well outside the interference zone of the fleet. Do not cross till late, hold low in clear air until the last possible moment. The farther laterally one starts the slicing up the easier the breakthrough will be. If it is necessary to cross under the interference of several boats, a lead of at least two boat lengths will be required to come out ahead.

If meeting another boat on the opposite jibe, plan to retain clear air and control. If behind, jibe onto his wind and seek the inside overlap or force him to sail away from the rhumb line in order to retain clear air. If ahead, jibe and keep ahead and beneath, forcing him away from the mark, so that a subsequent jibe will take you back nearer to the mark with the follower outside. If the initial jibe is preferable it may be best to maintain course for the mark without coming into the other boat's blanket zone, expecting her to slow consequent to being by the lee. Do not allow the other boat to jibe or continue into a position that will take her on a more lateral and faster course on the approach; stay with her so that her ultimate course is the same or lower than your own. If still astern near the mark, delay the luff till the last minute, swing up, blanket, bear away with spinnaker or wung-out jib retained to the last second, and seize the inside overlap.

It is essential to look farther ahead to the desired position after the rounding. In the 1964 Regionals I wanted to tack immediately but was pinned down by Sam Merrick, immediately astern, who had swung wide and come in close to the buoy. When the next leg is a beat and a tack is desired, it is essential to come in wide and luff high after the rounding so as to free one's transom for that tack. A quick tack suddenly attempted after rounding, particularly to port, is exceedingly dangerous as a closely following boat may luff sharply and catch one helpless in a trough. If ahead and no tack is indicated, a slower swing beginning closer to the mark is adequate; or, if overlapped, a wide turn to leeward to maintain a lee-bow position is needed. When a mob is rounding, it may pay to delay and come in just behind the inside boat, thus picking up all boats on the outside.

Again, planning is the essence of success. It is necessary to have planned the departure from the mark initiating the run prior to reaching it, the leg before initiating it, the approach to the leeward mark before beginning it, and the rounding and the departure from the leeward mark before arriving at it. And, once again, look over your shoulder—watch the competition particularly when it is between you and the wind!

300

J. Tactical Control Downwind

*"I have sailed or crewed on most types of modern boats,
even been aboard the famous old* Bluenose—*but of them
all, for sheer thrill, give me a 14-footer running with
spinnaker in a fresh breeze and long sea."*
—CHARLES BOURKE

Complete tactical control is possible from certain attacking positions
on the windward leg as no significant deviation to windward of the
close-hauled course is possible. The only escape from a boat close
abeam to windward or on the weather quarter is to bear away or
slow up, resulting in significant loss. On a downwind leg no such
complete control is possible as deviation away from the controlling
boat results in minimal increase in distance sailed. However, on the
run and, to a lesser degree, on the reach one side of the rhumb-line
course may be strategically preferred, one side may provide enhanced tactical opportunity for free air, spinnaker utilization, or
planing, or one side may permit the resumption of complete control
or a desired breakaway beyond the leeward mark. Inasmuch as wind
interference on the windward leg only operates astern, control tactics
are only effective against boats astern except for windward-quarter
(or close-astern) limitations on tacking. But downwind, as the blanket zone of sails operating beyond the stall operates ahead, it is
possible to control boats significantly in the lead. Thus partial control

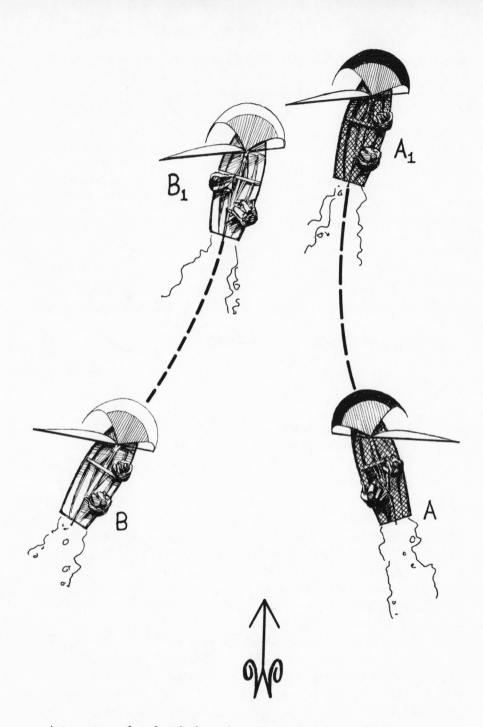

A turns to starboard and jibes when approaching **B** so as to be forward of
"mast abeam" upon completion of her jibe. Thereafter, **B** may not sail
above her proper course during the duration of the overlap.

techniques, which permit slowing of the competitor or acquisition of the preferred side of the course and deny its acquisition to the competitor, may be warranted to leeward.

1. PARTIAL CONTROL ALONG THE LEG: The competitor is induced to assume a less advantageous course or is prevented from subsequent acquisition of an advantageous course.
   a) *Leeward position*—Within three boat's lengths, may force competitor to assume a rhumb-line course
   ESCAPE—deviate farther to windward
   b) *Lee-bow position*—With luffing rights, may force competitor to deviate farther to windward
   ACQUISITION—from initially ahead position; from astern—entry into forward-of-mast-abeam position; from two boat's lengths to leeward; from a jibe—single or double
   ESCAPE—deviate still farther to windward
   c) *Starboard Tack*—May force competitor on the opposite tack to jibe or deviate
   ACQUISITION—jibe from port; jibe prior to leeward, port-tack boat's acquisition of luffing rights when being overtaken to leeward; jibe to starboard (from port) when meeting starboard tacker prior to her acquisition of luffing rights
2. PARTIAL CONTROL BY BLANKETING
   Weather-quarter position—Slow competitor to permit passing
   ACQUISITION—approach on apparent wind line of boat to leeward
   ESCAPE—luff or bear away; maneuver attacking boat into blanket zone of third yacht
3. CONTROL NEAR THE LEEWARD MARK: The competitor is blocked and forced to round second or in a controlled position
   a) *Lee-bow position*—With luffing rights may: force competitor to windward, followed by bear away or jibe away after overlap is broken; force competitor to the wrong side of mark, after hail, and accompany her until overlap is broken
   b) *Leeward position*—Without luffing rights, may provide control and interference with weather boat after rounding to close reach or to beat when rounding tack is preferred
   c) *Inside overlap position*—May force competitor to longer course around mark, permit immediate tacking after rounding to a beat when opposite tack is preferred and provide weather-quarter control position after rounding to beat
   d) *Close astern position*—May force competitor to continue

303

rounding tack when rounding to a beat and opposite tack is preferred

e) *Starboard tack*—Force competitor to the wrong side of mark, after hail, and accompany her until overlap is broken (May not force competitor beyond normal rounding turn if inside on opposite jibe *after* rounding)

Partial-control positions that permit the acquisition or maintenance of an advantage over a competitor should be sought at critical times such as at the initiation of the downwind leg, at crossings on the run, and particularly when nearing the leeward mark or the leeward finish.

VI. *Finishing* —

The Resolution of the Contest

A. One Last Beat

*"Small boat races are too short for the grand strategy;
more important are correct minute-by-minute tactics. Be
a platoon commander rather than a general."*
        —JACK KNIGHTS

That short final beat often shakes up positions and may all alone
determine the outcome of the race. Hardly seems fair, but race
committees seem to like the idea. To maintain a hard-won lead one
must capitalize on this last-leg confusion. At Corsica in 1963 we were
pinned by a close follower to the minor tack and forced to sail
almost parallel to the finish line when we should have tacked immediately. At Buzzard's Bay in 1964 we sailed off on the minor tack
looking for a header and, when that header appeared, overstood the
finish by 100 yards. To preclude such disasters a plan and a means
of (1) acquiring the shortest course to the near end of the line and
(2) the control of nearby boats on the approach must be evolved
before the leg is initiated.

The finish is the ultimate determination; here inches and milli-
seconds count. Nothing can be wasted, no chances taken with a
satisfactory position, no effort omitted to rectify an unsatisfactory
position. If in the lead, cover—*ahead and to windward*; avoid the
dangerous lee bow. If behind, save every inch; keep to the major
tack and tack again as soon as the lay line to the near end of the
line is reached. Any distance sailed beyond this lay line gives an
equivalent advantage to any competitor on that lay line. At the
Great Lakes Championship in '64 we thought we had picked the

lay line to the near end, but lost our position by inches to a Canadian on the opposite tack at the other end. There had been a shift, and we hadn't noticed.

Although the most downwind end of the starting line (the end opposite to the preferred starting end) may be determined in advance, if the committee sets a different line or resets the original one or if the wind shifts such information becomes worthless. Try to check the wind at the finish as other boats cross ahead or by the flags waving on the committee boat—and don't be too easily convinced. If a boat on the opposite tack suddenly seems to gain near the line, swing over with her. It is essential not only to determine the most downwind end of the line and to avoid overstanding it, but equally essential to be on the tack most perpendicular to the line on the final approach. If it becomes evident that one is sailing on a course at an angle greater than 45° to the finish line (or more nearly parallel to it), the near end has been overstood, and a tack should be made immediately. A finish line is not actually a line (except in the rare instance of one established precisely perpendicular to an exceedingly steady wind), it is a point, *i.e.* one end or the other, that must be determined by the finisher at the moment of his approach.

When a close finish is expected between two boats, the following possibilities exist for one of them: in the lead on the preferred, most perpendicular tack or on the minor tack, overlapped or crossing on either tack, or astern on either tack. The leading boat should continue on her approach tack until she can lay the desired end of the line, then tack, on the lee bow of all other boats that can lay the line. If she is overlapped or cannot cross boats on the opposite tack in the clear, she must sail the shortest course to the near end of the line as indicated but must retain control of all nearby boats. *Until she lays that near end she must avoid the lee-bow position*—unless fully prepared to accept the inherent risks. A boat ahead and to leeward is completely controlled; she has (almost) no choice but to continue, unable to tack. If a boat, not yet laying the mark, crosses close ahead on the approach, the follower should tack on her weather quarter. If close aboard on port tack or even at a moderate distance on starboard tack, the lee-bow boat may now be carried beyond the lay line—even beyond the opposite end of the line. The follower can subsequently tack at will when she has reached a position that will permit her to reach the line first.

When two boats are crossing near the line, the port-tack boat that has to bear away may still reach the line first if she is on the

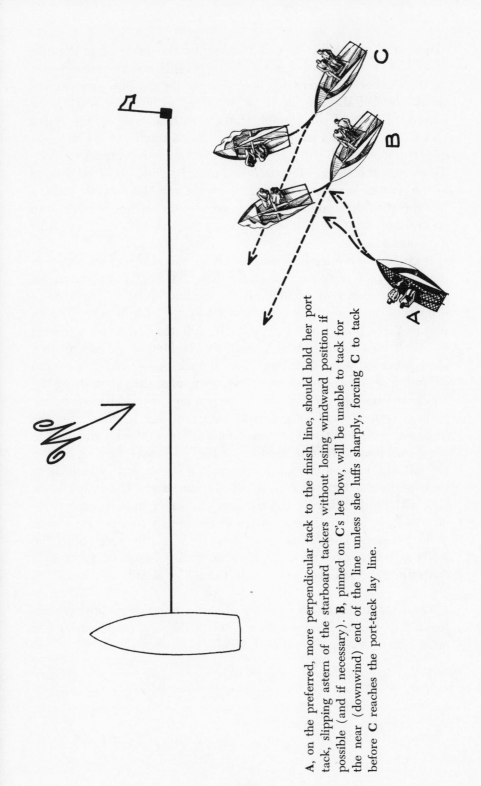

A, on the preferred, more perpendicular tack to the finish line, should hold her port tack, slipping astern of the starboard tackers without losing windward position if possible (and if necessary). B, pinned on C's lee bow, will be unable to tack for the near (downwind) end of the line unless she luffs sharply, forcing C to tack before C reaches the port-tack lay line.

major, most perpendicular tack heading for the near end of the line. If so, she should pass behind and continue; if not, she should tack on the starboard tacker's lee bow. Thereafter she may sail straight for the line, if she can lay it, or pinch up to lay it or to stop the windward boat, if she cannot. If the port-tack boat on the minor tack passes behind a starboard tacker who is unable to lay the near end, she may catch the starboard tacker when she returns on port. To counter this danger the starboard tacker should cover by tacking as the port tacker passes behind. She must keep clear while tacking but she should be able to pin her competitor on her lee bow and control her there until she can lay the near end and break away for a certain win.

If pinned on the lee bow short of laying the near end or sailing on the minor tack near parallel to the line, the breakaway maneuver is the sharp luff. It may be necessary to slow up by luffing so as to drop back into range, as a port tack to cross may be unsafe even two to three boat lengths ahead. The luff may result in stopping the other boat, head to wind, permitting tacking ahead in the clear after bearing away, may force her to tack, may force her to fall behind and to leeward, or of course, may miss, then permitting the windward boat to pass. If on the minor tack, the luff must be attempted prior to reaching the near-end lay line so that after the breakaway the leeward yacht may be the first to the lay line and to windward upon arrival there. Even if the luff misses, tacking behind the passing windward boat may permit a breakaway, which, if to port, permits a right-of-way return on starboard. If on the major tack with neither boat laying the near end, the gambit is even more effective as the windward boat will be forced to the minor tack or to leeward. The luffing boat may then readily reestablish the lee-bow position *on the lay line* after two subsequent tacks thus controlling the follower without ever crossing ahead.

The beat to the finish when competitors are close is always confused. But the proper resolution of the close, windward finish will often provide the one point that decides the series.

B. The Reaching Finish

> "There can be few more pleasurable sensations than the
> thrill of coasting down a long sea in a fresh breeze of wind,
> a sheet of spray on either side, holding the boat upright
> with every available muscle, a bunch of competitors
> 'breathing down one's neck' and the finishing line not too far
> away."
>
> —STEWART MORRIS

Sailing races are won and lost at the finish line—an artificial end
point injected into what is supposed to be a contest of speed. Fast
boats often win and boat speed is the major factor in staying ahead
throughout most of the race, but there are certain crucial positions,
the start, the turning marks, and the finish, imposed by the Race
Committee, that determine the final positions. Thus a race between
sailboats is not a mere contest of speed but a series of sprints from
one crucial point to another, the outcome of which is more often
determined by the management of the boat at these crucial locations than by its speed.

Salute rounded the weather mark in the lead (as she often did),
set the chute and held her 200 foot lead to the jibing mark. But
Salute made her gains to windward, and there was a long dead reach
to the finish line ahead. *Wild Goose* would be breathing down our
necks (or roaring past to windward on that reach), unless we arranged something. Taking the leeward position, playing the gusts,
and waiting till the end of the leg for the spurt wouldn't work this
time; once *Wild Goose* planed past, she'd be gone for good. Could
we hold the chute on that high reach? Possibly, but if it was too high

311

the resultant side force would stop us in our tracks and *Wild Goose* under jib would be over and gone before we could get the chute down. ("When in doubt about carrying the spinnaker—don't!" G. D. O'Day.) We could carry our spinnaker effectively at a higher angle than anyone else in the fleet, but the initial inability to defend our weather quarter was too high a price to pay. We must hold *Wild Goose* back and prevent her from reaching a blanketing position. We dropped the spinnaker, jibed, and came up high on the course in the temporary lull in which we had rounded. As a gust hit we bore away in a cloud of spray but worked back up as soon as it died to maintain maximum speed. *Wild Goose* was now around and plunging towards us. We worked every puff, hiking abruptly and sliding away as they hit but always coming back up farther and farther above the rhumb line. We were holding *Wild Goose* as we maintained speed in the lulls, higher on the wind than she. And now we had reached the position we had been seeking; up the spinnaker, pole against the stay! With two of us flat out, we swept down and away from *Wild Goose*. She couldn't break through to leeward now, and by the time she'd worked far enough to windward to set her chute, it would be all over.

Combination courses, saving the fastest for last, are useful on the reach as they provide dominance at the finish and speed with free air en route. One may bear off to set the spinnaker first on a light-air reach and then come in to the finish high on the wind with the jib. Or if forced to go high to get clear air initially one may continue until an optimal spinnaker angle is reached and then bear away under the chute. If the reach is too high for easy planing one should work up initially and then bear off for the line. If planing is only just possible in moderate air, the planing angle should be saved till the end by bearing off initially to a leeward position. Usually in these circumstances variable wind strength and direction will encourage working up in the lulls and planing off in the puffs whenever they appear. Slight increases in thrust then cause relatively large increases in speed, and finishing on a close reach will provide right of way over boats on broader reaches.

A susceptible helmsman ahead may sometimes be overtaken by constant threats to windward and to leeward. The overtaking boat, who controls the maneuvers, can make smooth, gradual course alterations while the helmsman ahead, who frantically notes the competitor in a different threatening position every time he looks astern, sharply swings and slows his boat from side to side. When close astern at last, wait for the leading skipper to look, make a feint to

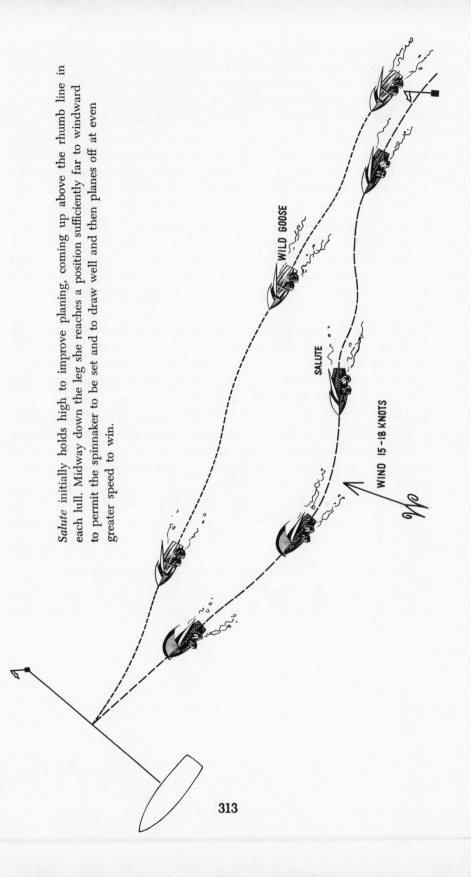

Salute initially holds high to improve planing, coming up above the rhumb line in each lull. Midway down the leg she reaches a position sufficiently far to windward to permit the spinnaker to be set and to draw well and then planes off at even greater speed to win.

WILD GOOSE

SALUTE

WIND 15–18 KNOTS

313

windward, which will force him into a quick luff, and, as he looks ahead to direct his crew, shoot off to leeward under his stern.

In planing conditions it may occasionally be possible to ride a wave or a puff through to leeward and so pass a boat ahead. To achieve this the leading boat must usually be drawn sufficiently far to windward initially so that the overtaking boat may keep its wind clear throughout most of the passing maneuver. By constant threats to pass to windward, the leader may be drawn gradually farther and farther above the course so that both boats will eventually finish on a run. This will permit the leeward boat's wind to be clear astern as she slips across the line ahead of her competitor to windward. A boat with a real propensity for luffing may eventually be carried so far up by threats to her windward quarter that both boats must jibe for the line thereby granting the overtaking boat clear wind on the opposite jibe!

Assuming that the optimal crossing point on the finish line has been chosen, due allowance should be made for the probability that the wind in the vicinity of the finish line will be less reliable in strength and direction than in open areas. It has usually been chopped up and deflected by boats of other classes, spectator boats, and by the committee boat itself. Often one has the feeling near the finish line that the boat won't move properly. The lighter the wind and the more boats are in the vicinity of the line, the more the wind disturbance and the more one should deviate from the ideal crossing point to allow for the effect of this disturbed air. Unless wind or tide variations or covering a competitor dictate otherwise, one should avoid an approach that leads through the center of the area most likely to be disturbed.

Maintain control, if possible, all the way along that last leg, but save the best for last, timing the blanketing, the slip through to lee- ward, the forced jibe, till the crucial moment of crossing the line.

C. Finishing under Spinnaker

*"We race for fun. To be sure there are times—special
series and crucial races—when all hands get pretty intense,
but in most racing we are out on a sunny summer afternoon
to see what we can do to make our boat go a little faster
than it has ever gone before and to guess correctly the wind,
the water and what the other fellow is going to do."*
—GREGG BEMIS

Timing is the key to success on the run. As in a basketball game, it
is not achieving the lead first that matters but achieving it at the
finish. As the offensive technique of running is the application of
the blanket, it is blanketing that must be timed (or avoided) for
the precise moment of crossing the line. The sudden loss of speed
occasioned by the loss of clear air (and the associated loss of ability
to wave ride) is soon recovered when, of necessity, the blanketer
shoots ahead to become vulnerable in turn.

At a Miles River Yacht Club Regatta we once rounded the jibing
mark with a scant lead for the spinnaker run to the finish. *Glastrocity*
and *Wild Goose* rounded close astern and maintained position
slightly astern and to leeward all the way down the leg. They reasonably held low to retain the advantage of a faster sailing angle
on the approach to the line, recognizing that clear air would continue until they had worked considerably ahead. *Glastrocity*, finding
that she would be unable to break past to leeward, however, elected
to trap us under a Lightning as we neared the line. She trimmed in,
came up across our stern and across the Lightning's stern (to wind-

ward of us). As we had been gaining on the Lightning all the while it seemed likely that we would enter her blanket zone before reaching the line and thus grant *Glastrocity* a clear advantage unless we responded. Despite the threat of *Wild Goose* (who delighted in the entire procedure), we elected to round up across the Lightning's bow (hoping that she wouldn't luff with us) so as to counter *Glastrocity*. The latter gained appreciably while we worked through the Lightning's lee and required a sharp luff to control when we emerged. We were now about to be blanketed by *Glastrocity* and would still be threatened by the Lightning if we fell off to leeward. Another sharp luff took *Glastrocity* up sufficiently above the weather end of the line so that we could jibe for it with clear air. As we jibed, allowing *Glastrocity* room between us and the mark, *Wild Goose* crossed at the opposite end and the gun sounded. We had preserved our lead by inches.

Several fundamental principles are herein well demonstrated. (1) Whenever possible keep to leeward (as did *Wild Goose*) and let the remainder of the fleet fight for clear air and participate in luffing matches to their mutual detriment. (2) Time the attack (as did *Glastrocity*) to the precise moment of the approach so as to stop the opponent just before the finish and thus shoot ahead at the line. (3) Whenever possible use a third boat to do the dirty work, *i.e.* lead the opponent into someone else's blanket zone. (4) When blanketed, break free as quickly as possible by a dramatic deviation to windward or to leeward; in our case we did it by a sharp luff and a jibe-away with clear air at the line. (The jibe-away is often the best technique as it provides not only personal clear air but switches the opponent into a blanketed and controlled position.) (5) Keep an eye on the boats to leeward when fiddling about for clear air to weather—if two boats to leeward break through while one is blocked to weather the loss may be greater than the prospective gain!

Two major rules restrict tactics on the run: the limitation on bearing away on a free leg and the limitation on the luffing rights of a leeward yacht. These restrictions may be successfully exploited if their applications are clearly recognized. The restriction on bearing away does not apply except between boats on the same tack; a jibe may permit bearing down upon a leeward yacht to control her and a subsequent jibe may provide the position maintenance. Such a double jibe may also provide the acquisition of luffing rights to a leeward yacht overtaking from astern. A subsequent luff may then produce a break-through to leeward that could never have been

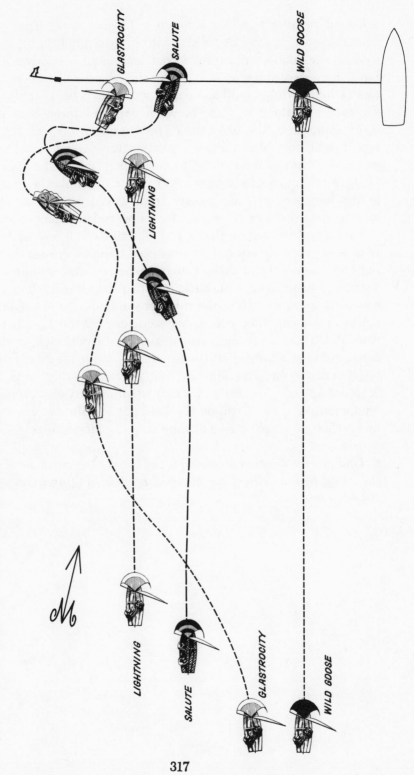

Wild Goose sails the preferred course in clear air to leeward while *Salute*, to windward, barely preserves her lead after luffing and jibing away from *Glastrocity*.

achieved by direct sailing through a blanket zone. The leeward overtaking yacht may establish control and limit bearing away as soon as she comes within three boat lengths of a windward yacht but is not establishing an overlap for the purpose of the determination of luffing rights until she comes within two boat lengths. Thus she may slip along in that "between two and three boat lengths zone" immune to the blanketing (by bearing away) of the windward yacht until she reaches a position forward of "mast abeam" when she acquires and may utilize her luffing rights. The application of these techniques to acquire clear air or to blanket a competitor at the line may provide victory from astern or prevent the last minute acquisition of advantage by an overtaking competitor.

The racing rules state that a boat finishes when any part of her hull, or her crew, or equipment *in normal position*, crosses the finishing line. Thereafter, it doesn't matter whether she continues across the line or capsizes or drifts back, but she must clear the line without committing any breach of the rules. If she fouls one of the finishing marks or a competitor before her stern crosses the line, her finish is invalid. Thus, if bearing away, assuming the port tack, or dashing across without allowing adequate room to an inside boat results in interference even after finishing but before clearing, it is illegal. A recent appeal (No. 99) states that when no part of a yacht's hull, equipment, or crew is still on the finishing line she has cleared it— and is then no longer racing or subject to the racing rules.

Time the application or avoidance of blanketing conditions, within the rules, to the critical moments of approaching and crossing the finishing line.

VII. *Synthesis—*

The Organization of a Plan for Victory

Synthesis

"There is nothing—absolutely nothing—half so much worth doing as simply messing about in boats."
—*The Water Rat*

AN OUTLINE OF ESSENTIAL CONSIDERATIONS

I. *The Week Before the Race*—Determine

A. The purpose of the race—victory in the race, series standing, trophy, sentimentality, or what? (If any indication that victory is not sought arises, expect to lose.)

B. The geography of the racing area

C. The prevailing wind patterns and the modifications produced by the geography

D. The prevailing current patterns and the modifications produced by the geography

II. *The Morning of the Race*—Determine

A. The factors that combine to produce the present wind and that can be expected to produce further modifications in the wind during the course of the race

   1. The strength of the resultant wind and its distribution

   2. The possible appearance of persistent shifts due to:

     a) Weather system movement

     b) Shoreline effects

     c) Thermal effects

   3. The probable time and location of such persistent shifts

   4. The possible presence of a vertically unstable oscillating wind

B. The factors determining the current in the racing area

   1. The strength of the current and its direction at various times during the course of the race

321

2. The distribution of the current in the racing area

C. The factors determining the wave pattern, its significance, and its distribution in the racing area

III. *The Hour before the Race*—Determine

    A. The race instructions and consider

        1. The starting time and the starting signals

        2. The course, how it will be signaled, and the means of signalling course modifications

        3. "Know Your Race Committee"

    B. A course plan and consider

        1. The preferred side of the course for the windward leg dependent upon

          a) Persistent shifts?

          b) Oscillating shifts?

          c) Current?

          d) Waves?

        2. The course and sail trim (or spinnaker use) for each reach or run dependent upon

          a) Wind strength and direction variations?

          b) Current?

          c) Waves?

    C. A starting plan and consider

        1. A means of reaching the preferred side of the windward leg

        2. The favored (most upwind) end of the starting line

        3. The effects of oscillating shifts

        4. The current—a primary determinant if of significant strength

        5. The waves

        6. The possible utilization of the port tack

IV. *The Management of the Race*

    A. The start

        1. Stick to the plan

        2. If starboard tack preferred, opt for the lee-bow position

        3. If port tack preferred retain a breakaway position

        4. Approach a "light and fluky" start from the middle of the line

        5. Keep moving in a sea; don't arrive early

    B. The windward leg

        1. Seek the new wind

        2. Stick with the major competition

        3. In light air—avoid the middle

4. At other times—avoid the lay lines
5. When on the outside of a persistent shift—tack back immediately
6. Use the compass to evaluate oscillating shifts, but do not be misled by its indications in persistent shifts or on short beats
7. Give primary consideration to the current if of significant strength (avoid unfavorable, utilize favorable)
8. Consider the sequential wind modifying effects of a nearby shoreline
9. Avoid areas of large waves
10. Maintain tactical control when approaching the weather mark or the lay lines

C. The reaches
1. Breakaway in clear air immediately after rounding to the preferred side of the course
2. Keep to leeward initially (unless the windward side has major advantages)
3. Keep upcurrent if unfavorable
4. Keep to leeward on a one-leg beat—don't tack
5. Keep her moving in light air, regardless of the direct course
6. If waves are present, ride them, regardless of the direct course
7. Consider the wind modifying effects of a nearby shoreline
8. Seize (or break) the two-boat-lengths overlap depending upon the nature of the next leg

D. The run
1. Breakaway in clear air immediately after rounding to the preferred side of the course
2. Keep moving until the breakaway is complete (delay hoisting the spinnaker till clear)
3. Be alert to the danger of capsize, particularly on the jibe
4. Don't be trapped in a blanket
5. Tack downwind in a favorable current
6. Adhere to the straight, most up-current course in adverse current
7. Retain tactical control at the initiation and end of the leg
8. Watch for the slowing at the end of the run—don't

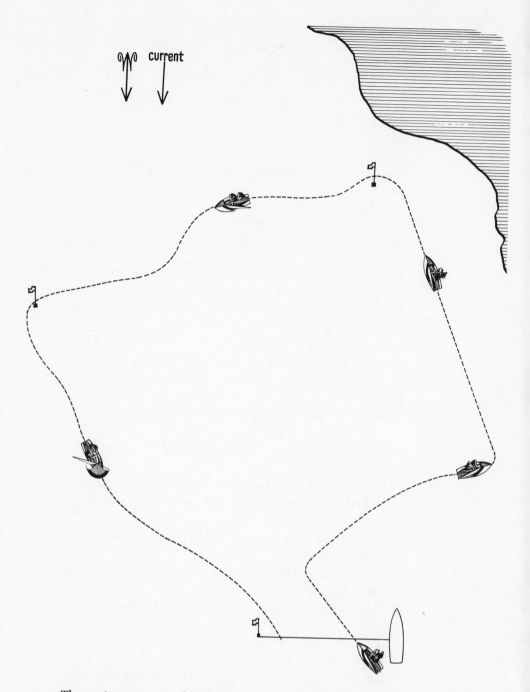

current

The entire race must be planned so as to utilize the variations in wind, waves, and current on each leg. The purpose of tactical adjustments is the accomplishment of the strategic plan.

      converge until the last second and then come in fast

V. *Underlying principles*
    A. Think and feel victory (if victory is what you desire)
    B. Keep the boat moving—don't become excessively preoccu-
        pied with tactics
    C. Expect to make a significant number of mistakes—don't
        become excessively preoccupied with their origin
    D. Constantly review the reasons for doing what you are doing
        and make no move without weighing the alternative
    E. Look over your shoulder—watch the competition
    F. Don't be greedy

N.A.Y.R.U. Definitions

Racing—A yacht is **racing** from her preparatory signal until she has either **finished** and cleared the finishing line and finishing **marks** or retired, or until the race has been **cancelled, postponed** or **abandoned**, except that in match or team races, the sailing instructions may prescribe that a yacht is **racing** from any specified time before the preparatory signal.

Starting—A yacht **starts** when, after her starting signal, any part of her hull, crew or equipment first crosses the starting line in the direction of the first **mark**.

Finishing—A yacht **finishes** when any part of her hull, or of her crew or equipment in normal position, crosses the finishing line from the direction of the last **mark**.

Luffing—Altering course towards the wind until head to wind.

Tacking—A yacht is **tacking** from the moment she is beyond head to wind until she has **borne away**, if beating to windward, to a **close-hauled** course; if not beating to windward, to the course on which her mainsail has filled.

Bearing Away—Altering course away from the wind until a yacht begins to jibe.

Jibing—A yacht begins to **jibe** at the moment when, with the wind aft, the foot of her mainsail crosses her center line and completes the jibe when the mainsail has filled on the other **tack**.

On a Tack—A yacht is **on a tack** except when she is **tacking** or **jibing**. A yacht is on the **tack** (**starboard** or **port**) corresponding to her **windward** side.

Close-hauled—A yacht is **close-hauled** when sailing by the wind as close as she can lie with advantage in working to windward.

Leeward and Windward—The **leeward** side of a yacht is that on which she is, or, if **luffing** head to wind, was, carrying her mainsail. The opposite side is the **windward** side.

When neither of two yachts on the same **tack** is **clear astern**, the one on the **leeward** side of the other is the **leeward yacht**. The other is the **windward yacht**.

Clear Astern and Clear Ahead; Overlap—A yacht is **clear astern** of another when her hull and equipment are abaft an imaginary line projected abeam from the aftermost point of the other's hull and equipment. The other yacht is **clear ahead**. The yachts **overlap** if neither is **clear astern**; or if, although one is **clear astern**, an intervening yacht **overlaps** both of them. The terms **clear astern, clear ahead** and **overlap** apply to yachts on opposite **tacks** only when they are subject to rule 42— **Rounding or Passing Marks and Obstructions**.

Proper Course—A **proper course** is any course which a yacht might sail after the starting signal, in the absence of the other yacht or yachts affected, to finish as quickly as possible. The course sailed before **luffing** or **bearing away** is presumably, but not necessarily, that yacht's **proper course**. There is no **proper course** before the starting signal.

Mark—A **mark** is any object specified in the sailing instructions which a yacht must round or pass on a required side.

Obstruction—An **obstruction** is any object, including craft under way, large enough to require a yacht, if not less than one overall length away from it, to make a substantial alteration of course to pass on one side or the other, or any object which can be passed on one side only, including a buoy when the yacht in question cannot safely pass between it and the shoal or object which it marks.

Cancellation—A **cancelled** race is one which the Race Committee decides will not be sailed thereafter.

Postponement—A **postponed** race is one which is not started at its scheduled time and which can be sailed at any time the Race Committee may decide.

Abandonment—An **abandoned** race is one which the Race Committee declares void at any time after the starting signal, and which can be resailed at its discretion.

Glossary

Aerodynamic force—the force developed as a result of the deviation of air flow produced by the sails

Angle of attack—the angle of the sails to the residual or apparent wind

Balance—the degree of equilibrium achieved by the aerodynamic force and the lateral resistances of the hull and fins resulting in forward movement of the boat with minimum drag, leeway, and forward resistance

Bow pressure wave—the resistance to turning and/or deviating effect of the water acting against the immersed bow

Drag—the frictional resistance of or turbulence produced by surfaces exposed to air or water flow or the force vector acting in the force direction

Feather—the act of heading the close-hauled boat closer to the wind (at a lesser angle of attack) so as to decrease side force and heeling

Forward resistance—the resistance, frictional and wave making, to forward movement of the boat that creates the major limitation upon displacement boat speed

Forward thrust—the element of the aerodynamic force acting to move the boat forward

Heeling moment—the couple of the aerodynamic force acting with lateral resistance to produce heeling

Lateral resistance—the resistance of the hull and fins to lateral movement (which permits the development of forward movement)

Leeway—the lateral deviation of the boat despite the lateral resistance that together with forward movement results in a crabbing forward course and that if greater than 4° results in marked increases in forward resistance

Pinching—the act of heading the close-hauled boat so close to the wind (at a small angle of attack) that forward movement is decreased below the optimum

Pointing—the act of heading the close-hauled boat close to the wind at a specific angle of attack; high—close to the wind, at a lesser angle of attack; low—less close to the wind, at a greater angle of attack; (footing—pointing low, resulting in increased forward speed at the expense of a less favorable angle to the median wind)

Sailing angle—the angle of the boat's course to the median wind, beating, close reaching, reaching, broad reaching, running representing progressively greater sailing angles

Side force—the element of the aerodynamic force acting to move the boat laterally

329

Skin friction—the resistance to water flow produced by the friction of the hull and fin surfaces

Stalling—the loss of laminar flow (and the production of turbulence) over the surface of sails encountering air flow at an excessively great angle of attack

Turning moment—the couple of the aerodynamic force acting with modifications of lateral resistance (rudder action) to produce turning

Wave making resistance—the resistance to forward movement produced by the dissipation of energy in the production of waves

Way—the forward movement of the boat; full way—maximum forward movement for the wind force available

Weather helm—the residual deviation of the rudder necessary to equilibrate the turning moment and prevent turning to windward; lee helm—the residual rudder deviation necessary to prevent turning to leeward

Windage—the frictional resistance of the above-water portions of the boat to air flow

COURSE

Favored end—the end of the starting line farthest to windward

Inside overlap—an overlapped position between another boat and a mark or obstruction; outside overlap—an overlapped position outside another boat when passing a mark or obstruction

Lay line—the course a close-hauled boat will assume so as to round a mark close aboard; starboard lay line—the course a close-hauled boat on starboard tack will assume so as to round a mark close aboard; port lay line—the opposite lay line to the starboard

Leeward—a position farther away from the area from which the wind is flowing—downwind; windward—a position farther towards the area from which the wind is flowing—upwind

Leeward end—the end of the starting line to leeward of boats crossing on starboard tack

Leeward shore—a shoreline toward which the wind is flowing; windward shore—a shoreline from which the wind is flowing

One-leg beat—a course requiring sailing close-hauled while permitting a close approach to the terminating mark without tacking

Premature start—crossing the starting line in the direction of the first mark prior to the starting signal

Rhumb line—the straight-line course from one mark of the course to the next

Rounding to port—passing a mark by leaving it to port, or on the port hand; rounding to starboard—the opposite

Two-boat-length circle—an imaginary circle whose center is a mark with a radius of two boat lengths representing the position at which the rights of an inside overlap condition are acquired

Weather end—the end of the starting line to windward of boats crossing on starboard tack; also the windward end

CURRENT

Adverse current—water flow developing a vector acting against the direction of boat movement

Favorable current—water flow developing a vector acting in the direction of boat movement

330

Lee-bow current—water flow developing a vector acting against the boat's leebow and resulting in a deviation of the boat to windward

Slack water—an area of diminished or absent water flow

Upcurrent—a position farther towards the area from which the current is flowing; down current—the opposite

Weather-going current—water flow acting against the direction of wind flow

TACTICAL RELATIONSHIPS

Across—the course of a boat intersecting ahead of another; beneath—the position of a boat to leeward of another; above—the position of a boat to windward of another

Backwind—the air flow aft of a boat that has been deviated by its sails

Balking—the action of a right-of-way boat to thwart or prevent a competitor from keeping clear

Barging—the attempt to pass between a leeward competitor and the mark at the weather end of the starting line

Blanket—the cone-shaped area of disturbed air flow extending to leeward of a boat due to wind obstruction

Clear air—the presence of air flow undeviated and unobstructed by other boats

Covering—the act of sailing between another boat and the next mark or an area of strategic advantage and/or the course modifications necessary to maintain this position

False tack—the act of luffing as if to tack followed by bearing away to the original course

Inside position—the position of a boat nearer to a wind shift, a puff, a mark or an obstruction than another boat

Leebow position—the position of a boat abeam or forward of abeam and close to leeward of another boat

Luffing match—the act of a leeward boat whose luff causes a windward boat to luff so as to avoid a disqualifying collision and which attempts to prevent her from passing to windward

Mast abeam—the position of a windward boat whose skipper in his normal position is abeam of the mast of a leeward boat, which restricts the luffing rights of the leeward boat

Passive sailing—the act of sailing the fastest possible course without regard to the presence of competitors

Short tacking—the act of tacking frequently, producing multiple short legs on each tack

Tacking to leeward—the act of deviating from the rhumb line course on the run necessitating one or more jibes to reach the leeward mark

Trapping—the act of acquiring a control position referrable to a competitor which forces her to assume a disadvantageous condition or course

Weather quarter position—the position of a boat abeam or aft of abeam and close to windward of another boat

Wind interference—the effect of the sails of one boat deviating or obstructing the air flow to another boat resulting in disadvantage to the other boat

WAVES

Crest—the peak of the wave composed of forward moving water

Slope drag—the horizontal acting force derived from the combination of buoyancy and gravity effects

Surfing—the utilization of forward acting slope drag to permit maintenance of position on a wave face

Trough—the nadir of the wave between crests composed of backward moving water

Wave back—the rising slope of the wave behind the crest

Wave face—the falling slope of the wave ahead of the crest

WIND

Channeled wind—the modified wind direction produced by the deviating effects of shorelines along a narrow body of water

Friction—the means by which surface contours deviate overlying air flow

Geographic shift—the direction deviation of air flow produced by shore contours, usually persistent in a particular area

Header—a wind shift that causes a close-hauled boat to assume a course at a greater angle to the previous wind; headed tack—the tack which is affected by a header

Heading—the direction of the course assumed, usually in relation to the wind direction

High—a weather system centered about an area of high barometric pressure which produces winds flowing in a clockwise direction about the center

Lift—a windshift that causes a close-hauled boat to assume a course at a lesser angle to the previous wind; lifted tack—the tack affected by a lift

Low—a weather system centered about an area of low barometric pressure that produces winds flowing in a counter-clockwise direction about the center

Lull—an episode of decreased wind velocity

Major header—a header of sufficient degree that the opposite tack provides a course closer to the direction of the median wind

Major tack—the tack that permits the boat to head more directly to the weather mark; minor tack—the opposite tack which heads the boat more away from the weather mark

Median wind—the median direction, midway between the extremes, of an oscillating wind; median wind line—the line from the weather mark parallel to the median wind

New wind—a wind derived from a new source appearing during the course of a race

Oscillating wind—a wind that varies in direction continuously between the extremes of a limited range, usually because of vertically instability

Phase—the period during which an oscillating wind flows from a direction to one side or the other of the median wind

Prevailing wind—the common direction of the wind aloft consequent to global pressure variations and the earth's rotation

Puff—an episode of increased wind velocity

Refraction—the deviation of wind direction produced by changes in surface friction so as to turn the wind more perpendicularly to a land-water interface when leaving shore or more parallel to a water-land interface when approaching shore

Residual wind—the wind remaining and affecting the boat when the true wind is modified by boat movement due to boat speed, waves, and current

Resultant wind—the true or actual wind resulting from combinations of prevailing, weather system and thermal winds as modified by topography, time, and temperature

Sea breeze—a thermal wind blowing from the water towards the land created by the decreased pressure of heated air over the sun-warmed land; land breeze—a thermal wind created by the pressure difference between warmer air over the thermo-stable water and cooler air over the thermo-labile land

Thermal shift—the deviation of wind direction due to the development of an air flow due to air temperature differences (such as a sea breeze)

Vertical stability—an air flow in which the temperature rises with the altitude producing stable layering of flow; vertical instability—an air flow in which the temperature falls with altitude producing rising (thermal) air currents, mixing of wind aloft and surface wind, and a puffy and oscillating surface wind

Weather system shift—the deviation of wind direction due to movement of the weather system or to the arrival of a new weather system

The Author

Dr. Stuart Walker lives in Annapolis, Maryland.

He is one of the world's leading small boat skippers. He has been a member of the United States team in the four-nation, International-14 Class races since 1961. He was the first American ever to win the Prince of Wales Cup — one of the most coveted championships in world sailing — and he is a winner of the Princess Elizabeth Cup in Bermuda, as well as countless, races, series, and trophies in the United States.